RECODING
AMERICA

RECODING AMERICA

WHY GOVERNMENT IS FAILING
IN THE DIGITAL AGE AND
HOW WE CAN DO BETTER

Jennifer Pahlka

METROPOLITAN BOOKS
HENRY HOLT AND COMPANY   NEW YORK

Metropolitan Books
Henry Holt and Company
Publishers since 1866
120 Broadway
New York, New York 10271
www.henryholt.com

Metropolitan Books® and ⅲ® are registered trademarks of
Macmillan Publishing Group, LLC.

Library of Congress Cataloging-in-Publication data is available.

ISBN: 9781250266774

Our books may be purchased in bulk for promotional, educational, or business use. Please
contact your local bookseller or the Macmillan Corporate and Premium Sales Department at
(800) 221-7945, extension 5442, or by e-mail at MacmillanSpecialMarkets@macmillan.com.

First Edition 2023

Designed by Kelly S. Too

Printed in the United States of America

5 7 9 10 8 6

To public servants everywhere. Don't give up.

The ultimate, hidden truth of the world is that it is something that we make, and could just as easily make differently.

—David Graeber, The Utopia of Rules

CONTENTS

RECODING
AMERICA

BEYOND *SCHOOLHOUSE ROCK!*

When California legalized marijuana use, the most visible change was the billboards. In San Francisco in 2017, suddenly it seemed like everywhere you looked a company you'd never heard of was plugging weed delivery to your door, fueled by investors eager to cash in on this land rush of opportunity. Half of the giant outdoor ads made no sense if you didn't know pot culture, but that didn't matter. Pot smokers were suddenly a coveted demographic in a city that often seems driven by commerce and novelty.

But there were other changes that were supposed to come with the new law, and they were as invisible as the billboards were impossible to miss. Thanks to Proposition 64, also known as the Adult Use of Marijuana Act, marijuana use would no longer mean prison, as it had meant for so many Californians for so long. Drug-related arrests had been a major source of the growth in the state's prison population, which now numbered around 130,000. Reducing that number was a big hope of the law's proponents, but current incarcerations were only part of California's problem. There were also a staggering eight million Californians living with criminal records from prior offenses. Many of those people now carried felony convictions for an act the state no longer even considered illegal.

Having a felony on your record can make it very hard to get a job. Most employers won't even consider you, and fields that require any kind of occupational licensing, from medical assistance to cosmetology, become off-limits. Former felons also can't join the military. And it's not just employment. With a felony record, it's hard to rent an apartment or get a home loan. Veterans with felony convictions are denied certain retirement benefits. Students with drug felonies can't deduct their tuition from their taxes, the way others can. Even minor pleasures like volunteering at your kid's school are off the table. Researchers have identified thousands of "collateral consequences" of having a criminal record.[1] That's a lot of barriers to building a stable life, and it seems especially unfair if you're someone who did time for something that's no longer even a crime.

One of those barriers, ironically, involved the nascent marijuana industry itself. People with felony controlled-substance offenses can't be licensed to sell in any capacity: they can't run a marijuana business, they can't work in a marijuana warehouse, they can't deliver pot to customers' doorsteps. That meant this rush of opportunity was limited to either people who never used weed or those who'd never been caught. Whites and people of color use marijuana at approximately the same rates, but people of color went to jail for it nearly four times more often, which meant that the new law would create opportunity disproportionately for white people.

Recognizing this, Prop 64 made past marijuana offenses eligible for expungement from people's criminal records. Once expunged, those convictions wouldn't show up on the background checks that kept these folks out of most jobs and limited their activities. But while this sounds like a simple matter of changing a field in a database, it was far more complicated in practice. The information needed for expungement could span court records, records from the arresting agency (which might be local, state, or federal police), jail and prison files, prosecutors' records, and probation records. If you had a conviction in more than one county, you would need to get all of the relevant materials in all the applicable jurisdictions. From those documents, you'd need to identify the docket numbers from your cases, then figure out which forms to complete and where to find them. You'd need to draft motions for each case and attach copies of the verified criminal history to each motion. You'd need to find out how many copies to make of these documents, where to send them, and how to pay the associated fees.

Prop 64 made hundreds of thousands of people statewide eligible to have their felony convictions expunged. But given the marathon of logistics, hardly anyone even tried to start the process. A year after the passage of the law, the San Francisco district attorney's office had a whopping twenty-three petitions to seal marijuana-related records. Not even twenty-three expungements: twenty-three people who'd gotten as far as filing the initial paperwork.

Voters had spoken. The law had changed. Marijuana was no longer a crime. The city was abuzz with a new chance for entrepreneurship. But the previously incarcerated were still felons. For them, things were the same as ever.

■ ■ ■

FORMER FELONS ARE by no means the only ones stuck between the promise of new laws and their reality. Just ask doctors who take Medicare.

Medicare, the federal government's medical insurance plan for seniors, has achieved remarkable success since its inception in 1965, when 48 percent of the elderly lacked health coverage. Today just 2 percent do. In approximately the same period, the

United States has enjoyed a fifteen-year increase in life expectancy, in part because of the greater access to care that the program provides. These are enormous accomplishments. But Medicare (and most of the rest of our health care system) has also been criticized for its payment structures and the sometimes perverse incentives they create. Most doctors get reimbursed simply for the number of patient visits they handle, procedures they perform, and tests they order: they get paid more when they do more, not when they do what would most help their patients. The US spends more than twice as much per capita on health care as most other developed countries, and Medicare is a big part of that discrepancy.

It would make sense to instead pay doctors more for better patient care and better outcomes, an approach known as value-based care. In 2015, Congress passed a major overhaul of Medicare meant to move the program in that direction. For the team within the Centers for Medicare and Medicaid Services (CMS) responsible for implementing the new law—writing the regulations it called for and designing the systems that providers would use—this was a chance to be part of getting health care in this country right. But for the program to succeed, the people who provided that care, from doctors and nurses to medical office administrators, would need to trust it. And as the CMS team found, among the many feelings that providers had about the new law, trust was not one. Fear, anxiety, and even anger, yes. But not trust.

One doctor in a public feedback session told the team: "As a practicing clinician for thirty years, I can honestly say that it's time to leave the profession if we stay on the current trajectory."[2] He had already spent a great deal of time struggling to understand what Medicare wanted from him: choosing among Medicare's assorted programs without being sure what effect the choice would have on his practice, submitting data about his patients without knowing if it was in the proper format, always worried that he and his team were making terrible mistakes that were going to mess up the payments and ruin his practice. None of this had anything to do with why he'd become a doctor; none of this helped him give his patients the best care he could. And now the rules were going to change again. The only thing he hated more than the current system was the thought of having to learn a new one.

He was not alone. Another doctor put it this way: "The federal government wants me to spend over $50,000 for an electronic health records system that doesn't work, takes more time for me and my staff, [involves] voluminous incoherent regulations. . . . It seems like the best course for solo practitioners that are over fifty-five is to either retire, close the office . . . or just collapse the practice and lay off most of the staff and only see private pay patients. Good God!"[3] A survey found that almost 40 percent of physicians in solo and small-group practices predicted an exodus from Medicare within their ranks. Many of those were in rural America, where fewer options for Medicare patients would be much more harmful than in a dense urban area.

Congress had passed the new law in order to improve the care patients received. But something was going awry in the course of moving from the written words of an act of Congress to its implementation by the administrative agency. Instead of improving care, the law risked driving doctors to stop taking Medicare patients entirely, thereby restricting patients' options and access. Republicans and Democrats had certainly disagreed on various provisions of this law, but neither wanted this outcome. If something didn't change, the law's effects on American health care would be the opposite of what its authors, and the people they represented, had in mind.

■ ■ ■

CHANGES IN MEDICARE reimbursement rules aren't the kind of thing most Americans pay attention to. But you couldn't miss what happened when our government tried to respond to a massive global pandemic.

In early 2020, the novel coronavirus that had ravaged China, Italy, and other countries began sweeping across the US. The virus was devastating: by the end of the year it had killed over 385,000 Americans and had had significant long-term health effects on countless more. But its impact went far beyond the havoc it wreaked on the infected and their families. The shelter-in-place orders needed to slow the virus's spread cost millions of people their jobs, and the health crisis was quickly joined by an economic crisis.

We knew little about the virus in the early months, which made the public health response challenging. But we did know about economic crises and how to mitigate their damage. While the scale of the pandemic's impact was almost unprecedented, the US economy experiences regular cycles of boom and bust. This is why we have programs like unemployment insurance—to reduce both human suffering and a further slowing of the economy. When COVID hit, the scale of job loss merited more than the regular aid. Congress authorized not only increased payments for regular unemployment insurance claimants but also special assistance to cover gig workers, a higher child tax credit, food benefits to help feed children who would otherwise have had access to free school meals, emergency rental assistance to keep people from losing their homes, and direct stimulus payments, among other measures.

Millions of Americans were grateful for Congress's willingness to act in this time of crisis. But many of those same millions heard the news that relief was coming their way and then waited. And waited. And waited. By April 2020, about half of households had received their stimulus checks.[4] By May, a survey of food-assistance recipients found that only 15 percent had received the pandemic supplement.[5] By June, only half the states had started delivering the food benefits for school-age children.[6] By July, the IRS had caught up significantly on stimulus checks, but an estimated five to ten million households were still waiting, and as many as six million remained blocked from filing taxes (and claiming critical tax credits) due to erratic behavior of the IRS's online tools.[7] By August, with a moratorium on evictions about to be struck down, only 11 percent of the $46 billion authorized for emergency rental assistance had been distributed.[8]

But the program that garnered the most ire was unemployment insurance, perhaps because it was well established before the pandemic and therefore expected to have the benefit of existing operations. By September 2020, millions of people who had applied for unemployment benefits in March, when the first shelter-in-place orders came down, were still waiting to hear back. Some didn't hear anything until well into the following year, while others who did get a response got stuck in a bureaucratic nightmare of confusing messages, requests for further documentation, and call centers that seemed never to actually answer calls. Suddenly, lawmakers in many states were reminded that their state-run systems for administering unemployment benefits were sorely out of date and called for immediate modernization. But twenty-two states had already "modernized"—meaning they had moved from decades-old mainframe computers to the cloud—and they fared no better.[9] Either the problem wasn't the out-of-date tech or the modernization efforts had failed. The US Department of Labor is still trying to sort out today exactly what went wrong and what might be done to avoid these meltdowns in the future.

All told, the various pieces of legislation that authorized the relief programs, including the CARES Act, the American Rescue Plan, and others at the federal, state, and local levels, are impressive in their scope, and their provisions no doubt saved countless lives and prevented a much worse disaster. But to those stuck between the promise of relief and the seeming impossibility of actually receiving it, the news of help coming from Washington felt like an epic bait and switch. Members of Congress weren't wondering where their next meal would come from, but they weren't happy either. They had put the pedal to the metal on economic relief and expected the engine of government to leap into action. Instead, their offices were overwhelmed with calls from desperate constituents who were on their last packet of ramen with nowhere to turn—and even the members who'd argued for a smaller relief package were angry. For once, thanks to an extraordinary crisis, Democrats and Republicans had (mostly) come together and acted with speed and resolve. But their best intentions were being dashed on the ugly rocks of implementation.

...

WHEN I FIRST learned that hardly anyone in California was likely to get out from under the burden of a marijuana felony despite a new law, I was a few years into what would become a long journey through those rocks of implementation. Haunted by the sense that government's struggles to participate in the digital revolution spelled real trouble for an already weakened institution and threatened already declining faith in both government and democracy, I had founded an organization called Code for America, which enlisted technologists to work with local governments. We'd had some successes as a fledgling nonprofit, enough to be growing fast. But my colleagues and I also spent five years realizing how much bigger the problem was than we had known. City and county governments all across the country partnered with us to improve the quality of their technology and design, but everywhere we went we found ourselves dealing with cases where policy results had failed to live up to expectations.

In 2013, a few years after I started Code for America, Todd Park, the chief technology officer of the US under President Obama, recruited me to be one of his deputies. Although terrified by the enormous task at hand, I asked my board for a leave of absence and warily accepted for a one-year term. I promptly relearned the lesson I had learned at Code for America: the problem was even bigger yet than I had realized. Three months into my new job, I watched the much-heralded launch of healthcare.gov, which would administer Obama's signature policy initiative, the Afford-able Care Act. The site immediately crashed. With millions to enroll and hundreds of thousands attempting to log on at any given moment, it managed on its first day to serve a total of eight people.

While getting the site to work absorbed practically every wak-ing moment for my boss and many of my colleagues, my job in DC took me farther afield. At the Departments of Education, Defense, Labor, Treasury, and Veterans Affairs—everywhere, really—I found the same glaring gap between policy intentions and actual out-comes. It was a sobering lesson in how government really worked, so different from the simplistic and incomplete model I had been taught.

Like many other Americans of my generation, I learned how a bill becomes a law by watching *Schoolhouse Rock!* In one three-minute segment, an adorable singing bill—literally a piece of paper rolled up and tied with a ribbon, but with arms, legs, a face, and Jack Sheldon's robust and soulful voice—starts out bored and neglected on the steps of the US Capitol ("Well, it's a long, long journey to the capital city, and it's a long, long wait, while I'm sitting in committee"). He finally makes it through all the steps of the legislative process, and the pin on his red sash magically becomes a wax seal with the word LAW stamped into it. Every-one celebrates! The tune was very catchy, and I knew the song by heart, but none of it meant that much to me until I understood what was in those bills. The Civil Rights Act, the Social Security Act, the Voting Rights Act . . . I eventually got the message. This is how change happens. This is how we fulfill the flawed but hopeful promise of America: we make it better over time, adjusting our laws to align more fully with our values and adapt to an ever-changing world. It's not a linear process, and laws can do things you think are good or things you think are bad. But ultimately, I believed, passing legislation and adopting new policy is how we improve our country.

It was the mid-1970s when I was watching that bill on Capitol Hill on our fuzzy black-and-white TV set with a giant antenna. Forty-five years later, thanks to a massive digital revolution, we can watch pretty much any video we want any time we want on a phone or tablet; "I'm Just a Bill" has over a million views on YouTube.[10] And as that revolution gave rise to social media (and in part because of it), Americans have become more divided than ever about which policies we should enact, about which of those needy animated little bills should make it through the journey to become the law of the land.

Yet despite increasing partisan gridlock, plenty of those bills *have* made their way into law. The 116th US Congress, which met during the last two years of Donald Trump's presidency— when Democrats held the House and Republicans held the Senate—enacted 344 pieces of legislation (1,229, if you count those enacted by incorporation into other bills), including the largest economic stimulus package in US history. Add to that the legislative output of fifty states and over thirty-five thousand local governments, plus propositions and other measures that in twenty-four states can become law through the collection of signatures and passage at the ballot box. Add to that executive orders and their state and local government equivalents, plus countless policies, regulations, and rules enacted by administrative agencies and other bodies under the authority of Congress in accordance with existing law. Even when Congress is supposedly incapable of anything, there's quite a lot of lawmaking going on.

Each of these documents is transformed the moment it is enacted, becoming more than just words on a page: backed by the weight of our representative democracy, it now compels action. When the words of a bill become law, they are suddenly magic, or so I believed. But the *Schoolhouse Rock!* video ended when a bill was passed. What was supposed to happen next was not clear to my preschool brain, but I now understand that some-where, someone (actually, lots of someones) must figure out how to implement and enforce it. Once regular words become magic words, someone has to write *more* words about how this new rule will work, and someone else has to make or amend forms that people can use to interact with the new rule. These forms become records, which have their own magic. It says here that you are married. It says here that you are eligible for health care. It says here that you must go to jail.

In the past, this all happened on paper. Stacks of paper with words and numbers and official seals got you things, like money or food stamps or even freedom. Now, though, those records are rarely magic without a digital element. Today, if someone tells you, "It says here you are a felon," it's usually a screen they're looking at. Conversely, if the law changes and the act that made you a felon is no longer a crime, nothing is really different for you until the database is updated. The magic of law is now inextrica-bly tied to the bits and bytes of computer code.

Of course, the government is not alone in maintaining data-bases. Every one of us is a record in thousands of them, mostly kept by private companies. Every time you make a purchase with your credit card, click on a link in an email, or glance at a photo on Instagram, part of your record updates in some database some-where. It happens dozens of times a day to most of us, whether we're working, shopping, managing our finances, engaging in

causes we care about, or just texting our friends. Sometimes these
updates help us, like when we pay a credit card bill on time and
our credit score ticks up a notch. Sometimes they can hurt us, as
when companies use all this data to engage in discrimination or
to target us with ever more insidiously effective ads. But whether
for good or for ill, the essence of the digital revolution is that
it has become easier to implement ideas of all kinds—business,
cultural, and social.

Inside government, however, the digital revolution has played
out very differently. Even as our expectations about the immediacy
and accuracy of services have skyrocketed, the implementation of
laws has become anything but easier. The famous slowness of
bureaucracy is a key reason, but all too frequently, what now
widens the gap between policy intentions and actual outcomes
is the messy task of implementation through digital technology,
and the ways government makes working with that technology uniquely complex. It has gotten so difficult to deliver on
the promise of legislation that the magic words are losing their
magic. Today, when the *Schoolhouse Rock!* characters cheer our
little bill's becoming law, they are celebrating prematurely.

■ ■ ■

THERE IS PLENTY of blame to go around when policies fail. Intentional sabotage by opponents of a policy does happen, and there
is a rich history of interest groups lobbying for administrative burdens that purposely make government services harder
to use.[11] But no enemy of California's record expungement
designed the process to keep former felons from relief; no enemy
of Medicare doctors was trying to drive them insane with confusing data systems; no enemy of the American economy sought
to keep stimulus money from reaching millions of households.
If anything, all those failures stemmed from a *lack* of design.
And all resulted in outcomes that no one wants—not the left,

not the right, and not the average American who identifies with neither. The reality of occasional sabotage should not blind us to our self-inflicted wounds.

To be sure, there have also been reasons for celebration. My White House colleagues worked closely with hundreds of dedi- cated public servants at the Centers for Medicare and Medicaid Services and eventually got the healthcare.gov website to work. For my part, I left DC having laid the foundation for a new unit within the White House called the United States Digital Service (USDS), which helps federal agencies make better use of tech- nology. When I returned to Code for America, one of the goals we set was to bring the magic words of decriminalization laws to life through a project called Clear My Record. By helping dozens of state and local governments translate legislation into changes in databases, it has helped millions of people shed the burden of their outdated convictions. Code for America and its partners have also made it easier for people in need to access our nation's social safety net, to send their children to school, and to receive much-needed tax credits. With and without our help, many pub- lic servants across the country are finding ways to close the gap between policy intentions and real-world outcomes.

But our progress is hampered by a poor understanding of the problem. Seeing the effects of this gap, public- and private- sector leaders, advocates, and pundits have come up with a host of solutions. "Government needs to spend more on technology," they say. Or "government technology needs to be modernized." Or "government should leave technology and service delivery to private-sector vendors." Or "government technology should be subject to stricter oversight." But the reality of how and why gov- ernment is failing to deliver on policy promises in the digital age is much more nuanced than these quick fixes suggest. Over the past twelve years, I've seen how more money, more technology, more outsourcing, and more oversight have played out, failing again and again. A deeper understanding of the dynamics is needed.

One reason these common prescriptions sound attractive is that they are partially right. More money can be useful, of course, and is often necessary—but having big budgets from the start can be deadly, since they often require an entire megaproject to be planned up front, reducing the ability of the team to learn as it goes. More modern technology can be handy—but successive layers of policy, regulation, procedure, and process that have accrued over decades encumber our digital services and make even the most modern technologies opaque and hard to use. More outsourcing can help with some aspects of service delivery, and contractors are a valuable piece of the implementation puzzle—but government can work well with these critical players only when it can bring its own basic digital competency to bear as well.

As for the call for more oversight, it is right only in the most abstract sense. Of course neutral third parties should serve as a check on any project paid for with taxpayer dollars. But it's already common for government technology teams to report to six, seven, eight, or even more separate oversight bodies, and that's *before* they get flagged for an investigation by an agency inspector general, audited by the Government Accountability Office, or called before a congressional committee (or the state or local equivalent of any of these). There are obvious harms from this excess: it worsens an already debilitating risk aversion, and when these bodies issue conflicting guidance it creates confusion and derails progress. But the bigger problem is that all that oversight hijacks the time and attention of the teams supposedly delivering the product or service. When all your time is spent answering questions and writing reports for other people inside government, it's mighty hard to be focused on the people outside government you're supposed to serve.

Spending more on blockbuster projects, pursuing the latest technologies, outsourcing more aggressively, and ramping up oversight doesn't help. But it's worse than that. These supposed solutions hurt, making it even harder to deliver on policy promises. The fundamental causes of government's ineffectiveness are not mechanistic: there is no one glitch in an otherwise functional machine that, when removed, will let it operate as intended. There is not even really a machine at all. These dysfunctions derive from core issues that are human rather than technological, complex rather than just complicated.

Chief among them is a structure and way of thinking deeply rooted in American culture: hierarchy. In today's world, making our laws and policies into reality will almost always involve some sort of digital technology, but what's valued in government isn't the nuts and bolts of implementation but the rarefied work of policymaking. Digital work, which in our larger society commands so much attention (whether it's lionized or vilified), in government is reduced to an afterthought. It's not what important people do, and important people don't do it. They hand it off to people many rungs down the ladder, or to companies hired to do it for them. At times it almost seems that status in government is dependent on how distant one can be from the implementation of policy.

There is a debilitating distance, too, between the people creating government systems and the people who use them. The digital revolution has disintermediated many sectors of our economy and society; you can now buy tickets from an airline instead of going through a travel agent, for instance, or get in touch directly with artists selling their wares on Etsy. But in government, countless bureaucratic processes and procedures—most notably, lengthy and burdensome procurement requirements—have had the opposite effect, putting ever more layers between the people creating the services and those who use them.

These levels of remove are deeply problematic. Policy is often ambiguous—either a statement of intentions without clear instructions on how to go about achieving those aims or a set of overly specific directives that can be fulfilled without achieving the real policy goals. The temporal, organizational, structural, and cultural gaps between policy and tech teams, and between tech teams and the users of that tech, make it hard to try out strategies, learn what works, resolve ambiguities, and readjust. Instead of active collaboration and co-learning, implementing government policy through digital technology resembles a game of telephone, in which each party in sequence fumbles the translation a bit until, many stakeholders later, the message is mangled beyond recognition.

The comedy of telephone is that messages go only one way. That is also the tragedy of much failed government service delivery. Because digital is seen as a mere implementation detail, separate from the important work of creating policy, it is assumed that digital teams should simply follow orders from above and not exercise their own judgment. The people implementing policy may (or may not) try to engage in problem solving, but they are constrained by the directives they received, which frequently make no sense for the on-the-ground conditions of implementation.

Formally, the tech implementers are not charged with building services that meet users' needs or achieve policy goals. Their job is simply to meet a predetermined list of requirements. These are often exceedingly specific, but nowhere in government documents will you find a requirement that the service actually works for the people who are supposed to use it. The systems are designed instead to meet the needs of the bureaucracies that create them—they are risk-mitigation strategies for dozens of internal stakeholders. And they often fail even at that task; trying to be all things to all people, they're unable to make any reasonable tradeoffs for the sake of usability.

· · ·

THE NEED TO understand the deeper causes of this dysfunction is increasingly urgent. In 2008, the National Academy of Public Administration surveyed its senior fellows—people who have spent their entire careers as policymakers in federal government and achieved great honors—and found that only 16 percent of them consider government proficient at designing policies that can actually be implemented.[12] In the years since then, the situation has for the most part only gotten bleaker. It's no coincidence that the trust Americans have in their government is now fraying and breaking. And the implications of that broken trust go beyond the harms of failed service delivery.

Everyone who cares about American democracy should care about this crisis. Joe Soss, a professor of political science at the University of Minnesota, found in the 1990s that participating in means-tested programs—benefits that you must prove that you are poor enough to qualify for—significantly reduces the chance you will vote.[13] Applying for those programs can be a lot like applying for record expungement: hard to start, confusing, often insulting, and impossible to succeed at for many people. "Because clients interpret their experiences with welfare bureaucracies as evidence of how government works more generally, beliefs about the welfare agency and client involvement become the basis for broader political orientations," Soss explains. People's experiences with the bureaucracies of the criminal legal system, the child welfare system, or the immigration system offer much the same evidence. Even the process of getting a construction permit, registering a vehicle, or just filing taxes can erode faith in our system of government. We can't afford this downward spiral of poor service leading to alienation and decreased political participation, which in turn lead to poorer service. The implementation crisis threatens our democracy.

Elites understand policy. They are comfortable with it. They may also be comfortable with politics, which is often described as "how the policy gets done." The rest of us know about delivery. Delivery is how the intent of the policy gets done. It is what we, the public, experience when a policy is implemented. We know about it because it's the fabric of our daily lives. We don't so much think about it as we feel it. We are living it when we pick up our mail, pay our taxes, go to court, send our children to school, or pay a parking ticket—even when we drive on public roads. We take it for granted, to our detriment. But when it disappoints or, worse, frightens or insults us, it shapes who we are as citizens. Our government's failures to deliver create the conditions for a less effective government.

Reversing this vicious cycle starts with understanding how we got into this mess—why we have so little capacity to deliver within government relative to our ambitions. We have to examine and challenge the underlying structures, assumptions, and values that drive the larger system of government in which the bureaucracy of implementation operates. We must recognize the limits of simply ordering change from the top rather than enabling change from all directions. Instead of seeking quick fixes, we must accept that increasing government's capacity to function in a digital world will be long, hard work.

It will be long and hard in part because our government was built for earlier eras in our history, and we can't make it purpose-fit for today's world by merely changing the tools that bureaucrats use to do their jobs. As Clay Shirky, who writes about technology and society, puts it, "A revolution doesn't happen when society adopts new technologies—it happens when society adopts new behaviors."[14] The same is true of government. Although government must adapt to an increasingly digital world, the heart of the adaptation isn't mobile apps, cloud computing, or even artificial intelligence. It is a willingness to put the needs of government's many users ahead of the needs of the bureaucracy, and to learn while doing. The good news is that software and our government have something very important in common: they are made by and for people. In the end, we get to decide how they work.

PART 1

The Waterfall

1

ARCHAEOLOGY

Over the past decade, I have seen technology services fail at all levels of government. Sometimes it happens loudly and spectacularly, as when healthcare.gov crashed on launch; sometimes it's quietly and persistently, in ways that few seem to notice, as when benefits for the poor are routinely so hard to access that people in need simply go without. The circumstances of these failures differ by jurisdiction, by geography, and by policy domain, but the forces behind them are remarkably consistent. And of all the tech disasters that I've witnessed and tried to help untangle, the one I've come to see as most emblematic of these forces—and the ways we consistently misunderstand them—is the story of California's unemployment insurance in the first year of the pandemic.

I had not planned to spend the pandemic poring through online support forums for benefits applicants and watching members of the California State Assembly excoriate the leadership of the state's Employment Development Department (EDD) in tense hearings. After ten years running Code for America, I had stepped down from the organization in January 2020, looking to take some time away from the problems of government and technology. Six weeks later, we were sheltering in place. I was secretly grateful for the travel restrictions, and even for the eerie quiet. I had needed a break, and as scary as COVID was, it was giving me one.

The pandemic was less kind to others, to say the least, and not just those who died or whose health suffered. Millions of people were suddenly out of work and in desperate need of support. For many, their first recourse was filing for unemployment insurance. Unfortunately, it turned out to be *too* many. Confronted with what was in many states a tenfold increase in claims, the systems that administered unemployment crumpled under the weight.[1] My home state of California was no exception. By July 2020, the state's unemployment insurance had paid out about $50 billion since the lockdowns began, and about 4.4 million Californians were receiving benefits.[2] But hundreds of thousands of others who needed help were not. Many had gotten confusing letters in the mail indicating that EDD had received their application but something was wrong with it; others had heard nothing at all. Applicants were calling the EDD in record numbers, but only a tiny fraction of the calls were even being answered (I would later learn it was about one in a thousand) and when calls did get picked up it was by newly hired staffers who had no training or access to EDD systems and could only encourage the callers to continue to wait.

Some of the desperate applicants, unable to reach the EDD, tried calling their state representatives, and soon the offices of every member of the legislature were swamped. Each office has staffers dedicated to "constituent response," who are used to hearing from the public about problems with various government agencies and figuring out how to resolve the issues. But now, so many people were calling about unemployment that other staffers, whether they normally did legislative analysis or scheduling or anything else, were roped into answering the calls too. Even then, the offices couldn't keep up. Moreover, very quickly they found they couldn't help much, either. The EDD had limited each office to escalating just a few cases a week. For everyone else, all that the staffers could do was ask these people with no income and dwindling savings to be patient. The legislators were furious.

As the media increasingly profiled the plight of unemployment claimants, Governor Gavin Newsom announced a task force[3] to help the EDD, chaired by the most valuable member of his cabinet, Yolanda Richardson, his secretary for government operations. Richardson had led the state's pandemic response efforts, helping state agencies transition to remote work and securing supplies of personal protective equipment and COVID testing materials. Shortly after the task force wrapped up, Newsom would put her in charge of California's vaccine rollout. She was a skilled and accomplished operator. But the task force also wanted a co-chair from outside government, someone with technology experience, and mine was the name they chose. I was relishing my downtime, but watching the crisis from afar was heartbreaking, and I reluctantly accepted.

At my suggestion, the task force hired a former White House colleague of mine, Marina Nitze, to lead the on-the-ground analysis. Marina's government experience included helping clear one of the worst backlogs at the Department of Veterans Affairs; she had been appointed the chief technology officer of the VA when she was just twenty-eight years old. Working with Marina would be three software engineers who had all once been part of the team that keeps Google up and running, then had come to DC to help get healthcare.gov back on track.[4] The problems at the EDD were big, but Google serves hundreds of millions of people every hour with astonishing reliability and speed. Privately, some California officials told me they thought the EDD staff was just incompetent at technology and our team would find the problems easy to fix.

I understood why they thought that. Today, most people have enough experience with technology to have a mental model for how computers work. They understand that at their bank or on their food delivery app, they have an account that they can log in to, where they can do things like download a statement or order takeout. Companies routinely analyze data across millions of accounts to decide things like who should be offered a credit card or who should be shown an ad for a new movie. The EDD, it seemed, also got the information it needed from claimants when they created their accounts. Everyone seemed to believe that it was simply a matter of finding a faster way to process that information and give benefits to the right people.

But none of us on the task force thought this would be easy—not Marina, not her colleagues, and certainly not me. Privately, we wondered if we could help at all. Nothing we had seen in the government systems we'd worked on conformed to the model others seemed to assume. Some former colleagues had advised us not to get involved, worried that the administration was just looking for others to fail in order to spread the blame. The fact that our task force was being convened for just a few weeks spoke to the absurdity of the premise: the problems the EDD was experiencing were decades in the making, and they would not be solved so quickly. Still, we would try to do our best. Marina loaded her laser printer into her car (because reading detailed reports is still easier on paper than on-screen) and drove from her home in Seattle to the EDD's offices in Northern California. The team got to work.

...

WE KNEW THE first thing we needed to do was to define and count the EDD's backlog of unemployment claims. The department had publicly said that 239,000 claims were backlogged, but state legislators were convinced it was much higher based on what they were hearing from their constituents. They also angrily noted inconsistencies in how the department was reporting on the number of pending claims each period. Without a clear and consistent definition, each report was comparing apples to oranges, and we would never know how fast the backlog was shrinking—or growing, as the case turned out to be.

Counting is something computers are supposed to excel at. If tickets for a concert are sold through an online service, for instance, it's elementary for the program to spit out the total count. Similarly, if all the unemployment applications that come in are put into a computer system, then somewhere there is clearly a record of all the applications that have come in but haven't been processed, and that is obviously the number we were looking for. How hard could it be?

Many of us have at some point run a report that didn't account for all the right factors and gotten an inaccurate number. If I'm looking for total attendance at the concert, for instance, it's not enough to know how many tickets were sold online. I also need to include any tickets that were sold at the door, exclude people who bought a ticket but didn't show up, and so forth. And most of us understand that the systems at a place like the EDD are often archaic and less easy to use than the typical software we've been exposed to.

What most people don't appreciate, though, is just how difficult it can be to make computers do something as simple as counting the number of applications when there isn't one system in question but many and those systems have accrued in layers over the decades. Tony Scott, a former US chief information officer, uses the metaphor of layers of paint. Because each successive leadership at an agency usually gets the budget or the mandate to deal only with the most pressing technology crises at hand, and because tech investments must always be pitched as adding some new capability to the system (rarely just renovating what already exists), each piece of the system gets built in different technology paradigms from different eras. But every new piece depends on everything that came before, so each successive layer is constrained by the limitations of the earlier technologies. The system is not so much updated as it is tacked on to. Over time, new functionality is added, but the system never sheds the core limitations of the foundational technologies. At the same time, it becomes enormously complex and fragile. Updates require caution, as any change in one layer can have unforeseen consequences in the others. It becomes harder and harder to support the technologies in the lower, older layers, while the more recent layers require constant updates and patches. The paint cracks.

Along with Marina, several of us had spent time at the US Department of Veterans Affairs, where the technology layers date back to the sixties and even earlier. The architecture diagram for just one benefit system at the VA was so complex that it was displayed on a wall twenty feet long and eight feet tall. Even at that size, many of the elements were printed in a font so small you had to be right up next to the wall to read them. When I first saw it, I found myself paralyzed. Moments like that served to remind me that when people talk about government technology and ask "how hard could it be?" the answer is almost always: really, really hard. We think that the technology that runs our government has been designed to perform specific functions. In fact, it has merely accreted.

There were decades' worth of layers at the EDD, too, and they had started cracking even before the stresses of the pandemic. As we dug into them, we started to think of the hodgepodge of technology not only as layers of paint but as the layers of sediment you might excavate in an archaeological dig. And while you don't need to be a programmer to understand the EDD's problems, it's worth examining these layers to appreciate just how greatly government technology differs from what legislators and the public imagine it to be.

The oldest layer of technology at the EDD is something called the Single Client Database, running on an IBM mainframe.[5] Its exact origins are murky. Some of this layer is written in COBOL, a programming language invented in 1959, but the EDD probably began using the system in the 1980s. The Single Client Database was designed for green-screen terminals, the monochrome displays with green text on a black background that you may remember from movies like *WarGames*. Today, it's mostly operated with green-screen emulators, which reproduce the same display on the kinds of PC you can pick up at your local Office Depot, since those are a lot cheaper and easier to find than vintage hardware.

In the 1990s, resourceful claims processors at the EDD took advantage of those Windows desktop PCs running the green-screen emulators. They started writing scripts to automate some of the most repetitive routines they had to do every day. These scripts became known as *macros*, a word I learned using Word-Perfect and Lotus 1–2–3 on a PC back in the nineties. I loved building those little shortcuts: instead of typing out the inordinately long name of the organization where I worked, for example, I only had to hit Alt+F10, then a single key I'd chosen, and there it was. What the EDD employees were doing was more complicated than that, but the basic idea is the same. If a claims processor frequently needed to reassign a work item to a new queue, for instance, and it took twenty different small actions to accomplish that on the green-screen interface, a macro would let them do it with just a few keystrokes. Outside of writing new COBOL code, macros are the only way that the EDD can automate significant new workloads in this layer. Since there are fewer and fewer

COBOL programmers around (and they are consequently more and more expensive to hire, if you can even get them), the EDD's own staff wrote a lot of these macros, to the delight of their fellow overworked claims processors, who appreciated any shortcut.

Eventually, a few of the macro writers learned new computer languages like Visual Basic, C#, and the .Net programming environment, which gave them the ability to automate more complex tasks and run larger batches. Today, the green-screen emulator used by an EDD claims processor has several rows of brightly colored buttons that provide access to dozens of these macros. Without them, claims processing would take even more time than it does right now. But the addition of these many macros also means that to maintain and update the EDD system, you need people who know not only Visual Basic and C# and so on but also how all these particular macros operate. The only place someone can learn that is by working at the EDD. And given how chaotically this layer of technology developed over several decades—with new macros written every time the department needed to implement a new workflow or respond to some change in the rules or regulations—it can take many years on the job to get up to speed.

The next layer, by contrast, is only a residue. Around 2002, the EDD entered the internet era by making its paper application form for unemployment benefits available online through something called eApply4UI. This went away in the 2010s, though a Google search for eApply4UI still returns a few thousand results, including a lot of downtime notices. Assorted websites from legal aid groups, workforce agencies, and others still erroneously point to it. Since it is no longer used to accept applications, it wasn't relevant to our challenge of tallying up the backlog, but its transitory existence means that the EDD essentially lost a decade of progress when it abandoned eApply4UI as a failed experiment.

During the next decade the department tried to catch up. Seeking to "modernize," it added three major new systems, largely through contracting with the consulting firm Deloitte. The first of them, California Unemployment Benefits System (CUBS), provides another way of accessing the Single Client Database, the one that runs on the IBM mainframe from the 1980s. CUBS allows claims processors to do many of the same maintenance tasks that were done through macros or directly on the mainframe in a web browser window instead. The second system, Benefit Claim Information System (BCIS), has a very similar web interface, but it was contracted for separately and uses its own database. It was developed to manage "recomps," or recomputations of benefits, which aren't quite what they sound like: claims usually wind up in there because they got flagged for manual identity verification when they first came in and therefore never made it through to the system that would compute a benefit in the first place. The third system from this decade is UIOnline, a public-facing website that replaced eApply4UI and is now what most people use to apply for benefits. It has a lot in common with CUBS, but a claim filed through UIOnline won't wind up in CUBS if it needs to go to recomps for any reason.

With this grab bag of somewhat connected, somewhat separate systems in mind, let's return to our challenge of counting backlogged applications. Since CUBS and BCIS have separate data stores, a single applicant might have a record in both. Each of the two systems also has its own numerous "work queues" that list the tasks, or "work items," requiring human action to process an application. (CUBS alone has 153 different work queues.) Specific groups of workers at the EDD are granted the ability to handle specific kinds of work items, based on their levels of training. But because the work queues and types of tasks are not the same in the two applications, understanding how CUBS works doesn't necessarily help you master BCIS, and the definition of a back-logged application will be different in CUBS than it is in BCIS.

In addition, one of the effects of having IT systems built in archaeological layers is that workers can often perform the same action via different layers, meaning that there are multiple ways to accomplish a given task. Over the years, as different teams take different approaches, knowledge and habits become frag-mented. If one team encounters a problem and uses some par-ticular piece of the system—the browser-based CUBS, or the macros on the green-screen emulator, or direct access to the mainframe—to work around it, another team may not know how to run a report that accounts for that work-around and will inadvertently include the wrong records and exclude the right ones in its accounting.

And going through the work items was far from intuitive. While we were trying to determine the right way to count back-logged claims, for example, we came across a work item called "Stop Payment Alert—Claim Review." There were 730,023 open items of that type. It seemed alarming, but EDD staffers explained that this work item is merely an automatic system-generated notice and could be ignored—in fact, most of those claims were probably fine to pay. But there was a different alert called "Stop Payment Alert" (without the "Claim Review") that *did* mean what it sounded like and required attention. But nobody had cleaned up the automated system notices, so these work items cluttered the queues and threw off the reporting when staff didn't exclude them. We saw dozens of idiosyncrasies like this one.

In order to count how many backlogged unemployment applications there were, then, we would need to look not just at one system but separately at quite a few. We would need to make a count in each one individually and then figure out how they overlapped in order to deduplicate the combined list. We would need very specialized knowledge of the meaning of hundreds of work queues to even start discussing how to *define* a backlogged application, never mind running the queries that would pull every record that met that definition from multiple incompatible databases.

The number of people with such specialized knowledge is very limited. In the midst of a pandemic that has forced millions out of work, spurring Congress to overhaul existing unemployment programs and add entirely new ones, all of which need to be programmed into these fragile and complex systems, the demands on these employees' time are enormous. There is no easy way to suddenly have more of these people. And there is no easy way to explain to angry constituents and the people who represent them—whose personal experience with seamless online services gives them certain expectations about how technology should work—why this task is so hard.

■ ■ ■

THE CRISIS IN unemployment insurance during the pandemic led to lots of questions about why these systems hadn't been modernized in recent decades. Agency directors around the country blamed governors and state legislatures for not funding modernization. Legislators blamed their predecessors for inaction, vendors for their high price tags, and the agency directors for not putting forward credible modernization plans before the crisis hit. In fact, when Marina and I started our work, California's EDD was theoretically just weeks away from awarding a modernization contract that it had been working on for ten years. With the EDD in the spotlight, the legislature paid particular attention to this pending contract and noted, with horror, that the modernization effort was projected to take another eleven years.

The legislators were understandably upset, but it's odd that they seemed surprised. Their state had spent ten years and over

$500 million on a system to connect the courts with a common document management system—and then scrapped the entire effort.[6] It is also working on a modernization of its financial information systems that started in 2009 and has grown in cost to over $1 billion.[7] As of 2022, it remains unfinished. The EDD's IT modernization timeline was not exactly an outlier.

It wouldn't be an outlier in federal government either. The State Department's Bureau of Consular Affairs has been trying since 2009 to modernize and consolidate the systems that handle visa issuance, passport renewal, recording births abroad, and other services. It first projected a 2016 launch date, then announced a two-year delay. In 2019, it began a limited pilot of one component of the new system at six locations, out of hundreds of its embassies and consulates around the world. As of late 2021, the bureau still had not expanded that pilot and the other components still had not launched. The program's cost, originally estimated at $18 million, is now at least an order of magnitude higher. A report by the Office of Inspector General notes that it "was unable to determine the total cost of the ConsularOne modernization program with any precision. OIG's best estimate is that, as of mid-June 2021, the cost for ConsularOne ranged between $200 million . . . and $600 million."[8]

The ever-slipping timelines are pretty standard. In 2000, the IRS announced a plan to replace one of its core systems, called the Individual Master File (IMF), by 2006. But by 2009 that work was $37 million over budget with little to show for it. It was scrapped, and a new replacement project began, expected to be up and running by early 2014. That schedule, too, was revised several times over the following years. Then in 2019, the agency's CIO stated that the project was too broad and complex and that the focus would shift to updating only some parts of the system. In 2021, the IRS gave a new date for retiring—or perhaps mostly retiring—the IMF: January 2030.[9]

Why the continual date creep? To start, the IMF is the system that holds all individual taxpayers' data—our names, addresses, tax IDs, incomes, deductions, credits, refunds, all of it. It's massive, and hugely critical. It's been around since the 1960s, when it stored data on magnetic tape. For years, its structure was akin more to a massive spreadsheet than to a modern database. (As one overview puts it, "accounts were stored sequentially so that information for taxpayer number 100,000,001, for example, could be accessed only by skipping through the first 100,000,000 accounts.")[10] The IRS successfully shed that legacy, but much of the IMF is still written in assembly language, a finicky and labor-intensive way of programming computers specific to the hardware it runs on. You can't just hire a programmer off the street to work on the system. Not only is assembly language an increasingly rare specialty, but the IMF's particular kind of assembly language, and the complex business logic of its core processing programs, can take years to learn.[11] In the meantime, just as at California's EDD, many layers have been built on top of this code, constraining all sorts of other functions that depend on the core data store.

Contrary to popular belief, the public servants responsible for the interminably drawn-out modernization efforts are neither lazy, stupid, nor malicious. I've met hundreds of them, and they are overwhelmingly dedicated, conscientious, and often quite creative. IRS employees managed to send monthly child tax-credit payments to nearly forty million families and to mail out over $800 billion in stimulus checks during the pandemic, all while relying on systems that were never designed to change so quickly or handle such enormous volume. Like the wall-sized architecture diagram from the VA that still haunts me, the systems these public servants are trying to update are often complex beyond our ability to imagine. And then there's the complexity of all the rules these public servants need to follow to do that updating.

The California legislators aghast at the EDD's eleven-year estimate for modernization hadn't seen the archaeological layers we were about to unearth. If they had, they might have been less shocked by the timeline. And perhaps they would have had a bit more sympathy for the pickle the EDD was in at the moment.

· · ·

WHEN WE STARTED trying to get an accurate count of the back-logged unemployment applications at the EDD, we expected that it would take the better part of a week. Mikey Dickerson, one of the ex-Google software engineers on the task force, led the charge while the rest of us focused on other problems. Mikey was as qualified for this task as anyone could be: he was a top-tier engineer who knew government, and he was calm and analytical under pressure. He worked closely with EDD staff, running, tweaking, and rerunning dozens of database queries in a way that looked much more like an art than a science. He and staff worked long days and weekends. Over and over I asked if the EDD was blocking access or slow-rolling us, and over and over again Mikey said, "No, they're busting their butts. This is just hard."

The job took the entire seven weeks that the task force had been convened for. Mikey and the EDD team were refining the queries right through our very last day on the job. And the final number was not 239,000, plus whatever other applications had become backlogged during those seven weeks. It was 1.2 million.

As frightening as that number was, at least now the EDD had a replicable set of queries its team could run that measured the backlog consistently each week. They would be able to run them on their own, after Mikey was gone, and would be able to judge if any changes to the process improved or slowed their throughput. The EDD team now understood how to tell what direction they were going in, and we understood why it had been so hard for them to know in the first place.

When we speak of "legacy systems" in government, it does not mean simply that they are old. It means that we are grappling with the legacy of decades of competing interests, power struggles, creative work-arounds, and make-dos that are opportune at the time but unmanageable in the long run.

But the archaeological layers of technology are only part of the story. We are also struggling with the legacy of the systems of government that created these archaeological layers. Marina and I knew from our time at places like the VA that as fragile as the tech systems were, they would not be the EDD's biggest problem. Not by a long shot.

2

SEVENTEEN YEARS

A few days into our work as a task force, Marina Nitze arrived at one of the EDD's many offices, a nondescript building with no visible signage of any kind in an office park near Sacramento. There was not a soul in sight, but an aggressive turkey lurked by the entrance and lunged at her each time she approached. When you're given a near-impossible task like clearing a backlog of 1.2 million unemployment claims, an obstacle like an angry turkey feels like a fitting warm-up act. Marina retreated and advanced a few times until she was finally able to dash through the doors.

Inside she found someone I'll call Carl, an upper-middle manager at the EDD, and a couple of members of his team. The conditions that Marina and her colleagues had set for taking on this project had been largely about access: they could get results only if they were allowed to see how lots of different parts of the organization worked at a tactical level. The PowerPoint presentations commonly given to executives are sorely insufficient.[1] Spending time with frontline staff, watching them work, and asking questions about how and why they do what they do are critical.

One of Carl's staff members was planning for a session he had to run the next day to train a batch of new EDD hires over Zoom. Training people by videoconference is always difficult, but by that point Marina knew how complex and unintuitive the layers of the EDD systems were. The new hires would not be learning all those layers, but even the small bits they'd be introduced to in the training were hard to teach. Unlike with a browser or desktop application, which has the kind of graphical user interface most of us are used to, when you're showing someone how to use a mainframe you can't point and click your way around it to show people what you're doing. The macros are all just keyboard shortcuts, which don't show up on the screen. Marina listened intently, nodding, asking questions, and making it clear that she understood how hard the work was even under normal circumstances, let alone amid this crisis. She genuinely felt for the employees, who were stuck in a terrible situation, but she was also intentionally building rapport.

Carl watched the conversation for a while. Then, almost secretively, he told Marina that he'd been checking his inbox while he was in the meeting and he was getting literally a thousand emails an hour. Marina asked to see them. Carl had recently been assigned four hundred new hires to help with the workload, and in email after email these new employees were explaining that they'd done as instructed in their recent training: they'd taken a few work items from the queue and tried to process them. But they didn't have the permissions in the system to do so. Because they also didn't have the permissions to *return* items to the queue, they needed Carl to go into the system and reassign those work items, one by one. Thousands of them.

It soon became clear to Marina that those thousands of emails were the tip of an iceberg. As she came to learn, the work of the claims processors is astonishingly specialized. The training manual is eight hundred pages long. And even reading through it does not give you the skills you need to do the job, since much of the knowledge involves work-arounds that are passed along from employee to employee but not consistently known across teams or even written down. In another office, where she met with a group of experienced claims processors, Marina encountered an employee who kept calling himself "the new guy." Finally, she asked him how long he'd worked at the EDD. "Seventeen years," he replied. What he meant was that, compared with his colleagues with over twenty-five years of experience, he was still getting up to speed on how the system worked.

The most complicated part of the EDD's process was the area called "recomps," where claims went if they got flagged for review. California had been able to pay out $50 billion in benefits in just a few months because straightforward claims—the ones where the department didn't see the need to verify the claimant's identity, for example—were processed largely automatically, on the digital equivalent of an assembly line. But if they got pulled off that assembly line, they would eventually end up in recomps, where the most experienced claims processors essentially worked through them by hand. Once there, they could not be put back onto the assembly line. Recomps was by far the biggest bottleneck in the system—the backlog was more or less all the claims that went to recomps.

What Marina learned was that not just anyone can work in recomps. It took three years of experience, schooling, and formal testing to progress from an entry-level accounting tech to an accountant I, and an additional three years to progress to each subsequent tier at the EDD, of which there were many. That seventeen-year veteran was indeed still making his way through those tiers. There was no way to fast-track the growth of a claims processor—not legally (since specific regulations covered what employees at each of these levels could do) and not practically, because the policies, processes, and procedures to be mastered were so complex. And that was before the pandemic brought unprecedented levels of change to all the rules. Even the most experienced claims processors were struggling to get their heads around the new programs and regulations, not to mention the move to remote work. New employees didn't stand a chance of being helpful.

Yet at the direction of the governor's office, the department had been on an astonishing hiring spree, adding over five thousand new staff since the beginning of the pandemic, mostly through an ever-ballooning contract with Deloitte. The legislature had pretty much opened up the wallet to the EDD to spend whatever it needed to clear the backlog. Indeed, they were pressing the department to hire even faster. After hearings on the EDD's failures, news reports led with the hiring numbers. The governor referred to them in press conferences as proof that relief was coming.

More people equals more productivity equals fewer backlogged claims, the logic went. But what the politicians didn't know was that these brand-new employees, with their days or weeks of training by Zoom, could not do the work that would reduce the backlog. Only highly experienced claims processors could do that. In fact, new employees could do almost none of the work assigned to them.

But it was worse than that. As Marina watched Carl scroll through the emails from the four hundred new hires in his group, she wondered who was training, and responding to, the other forty-six hundred new employees around the EDD. The answer was grim: pretty much every staff member with tenure and knowledge of how the arcane and complex systems worked. They all had inboxes full of requests from new employees, representing hundreds of hours of work just to read and respond to them. It was clear that the new employees couldn't help with recomps, the part of the system that was causing the backlog; it would be years before they were either competent or authorized to do so. But if the people who *could* help with it, the old-timers, were busy training the new employees, who was processing the claims?

With that question on her mind, Marina thanked Carl for his insights and took a break to go to the bathroom. When she returned, she closed her laptop and, preparing to go to the next meeting, started to put it away. In her bag, she noticed some neatly stapled papers that hadn't been there before. She smiled at Carl, thanked him, and left.

Marina waited until she was back at her Airbnb to look at the papers. They were the Daily Production Tally (DPT) sheets for Carl's team, recording the average time spent on a variety of key tasks. Quick analysis confirmed Marina's suspicions. The productivity of Carl's group had all but ground to a halt. Later, when Marina got the DPT sheets for some of the other groups (this time by request), she calculated that in those offices it now took two to five times as long to do recomps as it had in January, before the pandemic. It was right there in black and white: every new person the EDD hired made it *slower*—not faster—to get a benefit check to an unemployed Californian.[2] The backlog was growing unbounded not because of the bespoke and antiquated technology. It was growing because the policy and processes that govern unemployment insurance take seventeen years to learn.

. . .

THE POLITICIANS WHO jeer when a government agency like the EDD says that it will need eleven years to modernize its systems do not understand the nature of the technology in question. They envision a *system*, not a bunch of tenuously connected layers that function by way of awkward work-arounds. But they also don't understand that those archaeological tech layers are an expression of archaeological policy layers. The tech gets complex because the program and the policy governing it are complex. And like the tech, the policy is complex in part because it always accrues but is rarely reduced or reconciled. Like a hoarder, government rarely throws out the old to make room for the new.

In the cartoon world of *Schoolhouse Rock!* and high school textbooks, programs like unemployment insurance are thoughtfully designed by policy architects in Washington, DC, and then cascade down to states and local communities, where we feel their impact. States, in their role as the laboratories of democracy, can administer these programs in keeping with the unique needs of their citizens, as long as they comply with a binder of federal regulations provided by the US Department of Labor. In reality, there is no binder with those regulations—there is a *wall* of binders containing steady streams of correspondence from federal and state agencies going back to the 1935 Social Security Act, a mess of rules and oversight mechanisms that reference earlier rules and oversight mechanisms that reference even earlier ones. They frequently cross federal, state, and local jurisdictions and are subject to direction and influence from the executive, legislative, and judicial branches of each of those levels of government. These rules can grow to epic proportions.

One reason the IRS has so much trouble modernizing its systems, for instance, is that there are over seventy-three thousand pages in the statutes and regulations the agency must implement.[3] Between 2001 and 2012, the tax code changed 4,680 times, an average of once per day.[4] When former IRS commissioner John Koskinen would get called in front of Congress and its members would gripe about the tax system, he would shake his head and say, "I didn't write the tax laws, you did."[5] He had a point.

The law governing unemployment insurance regulations isn't quite as voluminous, and at the federal level it's fairly simple. But that doesn't mean that agencies that administer the benefit have any easier a task than the IRS. To start, though the statutes are minimal, the regulations that have been written to guide their implementation are not. One state labor commissioner testifying in a hearing, as tense as the ones I watched in California, brought a cardboard box holding over seven thousand pages of federal regulations and parked it conspicuously on the table next to his microphone. He implored angry state legislators to understand that they were "working their butts off" but it was all "just putting duct tape and Band-Aids on outdated federal policy." Fifteen hundred of those pages had been added just since COVID hit. "The problems lie in federal policies," he proclaimed, "not legacy computer systems."[6]

Part of the money for unemployment insurance comes from federal payroll taxes, and no state can afford to forgo this funding. So the federal Department of Labor (DOL), which writes those rules and regulations that state unemployment programs need to meet in order to receive the funds, has de facto control over some aspects of the program. But unemployment insurance is fundamentally run by the states. Each of the fifty states plus DC, Puerto Rico, and the US Virgin Islands passes its own laws and regulations governing eligibility, oversight, benefit amounts, adjudication in the event of conflict, and dozens of other elements. That means that each state program is unique in both its policy and its operations, and is controlled by a mixture of federal regulations (which are somehow supposed to apply equally to all fifty-three different programs), state law set by the individual legislatures, and policy set by the individual state departments of labor (which often interpret guidance from the federal DOL in different ways). They are accountable to the federal DOL, whose staff is trying to interpret and apply direction from Congress, but they also report to governors, get written up by state legislative analysts, and are publicly admonished by state legislators. If a state labor agency runs afoul of federal regulations, it risks losing federal funding, which would devastate its state's finances, but the direction from the feds doesn't always harmonize with state leaders' goals and desires. It can be hard to make everyone happy.

Federalism also makes the job of the DOL, which has to regulate each state labor agency to ensure compliance with federal law, exceptionally difficult. And when crisis hits, Congress looks to the DOL to help all fifty-three systems deliver the necessary relief and economic stimulus. It's a bit like trying to wrangle fifty-three IRSes.

For example, consider the most basic issue of coverage: whether a given worker is eligible to claim unemployment benefits. According to the DOL, to answer that question you must figure out, among other things, whether the worker's "employing unit" qualifies as an "employer." Under the Federal Unemployment Tax Act, that term originally applied to "employing units" that, "during any calendar quarter in the current or immediately preceding calendar year, paid wages of $1,500 or more" and to "employing units of eight or more workers on at least one day in each of 20 different weeks in a calendar year."[7] In 1956, that threshold was changed to four or more workers; in 1972, it dropped to just one worker. Today, about half the states use this federal definition, but the others strike out on their own. In Montana, the minimum payroll to qualify as an employer is $1,000 in the current or preceding year; in New York, it's $300 in a single quarter; in Iowa, any wages at all paid in the current or preceding quarter will qualify. In Massachusetts, thirteen weeks of payroll is enough to be an employer; in Arkansas, it's having a single employee for ten or more days.

The unemployment department in any given state would have had to update its systems as the federal definition changed, as their own state definition changed, or as their labor agency switched back and forth between the federal and state definitions. Few updates succeed in catching all past references to the former rule, so you will find artifacts of previous regulations strewn throughout documentation and code. That's probably how the EDD came to have work items for "Stop Payment Alert" and for "Stop Payment Alert—Claim Review" that mean two totally different things. Perhaps some law changed and program-mers coded a new work item to fit the new rules, but the original one persisted, most likely because it was still attached to active claims. Everything accumulates.

...

THE BUREAUCRATIC CONFUSION ultimately lands on the people try-ing to get the benefits they're entitled to. For example, one tenet of unemployment insurance is that it is for people who are "able and available for work." This means that you might apply for and begin receiving benefits, but if you happen to get sick enough that you wouldn't have been able to work if a job had been offered, even for one day, then on that day you are technically not "able and available." In California, your benefits are supposed to be reduced by one-seventh for each day of a week you cannot work due to an illness or injury.[8] (That's just one rule among many hundreds; you start to see why the request for proposals for a new system to run the EDD detailed some thirty-six hundred unique requirements.) Given that there are other programs that cover people who are too sick to work, such as disability insurance, it makes some sense that lawmakers might not want people claiming both benefits. But the policy, especially the granularity of docking by the day, feels miserly, and the administrative burden imposed on both the claimant and the bureaucracy is out of proportion to any savings.

Now put this rule into the context of a global pandemic. Not only did a lot of sick people need some sort of financial sup-port but there was a very common and legitimate reason why people might refuse work: their workplace did not protect them from COVID. Regulators saw this as a reasonable concern: some people on unemployment were particularly vulnerable if they were to get infected, and some employers were not taking many precautions in the workplace. Federal regulators temporarily changed the rules, allowing benefits to continue even if claimants had not continued to look for work. Eventually, they made those who had refused unsafe work eligible for a new program called Pandemic Unemployment Assistance.[9]

But the EDD's systems were hardwired to ask all unemployment claimants two questions on a biweekly basis: "Were you too sick or injured to work?" and "Was there any reason (other than sickness or injury) that you could not have accepted full-time work each workday?" Before the pandemic, if you said "yes" your claim was temporarily suspended pending a phone interview and eligibility review. During the pandemic, with the department accruing a backlog of 1.2 million claims, there were obviously no resources for these phone calls and claim reviews, so saying "yes" effectively meant you were cut off from your benefits. Yet instead of recoding the system to allow for a "yes" answer, the EDD just issued press releases and posted FAQs in which they essentially implied that claimants should lie. "The EDD has found many claimants are having issues answering the first two questions on the required bi-weekly certification," one such announcement said. "The usual requirement to look for work each week is temporarily suspended during the conditions associated with this pandemic. . . . Answering YES to these questions could disqualify you for benefits for that week." In other words, you could refuse unsafe work, as long as you didn't admit that you did. There was a new policy layer, but the old one was showing beneath.

The EDD team gave us several reasons for this inelegant hack. One was obvious: it was hard to update the system for all the same reasons it had been hard to count the backlog. Fixing these questions would take resources away from other urgent problems. And changing the system in the middle of such a maelstrom would require the department to keep track of who had answered the questions under the old scheme, and who under the new scheme, and which weeks were which, and how these mapped onto the shifting federal policies.

There was another difficulty: regulations regarding equity. In theory, the EDD could have updated the wording of the certification questions on its website to bring them more in line with the new federal guidance. But updating the paper version of the certification form was another matter. The EDD could issue a new form, but the old one was around at all sorts of advocacy and support agencies, some of whom would likely miss the changeover. It was also all over the web as a PDF. And there are a variety of policies at both the state and federal levels that dictate that the applicant experience should be the same across different groups and channels. If online claimants got a different question from paper claimants, it could violate these equity policies.

Of course, an online experience is by definition different from a paper application. A paper application is always going to involve either an in-person visit or an envelope and a stamp, for instance; an online application will just have a "submit" button. More importantly, web forms can make things easier for users in ways that paper can't, like hiding questions that are unnecessary for a particular user based on the answers they have already given. (If you don't have dependents, for instance, you don't need to see or answer questions about dependents.) But equity policies are often interpreted to mean that the questions asked across the different channels must be exactly the same, which is why you see government websites that clearly could leverage such branching logic but don't do so. The authors of these policies presumably didn't intend to make the user experience worse for most applicants. But when policies like this—often written at the state level to cover every service the state provides—land without context at places like the EDD, and accumulate alongside dozens of other poorly targeted policies, they end up slowing progress and making it harder to serve the public. They become clutter.

Public servants must frequently decide which of several incompatible regulations is more important to comply with. The conflict might be between federal, state, and local regulations or between older policies and new ones that overlap with them without clearly removing the previous rules. In either case, the answer is not likely to be determined by what's best for the people using the service. Rather, it's usually a combination of whatever seems most convenient (such as not updating an already fragile system at a time of crisis) and whatever seems like it will result in fewest lawsuits (advocates frequently sue government agencies over equity issues). In the case of the EDD's biweekly certification, the result was that in addition to the hundreds of thousands of people whose initial claims were sitting unanswered, there were also hundreds of thousands more who'd been found eligible but then been needlessly kicked off.

Even in the midst of the pandemic, I got to see yet more policy clutter build up. With the EDD in the media spotlight, a member of the California State Assembly introduced legislation requiring the department to make its application process and any follow-up communications available in over a dozen languages. Most of the languages were already required by a 1973 state law as well as multiple federal laws and regulations—one guidance memo on this issue from the federal DOL references eight relevant federal laws, one presidential executive order, and five federal regulations from such agencies as the Department of Justice and the Occupational Health and Safety Administration, in addition to the unemployment division's own regulations.[10] The EDD had been out of compliance for many years, which meant that getting the department to better accommodate these non-English speakers wasn't really a matter of law but of implementation. Nonetheless, the assembly member insisted on including it in his legislative agenda, piling on new requirements that largely but not entirely overlapped with existing ones.

Our task force recommended helping non-English-speaking clients in a different way, which removed a requirement instead of adding one. The EDD had long ago procured a phone-based translation service, but staffers had to jump through bureaucratic hoops to get permission to use it. Remove that need for permission, and EDD representatives could help far more claimants by using a translator. Indeed, given how confusing the application process was, having non-English-speaking applicants talk to someone on the phone, even through a translator, might have been better than making them wade through the application on their own, especially with the gotcha questions like the ones about being "able and available." But the people who would need to oversee the creation of systems to process claims in over a dozen languages were the same people who were urgently needed to clear the backlog. (In some cases, they were the same people who were burdened with requesting approvals to use the translation service—approvals that were, in our view, unnecessary.)

All of us on the task force believed that language access was critical but also that getting claims processed—and paid out—was the whole point of access. Why specify a particular way to help non-English speakers that also reduces the chances that their claims, once filed, will result in benefits? Why pile new policies onto a department that's shown little ability to implement the current ones? Why pass a law that will leave future EDD staffers even more beleaguered, trying to figure out how to comply with multiple overlapping policies on language access coming from various sources? And why force a rushed translation of obscure, unclear terminology? It was hard enough to understand what the EDD's forms and letters meant in English, which made them difficult to translate clearly into other languages. If you really wanted non-English speakers to be able to use the service in their native language, you'd give the department time to conduct a plain-language review in English first. You could help even more by simplifying the regulations, reducing the number of questions that have to be asked at all. Then, perhaps, you'd have a shot at a site that non-English speakers could reasonably use.

Part of the reason for these choices is that the assembly was furious with the EDD for its performance, and the bill—which passed unanimously—was punitive in tone. It was designed to make the assembly look like it was finding ways to hold the department accountable. But it was unlikely to actually help non-English speakers, and it added to the profusion of mandates that is one of the EDD's biggest problems. Lawmakers often have good intentions, but they continually add policy layers with too little understanding of (and, sometimes, regard for) how what they add will interact with the layers that are already cluttering the delivery environment. That's why a department like the EDD ends up with an eight-hundred-page training manual and a seventeen-year journey to becoming a competent but still inexpert claims processor.

■ ■ ■

LOOKING AT THE EDD's 1.2 million backlogged claims, one might be tempted to think that its failures were the result of a once-in-a-lifetime crisis and that unemployment insurance would operate adequately when things were normal again. But that kind of wishful thinking is contradicted by the very purpose of unemployment insurance, which exists explicitly to mitigate the worst effects of downturns in an economy that's always had boom-and-bust cycles. It needs to operate effectively at low levels during low unemployment and kick into high gear when more people are out of work. Although it wasn't as bad as the pandemic disaster, the unemployment program in California didn't perform very well during the last downturn either. During the Great Recession, the director of the EDD also spent a lot of time in front of the legislature getting yelled at for benefit checks that hadn't been issued to constituents.

Programs like unemployment insurance need to be able to scale up, and they need to be able to scale down. But even during good economic times, when the systems are handling relatively few claims, we tend to have shockingly low expectations for them. The federal DOL sets the goal for timeliness of payments at 87 percent, meaning that state labor agencies get a good grade even if one in every eight workers who apply has to wait over three weeks to receive a first payment.[11] Many states don't meet even that goal: California's pre-pandemic timeliness rate was 80 percent. The pandemic backlogs should not have been a surprise to anyone who was paying attention.

We seem to recognize this, briefly, after each downturn. After the last recession, Congress put $7 billion toward modernizing state unemployment systems.[12] Many state legislatures opened their pocketbooks too. But tech modernization, at least the way it's usually done today, has not helped much. Between 2000 and 2019, twenty-two states claimed to have "modernized" their unemployment systems in one fashion or another.[13] When the pandemic hit, those states should have been the bright spots in an otherwise bleak landscape of claims backlogs. They weren't. Some states still using mainframes, like New Jersey and Rhode Island, paid benefits much faster than others like Florida, which had ostensibly modernized.

None of the modernized states were able to avoid accruing backlogs, and few of them seemed to do much better than average in terms of scaling to meet demand. The problem is that the modernization projects all sought to "add functionality"—more layers of paint—or just to move to more modern infrastructure, particularly to the cloud. None of them targeted serving clients better or scaling to meet demand. If the people running the systems had set scale as a goal and truly analyzed their bottlenecks, they would have recognized the need to rationalize and simplify the accumulated layers of policy and process along with bringing in new technology. To be fair, none of them felt they had permission to.

So in addition to the billions spent on "modernization," when claim volumes go through the roof both state and federal governments throw more money at the problem to try to get through the crisis. During the pandemic, California not only received federal funds to help with emergency operating costs but spent hundreds of millions more from state coffers. Much of it went to hiring staff who inadvertently slowed the process and to emergency contracts with technology vendors like Deloitte, which built the ineffectual systems in the first place.[14] Such spending does nothing to help the EDD meet the next surge in need. But it does infuriate legislators who appropriated the funds in the hope of helping their constituents.

Discussions of modernizing the technology that runs unemployment insurance and other government programs can miss a critical point. A system can perform only at the speed of its slowest bottleneck. The only way to ensure that a system can scale up is to address its chokepoints. At the EDD in California, that's the recomps, those claims that need to be handled manually. As long as the training manual is eight hundred pages, as long as seventeen-year veterans of the department are still getting up to speed, making the tech better will be of only marginal help. Modernizing technology without rationalizing and simplifying the policy and processes it must support seldom works. Mostly, it results in much the same mess you had before, only now in the cloud. Many a tech modernization has gotten rid of the mainframes, the COBOL, and the green screens (or hidden them better) but has left the frontline workers just as confused and overburdened as before. Sometimes more so, because now they have to learn a new but still staggeringly complex system.

Lawmakers were furious at state-level bureaucrats for their failures during the pandemic, but it's the lawmakers who have insisted on petty provisions like docking a claimant's benefits because the person had a cold one day. You can have systems that do every possible thing policymakers can think of to ensure "program integrity" (in other words, making sure no one is getting a dollar more than they should) or you can have systems that scale. You can't have both. And most of what policymakers do to ensure program integrity ends up costing far more in administration than the program saves on paying out benefits. Those costs include the failure of the system when the benefits are most needed.

Nor is it just unemployment insurance systems that are doomed by overcomplexity. I once talked with a senior official in state government about a project one of her departments was about to bid out. This one had been in development for twelve years, and it was about to be released to vendors to bid with a $600 million price tag. When I told her I thought it would likely fail, she replied, "Do you think we don't know that? The last seven IT projects in this state have all failed."

The way government agencies build these systems is deeply flawed, but what's equally flawed is what we ask them to build. We keep hoping that if we can just get off the mainframes and the COBOL, things will be better. I thought that, too, when I first started working with government. But today, I'd bet on a legacy mainframe with a thirty-page manual over a modern system that takes decades to learn. If we want services that scale to meet people's needs, it's not just a matter of building new technology. It's a matter of clearing out the clutter it rests upon. The systems that run our government need to be built on a foundation of bedrock, not landfill.

3

CONCRETE BOATS

While Mikey was working his way through the maddening layers of technology to count the backlog and Marina was discovering the stultifying layers of policy, I was assigned to the top layers of the bureaucracy. My job was to work with the director of the EDD, whom I'll call Paula, to keep her informed about what we were finding and to get her perspective on it. We didn't want anything we would write in the task force report to come as a surprise to her and her team, and we didn't want any of her department's reactions to it to be a surprise to us.

Several weeks into our work, the technology and the policy both loomed as challenges, but we could see a way to deal with each, at least enough to get us through the current crisis. But our biggest challenge was about to become clear. It was one that Mikey and Marina and I had all seen before, on all sorts of ventures where enormous resources failed to achieve the project's goals. This problem, we knew from experience, would not respond to database queries or analysis of productivity reports, because it was not a symptom of haphazard technology and ineffective operations. It was, in many ways, their cause.

...

THE FIRST TIME I spoke to Paula privately, she made it clear that she knew her department needed help, and she truly welcomed the task force. She also let me know that she didn't need to be there and, understandably, didn't really want to be there. "I was planning on retiring and spending time with my grandkids, but there's a lot of vacancies and not enough people who know how this place runs," she told me. One of her deputies, someone she'd worked with for many years, was retiring in a few weeks, and I sensed she felt abandoned. Under the circumstances, I would have too.

Paula had spent her career at the EDD. She had started in the 1980s while she was still in college, on her way to a bachelor's degree in business administration. For thirty-seven years, she rose through the ranks of the department, serving in the Tax Branch, the Field Audit and Compliance Division, the Tax Processing and Accounting Division, the Integrity Accounting Division, and the Directorate's Office, all in roles heavily focused on compliance. At the end of 2019, when the administration offered her the chance to lead the department, unemployment in California was at a historic low. By the time her appointment was announced, in February 2020, concern about a novel coronavirus reaching the United States was slowly increasing. She'd been in her new role for just over a month when shelter-in-place orders led to an avalanche of job losses, and the EDD's workload skyrocketed.

It was not long before her name began to appear in front-page articles almost daily, and she was accused of everything from incompetence to intentional deception. Paula had a habit of trying to hide behind process, which didn't help her public image. When a member of the California State Assembly asked her whether the EDD's planned modernization would really take eleven years, for example, her answer was a dodge. "I can't speak to that," she began. "We follow the process set by the California Department of Technology. . . ." She was in a lot of hot water, with a lot of very powerful people angry at her, but she believed her ability to show that she was following established procedures was her best chance at avoiding consequences. That stance only further infuriated the assembly subcommittee. But she stuck to it in question after question.

Paula stayed on at the EDD amid the crisis, working long hours and withstanding enormous criticism, because she saw herself as a steward of a public program. Stewardship is a core value among civil servants, in part because of the frequent turnover in administrations, each of which brings its own priorities and approaches.[1] What looks like resistance to change is also a ballast, stabilizing against what amounts to fads rolling through government every time there's an election. I was always aware that I and the rest of the task force were around for what amounted to just a brief moment in Paula's long career. She had the benefit of a perspective I lacked, and she was committed. I respected that.

Paula and I would come to disagree on many things, but it was important for me to be able to look at the situation from her perspective. When systems or organizations don't work the way you think they should, it is generally not because the people in them are stupid or evil. It is because they are operating according to structures and incentives that aren't obvious from the outside.

I kept that in mind when I told Paula about our discovery that the EDD's big hiring spree wasn't clearing the backlog of claims and in fact was making it much worse. One might have assumed this would be welcome news. The hiring had been more or less imposed on the department by outside forces. Although Paula had never really pushed back on it, she had privately grumbled that it couldn't be expected to solve all of the EDD's problems. Now we had proof that she was right. I hoped Marina's analysis would be good news because it showed the path to restoring the department to its previous level of productivity. Given that it was impossible to train new claims processors in time to help, freeing up her seasoned workforce was critical to tackling the backlog.

That was not how Paula received the news. Well, that's nice, she said in effect, but there's nothing we can do about it. Hiring as fast as they possibly could had been the one consistent directive coming from everyone above them: the governor's office, the legislature, the federal Department of Labor, and every oversight body with jurisdiction over the EDD's operations. Telling all these stakeholders that they were wrong would not relieve the pressure on the department. It would just make the people up the chain look bad, which would further anger them. Moreover, Paula did not believe for a second that the governor's office would approve a plan to reduce staffing levels when the department was in the worst crisis it had ever seen. The optics, as they say, would be terrible.

This response was maddening to me. But it didn't make me see Paula as either foolish or malicious. It told me what I already knew from working with countless other public servants in similar situations. Paula was operating rationally within the system of beliefs and behaviors she'd spent her career in. She was stuck in a waterfall.

■ ■ ■

FOR DECADES, SOFTWARE developers have fought about how to manage their projects. The incumbent thesis was that if you wanted to manage something professionally, you structured it like a waterfall—or at least like a cartoon version of a waterfall, with several pools, each flowing into the next. There were separate, sequential stages each project had to go through: gathering requirements, design, implementation, verification, and maintenance. Different teams were generally responsible for each of the stages, and once a given stage was complete you didn't go back. Once the requirements had been set, for instance, it was critical that the design and implementation faithfully fulfill those requirements.

But many projects that followed the waterfall methodology failed badly, and it became clear that plenty of the most successful and meaningful pieces of software in the world were not built this way. In 2001, a group of developers got together to discuss the various ways software teams were working that didn't look at all like a waterfall and that were resulting in better software, happier users, and happier developers. They emerged from the meeting with a dozen core principles, which they dubbed a "Manifesto for Agile Software Development."

The manifesto rejected the precepts of waterfall project management. Whereas it's a major sin in the waterfall model to change requirements at a later phase, agile "welcomes changing requirements, even late in development." Whereas waterfall specifies a particular point in time when the software will be delivered before it moves on to verification, agile wants programmers to "deliver working software frequently, from a couple of weeks to a couple of months, with a preference to the shorter timescale." In other words, everyone gets to look at the software and try it out while it's still being coded. Whereas in waterfall, a separate team usually develops the requirements and then moves on to some other project, in agile, "business people and developers must work together daily throughout the project." But the biggest middle finger the agile manifesto gave to waterfall is expressed in the first of its twelve principles. Insinuating that those who followed a waterfall approach put fidelity to process over the usefulness of the product, the agile manifesto says at the top: "Our highest priority is to satisfy the customer through early and continuous delivery of valuable software."

Waterfall development is still very much alive and well, particularly in government. But most of the software that has changed the world around us in the past two decades was not made this way. Government's attachment to waterfall development seriously hinders its ability to build software that works well for the task at hand, whether it's distributing unemployment insurance or providing food benefits or processing tax returns.

More importantly, though, waterfall development of government software is a miniature version of a much larger dynamic that pervades all areas of government. Clay Shirky once quipped that "waterfall amounts to a pledge by all parties not to learn anything while doing the actual work."[2] And that implicit pledge was evident in Paula's response to finding out that her department's hiring spree was fatally stalling claims processing. As director of the EDD, Paula may have been at the top of a large department, but she was at the bottom of an enormous waterfall that started all the way in DC with Congress and the executive branch, flowed through the federal Department of Labor, cascaded down to the governor and his team, and on through to the labor secretary of California, to whom Paula reported. Other oversight bodies complicated the picture: the California Legislative Analyst's Office, for instance, evaluated the EDD's performance independently of the governor's office and the US Department of Labor, making this stream of the waterfall the aggregate of many sources. But whether fed by one source or many, waterfalls determine how information, insights, agency, and power flow. The flow goes only one way: down.

Our task force was assembled to deal with problems with the EDD's technology, which itself had been produced through waterfall development. But there was another, larger waterfall that wasn't really about technology—technology was caught in it. Blaming software that fails gets us little in the way of fixing the problems that government faces. More helpful is to understand the structures and culture that created the software, because they determine not just how the software works but how the whole system operates.

. . .

I REMEMBER WHEN this really hit home for me. It was the early spring of 2014, and I was working in the White House trying to set up the United States Digital Service. For months, I'd been trying to arrange the kickoff meeting for a project with the Department of Veterans Affairs, a sort of test case of the kinds of projects the USDS would take on. When the day finally arrived, I awoke to a snowstorm. There were hardly any cars on the street, but the bus was right on time, so I took it to Farragut Square and trudged through the snow to Cafe Soleil, about two blocks from both the White House and the VA. I was in luck. The others had made it too.

One of our group was a senior technology official at the Department of Veterans Affairs who had spent the past twenty-plus years in government technology roles. I'll call him Kevin. For the other two, it was their first day on the job in their first-ever government assignments. They were both software engineers—one taking a leave from Facebook, the other from Google—and they were here at my request to help with a problem. The Veterans Benefit Management System (VBMS) was maddeningly slow.

VBMS is basically a database of veterans' disability claims files. It has some obvious oddities. When you open it, for instance, there is no visible menu. You have to move your mouse to the edge of the screen to get a very thin line to appear, and when you click on it, it expands to reveal the menu. More importantly, while some parts of VBMS look like what you'd expect to see in a database, with fields like name, address, and other information, much of what's contained in it is not structured data but rather images of paper forms. It's a lot more like reading through old microfiches at the library than it is like doing a web search. You have to find the right file to open and read the words on the page yourself, because the computer only knows there's a file there, it doesn't know what's in it. This means two things: one, that the system is handling many large image files, which take up a lot of computer resources and slow things down, and two, that the people using the system need to open and close quite a few of these files to find the information they need to process a veteran's claim. They essentially need to flip through the claim as if it were a stack of paper on their desk, except that it's not on their desk. It's on a computer screen. And nothing will make you long to go back to a pre-computer world more than trying to look through a bunch of pieces of paper, only instead of thumbing through them, you click to the next page and wait. And wait. And wait.

Before we met with Kevin, we had been told that latency in VBMS was a problem. We all experience some latency in the apps we use, but if we have a good internet connection and we are connecting to a fast database, the latency may be so low we don't even notice it. In the case of VBMS, we'd heard that adjudicators could click on a file and then go start the coffee brewing and come back before the next page loaded.

As my colleagues and I got settled in at Cafe Soleil, we started peppering Kevin with questions about the system that we were to spend the next two weeks trying to help with. We were going to visit the coders developing the software, various people who used the system, and the officials within the VA who were managing the contracts for it. Like the EDD would be a few years later, the VA was under fire for a backlog of unprocessed claims (in their case chronic instead of sudden), and if those working the claims had time to go get coffee between clicks, that was obviously slowing things down. So that's where we planned to start. But Kevin started in a very different place. He said he was appreciative that the White House had offered help to confirm that everything was fine. "Latency's been solved," he told us. "As of last month, there are hardly any reports of latency." We'd barely gotten our own coffee, and he was telling us the thing we were here to work on wasn't a problem after all?

The three of us looked at one another and silently decided to put that question aside for the time being. We were to find out the next day what Kevin meant. Some work had indeed been done to speed up the system, but his office had sent a memo defining latency as a delay of over two minutes. If you clicked on a button or link, waited for a minute and fifty-nine seconds, and the page appeared, you were not to report latency. You could easily start a pot of coffee in that amount of time, or already be drinking a fresh cup of tea. But officially, that wasn't a problem; Kevin had defined it away.

Meanwhile, we shifted to asking Kevin about some of the requirements in the contract for VBMS. What was it the software was actually supposed to do? Why had the VA asked for certain things and not others? Kevin was cheerful and easygoing, and he seemed like the right person to help us understand the thinking behind the system. But there were whole categories of questions he would not answer. "That's a question for the program people," he said time and again.

Finally, a bit confused, I asked why was he so reticent to talk about what the system was designed to do. "I've spent my entire career training my team *not* to have an opinion on business requirements," he told me. "If they ask us to build a concrete boat, we'll build a concrete boat."[3] Why? I asked. "Because that way, when it goes wrong, it's not our fault."

Technically, I understood what he meant. There are a lot of stakeholders involved in building government technology, including the "program people" Kevin mentioned, who oversaw veterans' disability benefits, as well as procurement and contracting officials. Those other stakeholders give a lot of very specific direction to the technical teams, who can then feel as if they're merely to do what they've been told. But at the time we spoke to Kevin, sixteen veterans were committing suicide daily, an average of one every waking hour of the day. Many of them were still waiting for their backlogged benefits, including mental health support. There are few policies with greater support across the political spectrum than the provision of care for our returning service members, yet the VA was not able to get the job done. And here was one of the people charged with helping them, a senior official at the department, embracing the disempowerment. He was proudly abdicating responsibility in order to avoid blame. It was a gut punch.

(In real life, concrete boats do exist, and can float; hundreds of barges were built out of concrete during World War II due to steel shortages.[4] But it's hardly the best material for the job. And Kevin clearly wanted his teams to build whatever they were told even if it meant the project would sink like a rock.)

My colleagues and I pushed through that first meeting and spent the next two weeks talking to dozens of other people in DC, South Carolina, and Texas, where the software development teams working on VBMS were housed. Kevin may not have wanted his people to risk having opinions, but many of them had them anyway and many of their ideas were good. The developers cared very much about getting veterans their benefits, and they were also the ones who could see most clearly how policies and procedures put in place with the best of intentions sometimes backfired. They knew where the bottlenecks were and what to do about them—they just needed someone from higher up the chain to listen to them, and we could make that happen. It was a good test case for the digital services unit we were hoping to establish—it didn't take over from the agency, it simply helped an agency team get unstuck. After just two weeks, my colleagues had helped the developers make enough changes to get VBMS heading in the right direction.

But Kevin's words have stuck with me. I had come to DC

believing that if the tech teams could have a say in how things worked, we might have fewer failures of delivery. And many techies wanted a say, and wanted to get the job done right. But Kevin was operating under a completely different premise. The last thing he wanted was to have a seat at the table. Keeping his teams in order-taking mode didn't make them immune from criticism—there were constant headlines about the VA back-logs and ongoing fury from administration officials who wanted veterans taken care of—but it had been a winning strategy for him personally. Like Paula, he'd been promoted countless times, rewarded by a rule-bound civil service regime that values years of experience and a clean record but has little ability to judge competencies, leadership acumen, or a track record of meaning-ful results. Like Paula, he saw withstanding the criticism as part of the deal. In the end, he could say he'd just been following the established process. He'd just been doing what he was told.

■ ■ ■

A SURE SIGN of a waterfall organization is how the people within it treat data. In an agile, empowered organization, data is a use-ful tool for adjusting course. The people in the organization not only have access to data and the ability to understand it but have the power to decide what to do based on it. If the compass says you've drifted off course, no one summons the inspector general or calls for a hearing. You just turn the wheel.

In a waterfall organization, on the other hand, data functions less like a compass that helps you steer and more like an after-the-fact evaluation, a grade you get that says how well or poorly you did on something that has already happened. That's why there was such a big fight at the state assembly's EDD hearings about how many claims were backlogged. Paula wanted the backlog to be 239,000, not the 1.2 million it was eventually assessed at, because while the difference may only have been between a D and an F, that mattered to a leader who cared about the reputation of her department. For people stuck in waterfall frameworks, data is not a tool in their hands. It's something other people use as a stick to beat them with.

After Marina discovered that the new employees were dramatically slowing down the EDD, she wanted Paula to work with her on what she called a "burndown chart." This was essentially a giant spreadsheet that cataloged the backlog of different tasks and the people available to work them and modeled the impact of assigning people to tasks in a variety of ways. It was a way to manage the EDD out of Carl's problem—that experienced claims processors couldn't process claims while training new hires and that new hires were assigned to tasks they couldn't complete, while other tasks, like opening mail, remained hugely understaffed. At every meeting, Marina tried to get Paula to work with her on this tool. And for weeks, Paula put her off. To Paula, the analysis of the hiring problems didn't provide a useful new insight. It was just another grade, and a very bad one, and there was no point dwelling on it.

Intense as this disagreement was, it was nothing compared with what was coming.

Part of the challenge of counting the backlog was that not every application that the EDD receives is a valid claim for unemployment benefits. Some claims are filed but determined to be ineligible, for example, because the worker was fired for cause rather than laid off through no fault of their own. Some claims are begun but then abandoned, sometimes because the claimant has found new work, sometimes because the person has simply given up on completing the paperwork. And some claims do not actually represent an unemployed worker but are attempts to defraud the system, often by filing a claim using someone else's identity and getting the benefit in that person's name.

It was very hard to know which claims fell into which category. When you applied, the EDD had no idea if you were
who you claimed to be. For about 60 percent of the claims, the
department pretty much took your word for it. The other 40
percent were flagged for identity verification. Which bucket your
claim went into was decided in a way that to an outsider seemed
highly arbitrary. The EDD compared the name, date of birth,
and Social Security number you had provided with the corresponding data in a handful of other databases, like the Social
Security database. If what you had entered matched *exactly* with
those other databases, the EDD generally assumed you were the
person you claimed to be and sent your application on to be
processed. If it didn't, your claim was pulled off the line so that
the department could try to establish your identity with greater
confidence.

For lots of people with valid claims, the data didn't match. If
your name on your Social Security card was Alejandro, but you'd
put down Alex because that was how your previous employer
knew you, your claim was flagged. If you got a digit wrong when
you typed in your Social Security number, your claim was flagged.
(This error was common because almost half the claimants applied
using a mobile phone, but the UIOnline site worked very poorly
on phone browsers, and you couldn't really see what you were
typing.) If your last name was hyphenated, had an apostrophe,
or was more than twenty letters long, it was likely to be flagged,
because some of the other databases didn't accommodate those
characters. I met a lawyer from the California state government
who was providing legal advice to our team. He had filled out
an unemployment application on behalf of his mother, who had
lost her job when the pandemic hit in March, and provided her
first name, middle initial, and last name just the way she usually
signed them. But her Social Security card carried her full middle

name, so her application had been flagged for manual processing. It was now September and they hadn't heard anything back. His mother, who had had high hopes for her claim given her son's familiarity with the state's policies and procedures, was not very pleased with him.

The practice of flagging claims for minor discrepancies on applications may have made some sense in the past. If you're not who you claim to be, you might get information wrong about the person you're attempting to impersonate. It is possible that in the eighties and nineties, there was some correlation between inaccurate data about an individual applicant and attempted fraud, as people trying to use the identities of others got bits of information incorrect at a higher rate. Back then, of course, people didn't apply online. They came into offices and showed staffers their driver's licenses or other forms of physical ID. Remember that it wasn't until the early 2000s that the EDD started accepting online applications, first through eApply4UI, then through the UIOnline site that replaced it in the 2010s. Knowing whom you're dealing with is a very different question in person than it is on the internet.

Today, if there's any relationship between inaccuracy of the applicant data and fraud, it's an inverse correlation. Our world is awash in databases of stolen identities from breaches at credit monitoring services, retailers, and employers, and these stolen identities are freely traded on the dark web. Fraudulent applications using these sources will not get flagged: the data entered on the application will exactly match the sources the EDD checks against, because it is usually a copy of precisely that data. The data is also not likely to be accidentally entered wrong, because criminals with access to large databases of stolen identities will submit applications in bulk, automatically, using computer scripts. In other words, I am much more likely to get my own Social Security number wrong than a sophisticated criminal enterprise is, especially if I'm two-fingering it into a wonky, hard-to-see web form on a tiny keyboard on my mobile phone. Like the lawyer who'd included just his mother's middle initial, I'm a human, prone to human error. Organized crime is run by humans, but they don't do the typing.

The practice of flagging claims for identity verification based on mismatched names and Social Security numbers sounds archaic, but it was standard operating procedure across state unemployment insurance systems. It also turned out to be enabling massive organized fraud across almost all fifty states. And it had another effect as well. Because flagged applications must be manually processed and manual processing was the bottleneck in the EDD system, this practice was the main reason for the backlog.

The only way to stop the growth of the backlog was to send fewer claims into the manual process. The way to do that was to verify claimants' identities in some way that didn't rely on matching against Social Security and similar databases. The good news was that there were a variety of commercial offerings that would do just that. Our first recommendation as a task force was therefore very easy to make: procure and install an identity verification system as soon as humanly possible.

The California Department of Technology got to work immediately, and it worked at lightning speed by government standards. Under normal circumstances, selecting a vendor and integrating its technology into the EDD's systems would have taken upwards of a year, but this team pulled out all the stops and did the whole thing in seven weeks. It was heroic. The service they chose asked users to take a picture of their physical ID—driver's license or passport, for example—with their phone, and then to take a selfie. Using automated facial recognition, the system then compared the selfie with the uploaded document and also with photos in other available databases. (There was a range of protections built in to prevent people from using a photo of someone else instead

of a selfie.) It wasn't perfect by any means: it didn't help people
without smartphones, for instance, and we would find out later
that the app didn't work for some people, especially people with
poor internet connections, and they ended up in much the same
limbo as before. But it did work for lots of people, and once it
was in place, they would be able to verify their identity up front
and go through the automated process. If they ran into problems,
there would be a live human who could help them over video
chat in hours instead of months. The backlog would stop growing,
which would free up resources to individually help all those who
couldn't be verified through the app.

Even with that promise of dramatic change on the near hori-
zon, we still had a problem in the present: while the service was
being integrated, we were stuck with the current setup. The week
we agreed to move forward with an identity verification system,
189,575 claims were flagged for manual processing. If this rate
held over the course of the seven weeks that it would take to get
the identity verification system up and running, over 1.3 million
new claims would go into recomps. The backlog would more
than double.

That number could be reduced if the EDD loosened the criteria that were flagging claims for manual processing, but Paula
wouldn't hear of relaxing what she thought of as fraud prevention
practices. Those practices were not, in fact, preventing fraud. As
proof, Marina's team took claims that had been flagged for further identity verification during the previous quarter and looked
at what the EDD had decided to do with them after its manual review. Out of 183,167 claims, only 804 were judged to be
imposters. And even among those 804, many of them were likely
to be not actually fraudulent. People whose claims are denied
can appeal to the California Unemployment Insurance Appeals
Board, and the board overturns the EDD's identity verification
decisions around half the time.[5] So the real rate of fraud among

the flagged applications that quarter was probably just a few hundred people out of almost 200,000. In other words, only about 0.2 percent of applicants who were flagged for identity verification turned out to be committing fraud.

On the other hand, the claims filed in bulk by organized crime, with their perfectly matched data, were sailing through the system. Aiming to help gig workers during the pandemic, Congress had set up a new type of unemployment assistance that didn't require states to verify claimants' prior employment, making it much easier to get benefits. And applications to this particular program were spiking periodically in ways that didn't match the trends in regular unemployment claims and could not be explained by the normal patterns of legitimate claimants. For a few days in late August 2020, the EDD processed 120,000 new applications for it per day, strongly suggesting automated bulk submissions. Other states were seeing the same patterns.

In seven weeks, the new identity verification system was going to stop the bulk of that fraud. In the meantime, the question was whether at the end of those seven weeks Paula would have one big problem—a lot of fraud—or two problems: a lot of fraud and a backlog twice its previous size. By refusing to remove flagging conditions that we knew were catching almost exclusively valid claims, Paula was choosing the latter. She knew a backlash was coming when the staggering volume of fraud became known, and once again adherence to established procedures was going to be her shield. The line of questioning that would inevitably come if she did otherwise wasn't hard for her—or us, for that matter—to imagine. "So, Director, you're telling me that at a time when you were aware of large-scale attempted fraud in your program, you instructed your department to stop your long-standing fraud prevention practices?" One can see how "Yes, because they weren't working anyway" isn't a great answer.

In her role as steward of the program, Paula's safest move was to stick to whatever had been previously established, even as the proof mounted of its perverse effect. Our task force had learned quite a lot: that new hires were slowing everything down, that the flagging practices were both enabling fraud and creating the backlog. But just as Carl felt he couldn't simply speak out about the impact of the hiring spree and had to resort to stuffing reports surreptitiously into Marina's purse, Paula felt she couldn't simply tell everyone that new information necessitated new strategies and tactics. She knew that the tiers of the waterfall above her (and public opinion) would blame her for the disastrous performance of the department in any case, but the consequences to her personally were likely much worse if she deviated from accepted practices. The status quo was safer. That's how the waterfall's pledge not to learn anything while doing the work operates.

Waterfall culture is by no means the sole domain of government, and not all government organizations are run as waterfalls. Even the ultimate hierarchy, the military, can empower its workforce in an agile manner under the right conditions. General Stanley McChrystal put it this way: "I tell people, 'Don't follow my orders. Follow the orders I would have given you if I were there and knew what you know.'"[6] But Paula didn't give that direction to the people who reported to her, probably because she had never been given that direction herself. Following the orders as handed down had worked for her for decades.

But it wasn't working now, and we as the task force were not bound by the waterfall pledge. So when Paula refused to loosen the flagging criteria, we upped the stakes. If the department wouldn't take steps to keep the backlog from doubling while the new identity verification service was coming online, we told her, then it should stop taking applications altogether.

■ ■ ■

SHOCKING AS THE idea sounded, we were completely serious. Claimants trying to apply at that time had a 40 percent chance of going into the black hole of manual processing. If they waited just a few weeks for the new system, then as long as they could prove their identity through the new verification setup they would almost certainly go through the assembly line instead and start getting their unemployment benefits in a reasonable time frame. As for the 60 percent who would have been processed automatically, we pointed to an EDD rule that we'd never been able to understand the justification for: new applications normally sit for two weeks before anything happens with them. If the EDD could skip that step when the application form was turned back on, people who'd had to wait a few weeks to submit their claims would still get their benefits in almost the same amount of time.

We knew this option looked bad—very bad. We'd been asked to fix the system, not shut it down. EDD staff worried (needlessly, it turned out) that the federal Department of Labor might not even allow a shutdown. And the press, already understandably hostile to the department's explanations, was likely to ridicule it. But frustrated by the lack of any other options, we sprang the idea on a conference call with the governor's cabinet secretary. We wouldn't be shutting down the EDD's operations, we explained. In fact, we'd be speeding them up while the front doors were closed. And we'd stop the backlog from growing beyond all hope of clearance.

The cabinet secretary was open to our plan but asked for an analysis showing that turning off the application form would in fact free up claims processors to at least somewhat catch up on existing claims. The reality was that our maneuver would do very little unless Paula reassigned the bulk of her staff so that her most experienced team members could do their jobs. Fortunately, Paula realized that she had a unique opportunity here. While she would never have asked for a pause in accepting new applications, she was happy to take one, especially because it would mean that no more fraudulent applications would come in during that time.

Suddenly, Paula had an urgent need for Marina's burndown chart. She and one of her very capable team members called Marina on a Saturday morning and stayed on the phone with her all day. After eight hours, they had a working model in a spreadsheet. Every time you changed staffing levels in some area, it calculated a new date by which the current backlog would get cleared.

Marina remembers the sudden shift in Paula's thinking. "It was like she suddenly said, 'Oh, wait a minute. I can greatly influence the day when we work this part of the backlog down to zero by moving people over to this area, and then when it gets to zero, I move them over there. And every time I play around with the spreadsheet and make the allocations better, the dates move forward a bit,'" Marina told me. "I think prior to that, Paula had thought she really had no control over it, except to try to make the numbers *look* as small as possible."

Marina had seen this kind of fatalism before, many times. The VA, facing a very similar backlog in disability claims, had similarly been asked to project when they would be able to clear it. "They literally just drew a straight line heading down on a graph," she told me. "Oh, you want us to end it by August 2021? OK, here's a piece of paper that shows that." After that, the game is just waiting until the attention turns to other problems, which it always does. The reality is that this practice is frighteningly common in government, because it basically works, unless there is someone around like Marina asking to see the math behind your suspiciously straight line. Sadly, the tactic does not solve the problem for the people whose claims are stuck.

The spreadsheet got Paula what she wanted: the governor's office gave its thumbs-up to turning off new applications for two weeks while the EDD finished getting the new identity verification system going. That helped people in the backlog, because the EDD had resources to work on their applications during that time. It helped new applicants, because no one went into the black hole of the manual process. And it helped protect state resources, because no fraudulent applications came in. There was another benefit, too. Now Paula had control. She had a compass.

After two weeks, the EDD opened its virtual doors to new applicants again. The new identity verification system was now in place, and it kept all but a handful of claims from going into the backlog. It didn't stop all fraud, but the organized crime rings with their databases of stolen identities could no longer operate at the astounding scale they had been, and the state stopped bleeding billions of dollars.[7] And now that somebody else had delivered the bad news about the counterproductive hiring spree, Paula finally began both reassigning and reducing her ballooning staff. She tried various reassignments, watched what they did to productivity, and tweaked her tactics weekly. Instead of just taking orders from above, she had a compass and was steering the ship. When we wrapped up our task force, the spreadsheet calculated that the backlog would be cleared in about twelve weeks, near the end of the year. By January 2021, it was gone.

I credit Marina and her team with superpowers—both the empathy to build trust with people like Carl and the analytical acumen to build the first accurate picture of what was going wrong. But it wasn't IQ or EQ that the task force had and Paula's team didn't. And it wasn't newer and sexier tools to replace legacy technology, since the infamous COBOL code chugged along just the same the whole time. It was permission—permission to disrupt the waterfall.

Certainly Paula could have decided to do on her own any of the things we recommended. She could have come up with a consistent definition of the backlog so she could see the impact of changes. She could have asked for an identity verification system to be procured months or even years earlier.[8] We didn't invent the DPT reports that Carl put in Marina's purse; they were there all along, and Paula could have asked for an analysis of changes in the department's productivity. But Paula was the product of a system that values deference to the hierarchy and punishes risk taking. It had rewarded her with job security and successive promotions for thirty-seven years, just as it rewarded people like Kevin at the VA. State and federal civil service rules are a big part of that system, but they are simply the expression of a culture in which fidelity to flawed rules and practices is valued more than solving problems.

The state should not have needed a task force to tell the EDD what it already knew, and it shouldn't have needed us to secure permission to act on it. These things are never said out loud— neither the permission we had nor Paula's lack of it. But when we were gone, so was that permission. And soon after, for reasons that were not clear to me, a new backlog began to accrue.

If we want systems like unemployment insurance to work when we rely on them the most, we need more than better technology. And we need more than momentary permission to push insights back up the chain of a hierarchy. What we need has to do less with updating rigid 1950s code than with updating rigid 1950s thinking. We need a fundamentally different way of delivering on the promise of policy. We need to retire the waterfall.

4

FRIENDLY FIRE

If we want to do away with the waterfall, we have to learn how to recognize it. It can be hard to notice because it most often shows up not in what people say but in what they don't say, like when Paula stayed mum about the impact of the hiring spree because she knew no one wanted to hear it. It can also be hard to notice because each level of the waterfall can usually see only what happens just below and just above. Rarely does someone take a step back and trace a decision made at the highest levels of government all the way down to its impact on teams at ground level.

Coincidentally, one story of such a retracing itself starts with the need to get information from above—some twelve thousand miles up, actually—down to all of us here on the ground. Bits and bytes routinely travel such distances just fine. Orders from the top of a hierarchy, on the other hand, arrive the worse for wear.

· · ·

THE GLOBAL POSITIONING System has to be one of the most successful investments the US has ever made, and not just because

GPS-enabled map apps on mobile phones have saved the directionally challenged like me from perpetually getting lost. GPS also powers thousands of critical services that we take for granted today, like routing cell phone calls, sending electricity to our homes, and enabling us to get cash from an ATM. Even stock exchange trades now rely on GPS.[1] It's not much of an exaggeration to say we couldn't function as a modern society without it.

Like the internet itself, GPS started life in the military-industrial complex. In the 1970s, the Department of Defense decided that a robust, stable navigation system was critical to national defense, and it eventually developed a constellation of satellites that could establish one's location within six feet. GPS provided dramatically greater coverage and accuracy than radio or radar navigation, but it was supposed to be available only to the military. In 1983, however, the crew of Korean Air Lines Flight 007, flying from New York City to Seoul via Anchorage, Alaska, made an error in their navigational calculations and accidentally strayed into the prohibited airspace of the USSR. Mistaking the airliner for a spy plane, the Soviets shot it down, killing all 269 people aboard, including Larry McDonald, a US congressman from Georgia. Recognizing that GPS could have prevented this tragedy, President Ronald Reagan directed the Department of Defense to make GPS freely available for civilian use. As a common good, it became even more powerful than Reagan could have imagined.

Its power comes from a complex and interdependent ecosystem that has developed around the GPS satellites and the data they beam down to earth. But ecosystems don't sit still. Satellites have a life expectancy, and by the early 2000s many of the satellites GPS relied on were nearing the end of theirs. The need to replace them offered a chance to update their software and improve the accuracy and availability of GPS navigation signals. In 2010, the US Air Force awarded the defense contractor Raytheon a

$1.5 billion contract to develop the Next Generation GPS Operational Control System, known as OCX.

Six years later, Matthew Weaver of the US Digital Service found himself at Raytheon's headquarters in Aurora, Colorado. Weaver, as he is always called—he does not use his first name—had come to Washington, DC, to work on healthcare.gov during its crisis. As that effort was winding down, my colleagues and I convinced him to stay and join the USDS, to help other parts of the federal government with similar but less headline-grabbing problems. This was one of them. OCX was falling more and more behind schedule, and the top brass at the air force were frustrated. According to the original plan, the work was supposed to have been completed already. Defense Department officials had already revised their project budget from $1.5 billion to $3.7 billion and would soon revise it again to $5.5 billion.[2] (Since then, it has been revised once more, to $6.2 billion and a due date in 2023.[3]) The huge project was getting huger.

Weaver, though, was busy looking at something very small, called multicast user datagram protocol, or UDP.[4] He was focused on UDP because it was the obvious way to get data from the satellite monitoring stations to the master control station run by the Department of Defense. UDP is one of the low-level protocols that make the internet work, and it's built into almost every operating system in the world. It's simple and stable; the technical paper that describes it is less than three pages long.[5] It's a standard component of networking, a bit like a two-by-four is for a carpenter. You can walk into any lumberyard in the US and buy one, and it will get the job done.

But OCX wasn't using UDP on its own. The satellites generated UDP messages, but the control station didn't receive them directly. Instead, the contractor had written a piece of software to receive a UDP message, read the data, decrypt it, and then recode it into a different format, called XML, re-encrypting it to XML security standards. The software then used another network protocol, called SOAP (which is largely obsolete in the commercial world), to put this XML message onto something called an Enterprise Service Bus, or ESB. The ESB eventually delivered the XML message to yet another piece of software, at which point the process ran in reverse: the software used SOAP to retrieve the XML message from the ESB, decrypted and decoded it, copied it into memory, and parsed out the original data *just as it had been initially delivered via UDP.* Only then did the control station get to see what the satellites had sent.

Because the data was taking such a roundabout route from the satellites to the control station on the ground, it wasn't arriving quickly enough for the station to make the calculations needed. Recoding the data into different formats also meant the computers running the programs needed more memory and processing power. And the complicated arrangement was making the whole thing not only incredibly inefficient but also hard to debug. SOAP and XML messages are quite complex, while an ESB is an entire software suite in itself and comes in lots of incompatible versions.

Trying to solve the problem of too-slow data transmission had taken up months of engineering time, but the team was no closer to a solution. Using UDP alone would have made the entire job a snap—as easy as nailing a couple of boards together—but the Raytheon team told Weaver that the data absolutely had to go through an ESB. He decided to find out why.

It is tempting to assume that Raytheon had required the team to include an ESB in the system because it would make them more money. Problems like this were driving the program's cost overruns, which weren't great for Raytheon's reputation but very good for its billing. And the Department of Defense has an embarrassing history of paying contractors more for more lines of code—even though, as the UDP versus ESB situation shows, more code is seldom better and is almost always worse. (Indeed, when good software developers revise their code so it is easier to maintain and to understand, uses less memory, or runs faster, they usually shrink it in the process.) But that's not what was happening on the OCX project.

What was going on took some digging. Weaver's first clue lay buried within the air force's Request for Proposal (RFP) for OCX, an enormous document with seemingly countless addenda. There he found frequent references to something called the "DoD Architecture Framework." The RFP required that the OCX project be developed in accordance with this framework.

Every company that bid on the project knew what the DoD Architecture Framework was. According to the department's website, "it is the overarching, comprehensive framework and conceptual model enabling the development of architectures to facilitate the ability of Department of Defense managers at all levels to make key decisions more effectively through organized information sharing across the Department, Joint Capability Areas, Mission, Component, and Program boundaries." In other words, if you want to build something for us, it has to be built this way, because we think that if everything is built the same way we can coordinate better across a large institution.

The DoD Architecture Framework comes in two volumes, and it is the second one, weighing in at 284 pages, that addresses the subject of data transfer. The framework emphasizes something it calls "net-centricity": "The DoD is committed to making operations net-centric; that is, enabling the ability to share information when it is needed, where it is needed, and with those who need it." So far so good, and then it gets even more promising. "Open technology standards are preferred," it says. "As information and capabilities are provided . . . architects and engineers should ensure that they are done so in a manner that provides the most value, in convenient ways, to the broadest set of potential users." All this sounds like the Department of Defense is pointing its

contractors to the simple, straightforward UDP protocol, because
it is an established and convenient open technology standard that
provides a lot of value. (It was also, Weaver discovered, created by
a researcher funded by the Department of Defense.)[6]

But keep reading, and the DoD Architecture Framework moves
from general guidance to more specific instructions. Among them
is Figure 5–8, a diagram of a model system with a "sensor deployment location" and a "data processing location." It's exactly the
situation confronting Weaver and the Raytheon team, with sensors on the satellites and a control station on the ground. And
there, next to the diagram, are the fateful words: "Items shown
to help illustrate net-centricity include: 1) an Enterprise Service
Bus (ESB) . . ."

Figure 5–8 is not the last diagram to show an Enterprise Service
Bus, nor is it the last mention of ESBs in the DoD Architecture
Framework. Somehow, its authors have jumped from the very
reasonable notions of broad value and open technology standards
to specifying an Enterprise Service Bus. The bizarre setup Weaver
was wrestling with was not a brilliant way for Raytheon to shake
down the federal government for more money. It was a requirement set by the air force that the contractor was obliged to meet.
It was friendly fire.

• • •

THE IEEE STANDARD Glossary of Software Engineering Terminology offers two definitions of *requirement* in the programming
context. It can be something "needed by a user to solve a problem or achieve an objective" or something that "must be met or
possessed by a system . . . to satisfy a contract, standard, specifi-
cation, or other formally imposed document." Government sub-
scribes almost exclusively to the second definition. Requirements
are the foundation of software development processes in government, and the source of many of its failures.

A couple of years before Weaver went to grapple with OCX, another US Digital Service member, Mary Ann Brody, was assigned to the Department of Veterans Affairs to work on access to benefits. Back then, services for veterans were hard to find online, buried deep and scattered across hundreds of different websites. Some services weren't online at all. At first, Mary Ann and her colleague at the VA Emily Tavoulareas thought they would just start with the services that *were* online, like the form for applying for health care, and put them all together in one place. But then they did what any good technologist who cares about their users would do: they tried out each of the services they were going to aggregate. They went through the health care application process using their own mobile phones and their own computers at home. They also tried filling out the form on older computers with low bandwidth, because they knew that not every veteran has access to the latest hardware and high-speed internet connections.

The health care application wasn't a web form like the kind you use when you're booking a rental car or taking a survey. It was a paper form that had been put online as a PDF. If the computer you were using had a particular (and outdated, even then) version of Internet Explorer, and a particular (also outdated) version of Acrobat Reader, and it was set up to open PDFs in Reader by default, you could click on the link for the form on the VA website and it would appear in your browser. You could then type your information into each field on the form, save it, and send the completed document to the VA electronically. The computers inside the VA ran that exact combination of Internet Explorer and Acrobat Reader and were set up to open Reader by default. Whenever anyone inside the building clicked on that link on the website, the form would load. It worked fine.

But outside the building, very few computers were set up that way. Some of the older computers Mary Ann tested were running even earlier versions of the software. Others were running more recent versions than those inside the VA. The team tested the application on all kinds of computers running all kinds of common combinations of software. In none of the tests did the application open in the browser.

Yet when the team approached VA management with a plan to redo the form, they were told there was no need. The vendor that had been hired to build the application had fulfilled all the specified requirements. The contracting officer in the VA had signed off on the completed project. Officially, there was nothing to fix. It was a bit like the scene in *30 Rock* when TV executive Jack Donaghy briefly goes to work in government. He arrives at his new office to the sight of water dripping onto his desk and points out to one of his new colleagues that the ceiling is leaking. "No, it's not," says the colleague. "We've looked into it and it's not. I'll show you the study."

By any reasonable definition, the form didn't work. But the way we build government technology is to specify the requirements and fulfill the requirements. That had happened. There had been no requirement to test the software outside the building and no requirement that the software actually work. So the team was stuck.

It was a veteran named Dominic who unstuck them. He had tried to get health care through the VA website dozens of times since he'd left the army, and he kept running into the same problem Mary Ann and Emily had just documented. In his mounting frustration, and in increasingly urgent need of medical care, he wrote to President Obama asking for help. When Mary Ann and Emily went to the presidential correspondence office looking for veterans in the area to interview, Dominic's letter was among the ones they were given. They reached out and arranged to meet.

Dominic told them that he had served in both Iraq and

Afghanistan. Now he worked at a discount store called Five Below and struggled with stable housing. He wasn't sleeping on the streets, but he was bouncing from a friend's couch to a girlfriend's to a short-term apartment lease. He had a kid with special needs, who took up a lot of his time. And because his store job didn't offer health insurance and he couldn't get through the VA application process, he hadn't seen a doctor in eight years.

Each time he tried to apply, Dominic would find a computer with an internet connection, sometimes at the library, sometimes borrowing a friend's. Each time he would click on the link for the application form, the screen would go white and all that would be there was a long message he didn't understand. It told him that the software his computer was running—no matter which computer he was using—wasn't right. Dominic didn't have permission to change the software on his borrowed computer, and even if he did he didn't know how. So he would call the VA. Each time, the people at the VA call center would be of no use. "That form works fine," they would say. "You must be doing something wrong."

Mary Ann and Emily listened, and then they asked if they could watch him try to apply for health benefits. They also asked his permission to record his voice and what was happening on his screen.

Dominic did what he'd done every time he'd tried to apply. Mary Ann noticed how easily he navigated to the right page and how well he seemed to know his way around the VA website. When he clicked the link and the error message appeared as usual, he was unsurprised. He tried clicking a link in the error message and got another error message, this one about his connection not being secure ("Attackers may be trying to steal your information!"). In the recording you hear Mary Ann asking dryly, "Is this what you expected to happen when you clicked on that?" "That?

No," Dominic replies. "It's like it takes you around the corner and over the meadow and tries to lead you into a back door that's blocked with spikes and IEDs."

Mary Ann then asks him what he usually does when he sees the error page, and he tells her about his many futile calls to the VA. "One of those . . . I called the VA, and the woman told me after she had me on hold that she couldn't help me. And I remember I was off that day, I didn't have to go to work, and I was just sitting there in front of the library thinking, 'Wow, you people just told me to go fuck myself.'"

His language is strong, but the Dominic you hear in the recording is charming and patient. He has a great sense of humor, which is especially remarkable when you consider not only how many times he'd already tried and failed at this task but also the profound betrayal he was suffering. He'd gone into war zones on behalf of the American people with the promise of health care and other benefits, and the government wasn't holding up its end of the bargain.

Dominic's charm made a difference. The team managed to get time with deputy secretary Sloan Gibson, the second in command at the VA, and insisted that he watch the video of Dominic. It had its intended effect. Suddenly it didn't matter what the paperwork said. Sloan put his head on his desk and said, "Oh my God, this is so embarrassing. Can you get me this young man's name? I want to call him and make sure that he gets health care." Mary Ann and Emily's team back at the VA had already developed a new version of the application form, and Sloan gave the orders to let them launch it. When Dominic tried it, he couldn't believe it had come from the VA. He told the team it was "easy to read, straightforward, so much better." The IEDs and the spikes were gone.

But even this victory could have been short-lived. As Mary Ann and Emily suspected, Dominic had not been the only veteran who couldn't access the previous application form. When the new form went live and worked on the vast majority of computers, the number of incoming health care applications jumped by a factor of ten. While the team celebrated, the blowback began. None of the systems that processed the applications were ready for ten times the volume. People all over the building were suddenly drowning in work, which was particularly bad because the VA was already facing fierce criticism for a myriad of other backlogs. Now there was going to be another one. Bureaucrats across the VA started calling up everyone in power: *Revert to the old application form!*

The inability to apply had been largely invisible, both in the press and inside the building, but the backlog of unprocessed applications starting to build up was very visible. What can look from the outside like solving a problem can feel for those on the inside like creating one, as I learned when Paula was unhappy to hear that she could clear *her* backlog by getting rid of most of her new hires. To many people inside the VA, fixing the form had broken their system.

Sloan held steady despite the cries to revert. The only way forward, he declared, was to fix the department's capacity to process these new applications. (The tech team was already working on that as well.) Mary Ann attributes Sloan's resolve to Dominic's video. It brought into sharp focus the way many veterans were experiencing the process of applying for health care—not just what happened but what it felt like. The team could not have gotten unstuck by arguing about the technicalities of contract requirements or the processes that had or had not been followed. They had to pull people in the department outside the walls of the building and make them see what things looked like from the perspective of those the VA was meant to serve. They succeeded by changing the frame of the debate. The outcome mattered more than the process.

...

WEAVER'S TEAM WAS stuck too. They knew how to fix the software and get data from the satellites back to the ground in time, but they didn't have permission to take out the ESB that was jamming things up.

Eric Schoonover was one of Weaver's colleagues on the OCX project. He now works for a startup defense contractor, and he has become accustomed to what he called "the weird ESB imperative." "I've spent a lot of my time just relabeling presentations," he says. "I would create a PowerPoint that described what we were doing, and then somebody would say, 'You don't have an ESB on here.' So I would just relabel one of the boxes 'ESB' and then go through the PowerPoint again." No one ever asked Eric which software components were using the ESB, or even if there was anything installed on the machine at all. Today, Eric's ESBs are all fictional.

Weaver would have loved to just buy a computer, write "ESB" on the side of it, and tell everyone that the problem had been solved. But that was not an option for the OCX team, at least not at the point when he and Eric were sent to help out. The more trouble a project is in, the more oversight it gets, and more oversight almost always means stricter compliance with requirements, not finding creative ways around them. Generals were visiting and checking in on the project. Weaver's colleagues got busy helping with a variety of other issues facing the Raytheon team, but no one could ditch the ESB. In the meantime, Weaver still wanted to know where the ESB requirement had come from in the first place, so he did a little more digging.

What he found was another entire Rube Goldberg machine, this time of policy rather than technology. Raytheon required its developers to use an ESB because the air force required it of them, and the air force in turn required it because the Department of

Defense required it of the developers. But why did the DoD require it? Naturally, the answer lay one tier up the waterfall.

It turns out that the DoD Architecture Framework, the source of the requirement in the air force's project, is itself derived from a higher-level document: the Federal Enterprise Architecture.[7] The FEA is the work of a body called the Chief Information Officers Council, a group of more than thirty CIOs of federal agencies, departments, administrations, and branches of the military. The council was officially established by an executive order issued by President Bill Clinton. But why did the Clinton White House establish the CIO Council, and why did the council publish the FEA? For the answer, we have to look to the ultimate source of the law of the land: Congress.

In 1996, Congress passed the Information Technology Management Reform Act, part of what became known as the Clinger Cohen Act. Among other provisions, the law required each federal agency to have an "Information Technology Architecture." There was a sense that the technical architectures of the various agencies should be coordinated in some way, and the thirty-odd members of the CIO Council got the job. The result seems to have been a classic example of design by committee. However the document came together, the 434-page Federal Enterprise Architecture, released in 1999, requires that federal technology solutions have a "service-oriented architecture." And one of the elements of a "service-oriented architecture" that it shows is an ESB.

Having followed the thread up to Congress and its 1996 law, we can now trace it back down to the White House, to the CIO Council and its Federal Enterprise Architecture, to the Department of Defense and its DoD Architecture Framework, to the ESB requirement in the air force contract that Raytheon and now Weaver were stuck with. As with so much detective work, it can be satisfying to solve the puzzle but truly unsettling to see the answer. The CIO Council had wanted to be very precise.

Raytheon wanted to be very thorough. Everyone in between wanted to ensure full compliance with the directives they'd been issued. No one was trying to sabotage the project, and there was nothing like gross negligence in sight. In fact, if anything, the OCX team was trying to do its job too diligently. Everyone was operating just as they were expected to in the waterfall system, from the lawmakers in Congress to the engineers in a room in Aurora, Colorado. Yet Weaver could only conclude that these best of intentions had "doomed federal IT projects to massive, predictable failures for at least twenty years."

This happens over and over in our dysfunctional waterfall system. "Friendly" bullets ricochet not just within the air force but from the Hill to the White House to the Pentagon and back again. They ricochet to other agencies, too, and around state and local government in much the same way. Everyone is trying to help, everyone is trying to do the best they can. But we just keep shooting ourselves in the foot.

The developers never did get around the ESB requirement. Weaver and his US Digital Service colleagues taught them faster ways to test and deploy software, which turned out to be quite helpful, but they never figured out how to make the Rube Goldberg machine work. Eventually, time ran out for the satellites that were wearing down in space. The air force had to launch new satellites whether the new software was ready or not, so it went ahead without some of the software updates. The new satellites have all the next-generation sensors and other kinds of updated hardware, but without the software to go with them, GPS users aren't getting the improved resolution and other benefits that these hardware upgrades were supposed to bring. GPS still works, but the US government has spent many billions of dollars for satellites that in many regards do the same things the old ones did. And all because of a requirement that cascaded down the waterfall all the way from Congress in 1999.

■ ■ ■

THERE'S ALSO A deeper message in this story. It's true that many laws and policies fail because they are overly prescriptive and lock implementers into a narrow set of options. But that is not quite what happened here. In fact, neither the Clinger Cohen Act nor any other law explicitly *required* an ESB. Nowhere in the Federal Enterprise Architecture does it say "thou shalt always use an enterprise service bus." There are five mentions of "enterprise service bus" in the document, but all of them are in charts or diagrams listing various application components that *could* support interoperability. ESBs became mandatory in practice within the Department of Defense through overzealous interpretations of law, policy, and guidance, combined with lack of technical understanding.

How does this happen? When there are big, visible delivery failures, like healthcare.gov or the unemployment insurance crisis, public servants are trapped between two distinct systems of accountability. In the first, politicians will hold the public servants accountable for *outcomes*: whether the website works to enroll people or whether benefits are actually getting to claimants. In this system there will be hearings. (Congressional committees held ten separate hearings on healthcare.gov in a single month in 2013, all as the people being called to testify were otherwise working night and day to get the site back up.)[8] Angry politicians will summon bureaucrats to the Hill, or the state capitol, or city council chambers, and their staffs will help them prepare incisive questions that show that they are paying close attention to the problem. These hearings will likely be televised or webcast, and a few sound bites might appear on the evening news or circulate on social media.

In the second system of accountability, various parts of the administrative state—the agency itself, the inspector general, the

Government Accountability Office—will hold these same public servants accountable to *process*. Procurement and planning
documents will be reviewed for any gaps, any skipped or partially skipped steps, any deviance from standard protocol, even
if that deviance is legal, just nonstandard. If an ESB is thought
to be "best practice"—even if it is not at all best practice—why
wasn't it used? If anti-fraud practices had been previously established, why weren't all of them deployed? If the vendor has been
hired under an Other Transaction Authority (a streamlined path
for procurement that Congress approved to give agencies flexibility to exercise judgment), why was this exception allowed and
a more thorough and standard process not followed? And who
signed off on all these decisions? Angry politicians will sometimes ask such questions too, but they are less familiar with the
many administrative rules and requirements. They tend to focus
more on the issue their constituents care about: Why isn't the
thing working?

The accountability trap is a damned-if-you-do, damned-if-
you-don't situation. The first system is extremely uncomfortable
for the public servants subjected to it. No one wants to be called
up to testify in a televised hearing. No one wants to be in the
video clip as a stone-faced bureaucrat with no good answers,
being yelled at by a righteous—or self-righteous—politician
fighting the good fight on behalf of the aggrieved public. In front
of the cameras, you can't say things like "it doesn't work because
we were forced to use an ESB." You would look like you were
trying to throw someone else under the bus, and the legislators
wouldn't understand what you were talking about anyway. Your
job is simply to endure the hearing, produce as few viral sound
bites as possible, and not incriminate others.

As painful and sometimes humiliating as these hearings are,
if you're a career civil servant, it is the second system of accountability that matters most to you. Legislators can't fire or officially

reprimand you, no matter how bad a job they think you did (although they can put political pressure on the administration to do so). They can't make you ineligible for promotions and raises. On the other hand, violations of policy, process, and procedure—real or perceived—can do all of that, even if there is no hearing. It is the job of many other public servants to make sure that happens. The people under scrutiny want to avoid these repercussions for the obvious reason that being fired or demoted affects their livelihoods, but many also simply want to continue doing their jobs. They believe in what they do, and they believe that they are still the best shot the agency has at fulfilling its mission. They are often right.

These dynamics kick into overdrive when technical issues are in question. Even the most competent tech team can hit resistance when trying to explain, for instance, why there should not be an ESB in the software they are building. A team could point out that it was only suggested, not required, and Weaver tried to do just that. But the reality is that the ESB became incrementally more codified as the Federal Enterprise Architecture gave rise to the Department of Defense Enterprise Architecture, which gave rise to the Air Force Enterprise Architecture, which gave rise to some large number of additional guidance documents within the air force and ultimately to the request for proposals and accompanying requirements documents that were issued when the OCX contract was awarded. Arguments about what is or isn't required happen all the time, but they are much less likely to lead to a suffocatingly risk-averse answer when the people involved in the argument understand the domain. Here, aside from the tech team, it is highly unlikely that anyone else in the debate—likely to be dozens of people in dozens of different roles—had any basis on which to judge whether an ESB was a good thing or a bad thing in this context. Thus, to nix the ESB, dozens of people in dozens of different roles would all have had

to agree to jeopardize their jobs over a recommendation they
didn't understand. These discussions tend to function as a vetoc-
racy, in which it takes all thumbs up in order to accept the risk,
and only one thumbs-down to stick with the less-risky option.
The ESB stays.

This drama plays out repeatedly in the area of cybersecurity.
The Federal Information Security Management Act, or FISMA,
provides a menu of some three hundred distinct "controls" that
tech teams can choose from to secure government software
and data from hackers. Competent developers should, in theory, create an informed, thoughtful security plan that chooses
the controls most relevant to the circumstances and focus their
efforts on implementing and testing those choices. But it's the
rare compliance officer who will take the risk of allowing anything less than all three hundred. So even if you have a skilled
security team, they'll have to march through a massive checklist,
much of it meaningless for their project, instead of focusing on
the specific controls they believe will actually secure their system. Implementing all three hundred and verifying that they
are implemented will add months, sometimes even years, to the
development schedule, making compliance extremely costly.
It will also detract from the time spent on both features and
testing—and testing, of course, is critical to the real-world security of software. FISMA, as written, is a fine law. But as prac-
ticed it often impairs the security of our systems. As Weaver
concluded from his work on the satellites, "almost all the outcomes generated by technical policy will be unintended consequences."[9]

In the business world, they say that culture eats strategy for
breakfast—meaning that the people implementing the strategy, and the skills, attitudes, and assumptions they bring to it,
will make more difference than even the most brilliant plan. In

government, culture eats policy. Even when legislators and policymakers try to give implementers the flexibility to exercise judgment, the words they write take on an entirely different meaning, and have an entirely different effect, as they descend through the hierarchy, becoming more rigid with every step. When rules rarely have their intended effect, more rules are not likely to improve outcomes.

■ ■ ■

IT IS TEMPTING to see both these stories as cases of specifying the wrong requirements. In Dominic's case, perhaps requiring a more common combination of software on users' machines would have allowed more access for more veterans. Certainly the OCX team would have had an easier time if the CIO Council had chosen something other than the ESB. And both cases share the problem of freezing technology requirements at a single moment in time. It was inevitable that the public would upgrade to newer versions of Acrobat Reader and Internet Explorer and increasingly adopt alternatives like Safari, Chrome, and Firefox. ESBs, meanwhile, were just past their prime in 1999 when the CIO Council effectively locked much of software development across federal government into this architecture. In the decades since then, they have largely been superseded altogether. It's a classic government problem, what my friends describe as "yesterday's technology tomorrow."

It's not just that the requirements pointed to soon-to-be-outdated technologies. Most web developers today don't worry about which browsers their application will run on, especially those who are building applications as simple and straightforward as a web form. There are many ways to build apps that will work on virtually any contemporary web browser. A native web application also means there's no need for Adobe Acrobat

Reader and therefore no need to worry about which version of it someone has installed. The problem is not that whoever wrote the contract for the VA health care form chose the wrong browser in their requirements, and it's not that the CIO Council chose the wrong architecture when it specified ESBs. The problem is that it specified those things at all.

Government's obsession with requirements—voluminous, detailed requirements that can take so long to compile the software is obsolete before it's even bid out—stems from a delusion that it's possible to make a work plan so specific that it requires no further decision-making. You hand it off and the developers just do exactly what they're told. Why not let those developers choose the best tool or platform for the job? In part, because they sit at the bottom of the waterfall. Technologists have had an astonishing impact on our world in recent decades, for better or worse; they sit at the top of the social structures of Silicon Valley, running companies and calling the shots. But the goal in government seems to be to drain the job of software development of any opportunity to exercise judgment. (To be clear, as we'll see later, this goal is seldom if ever achieved.) This is a terrible way to manage most things, but it's particularly destructive when hardly any of the people writing the work plan have much basis for their decisions either.

The redesign of the health care application form at the VA was a triumph of outcomes over process. Sadly, though, process usually wins, as it won on the satellites. That public servants get held accountable to process over outcomes is well known; I do not presume to know how to change this, though I desperately wish I did. What I do know is that the perverse effects of glorifying process are far greater in technology, for the simple reason that there are so few people in government who understand tech. Rigid, overly specific interpretations of law and policy are hard to avoid when those doing the interpretation can't evaluate the work for themselves.

So why *do* we have so little tech expertise in government? And why do we treat the experts we do have with so little regard? It wasn't always that way.

PART II

Mechanicals
at the Gate

5

THE KODAK CURSE

In the early days of computers, the US government dominated the nascent industry. What other entity had such a need to count, to store information, to process data? The first punch cards used in computing were the brainchild of Herman Hollerith, a former clerk at what is now the Census Bureau, who designed them explicitly to speed the tabulation of the 1890 census. (He succeeded: despite the country's growing population, the counting was completed eighteen months faster than for the previous census.) The first programmable, electronic, general-purpose digital computer, the ENIAC, was built to calculate artillery firing tables for the US Army and then immediately used to study the feasibility of the hydrogen bomb, kicking off a long history of connections between the military and computing advances. The predecessor to COBOL, the computer language that still powers mainframes at California's EDD and many other agencies, was developed by navy rear admiral Grace Hopper (who is also the source of the ever-useful phrase "it is easier to ask forgiveness than to get permission"). By the mid-1960s, the federal government purchased over 62 percent of the output of the entire US computer industry.[1]

The field of user experience design, the discipline most responsible for the ease of use (and occasional delight) provided by modern consumer software and web apps, also has its roots in the military. During World War II, the need for air dominance spurred the design of new aircraft that could outmaneuver the enemy's forces, but as these planes began to be deployed an alarming number of them crashed due to pilot error, often during training. Air force lieutenant colonel Paul Fitts, who also happened to have a PhD in psychology, began conducting detailed interviews of the pilots who survived the crashes and near-crashes, in a practice that modern user experience researchers would find very familiar.[2] He and a colleague, Captain Richard Jones, found that the design of the airplane cockpits made it easy to confuse critical controls, especially in moments of stress. In one example, the prop control, which adjusts the load on the engine, was right next to—and the same size and shape as—the mixture control, which regulates the amount of fuel added to the intake airflow. Mistaking one for the other during takeoff had sent the pilot careening toward a fence when he should have been rising off the runway.

These "pilot errors" were far too easy to make, and Fitts and Jones showed that even the most experienced pilots were making them. The planes met the requirements that had been set for superior performance, but because their designers hadn't accounted for how humans would use them, many of these fancy new machines never even made it into combat. Another air force lieutenant, Alphonse Chapanis, documented similar design flaws that caused similar crashes. Chapanis crafted new knobs for the controls that pilots were mixing up, making each a distinct shape and texture to make it easier to distinguish them by both sight and touch. All this work by Fitts, Jones, Chapanis, and others laid the foundation for what we now call human-centered design.

When the next button you need to tap on your phone is the one your eye is drawn to or when you get a dialog box double-checking before you delete your data, you have these uniformed service members, and the government that employed them, in part to thank.

By the twenty-first century, though, cutting-edge computing in the US had largely become the domain of private industry.[3] As for everyday usability, consumer software products had picked up the lessons of Fitts and Chapanis and run with them. It was now easy for regular people to do for themselves all sorts of things that trained professionals had previously done for them, from booking flights to editing video. Meanwhile, government software often felt like those planes that met the technical requirements but hadn't accounted for how humans would use them, putting the prop control right next to the mixture control, confusing and confounding their users with poor wording and design.

Somehow, the US government went from being a technology pioneer to seeming digitally incompetent. What happened? In a certain sense, the digital revolution had bad timing.

. . .

BY THE MIDDLE of the twentieth century, computing had become a commodity, if a specialized one. In 1965, Congress passed the Brooks Act, also known as the Automatic Data Processing Act, a name that now evokes visions of bulky mainframe computers. The law specified that technology acquisition in the federal government should go through the General Services Administration (GSA), the agency that handles the government's real estate and procurement services, sometimes known as "America's buyer."

The following year, the White House Office of Management and Budget released a memo called Circular A-76. It built on previous policies stating that the federal government "will not start or carry on any commercial activity to provide a service or product for its own use if such service or product can be procured from private enterprise."[4] The message was: if someone outside government can do your job, and especially if they can do it cheaper, we're giving it to them. The memo is important because it formalized the distinction between functions that are "commercial" and those that are "inherently governmental," a difference whose meaning has been debated ever since. In the former category, it included everything from bus service and vending machines to medical care, geological surveys, and the maintenance of weapon systems. In the latter, it placed "management of government programs requiring value judgments."[5]

One of the categories A-76 lists as commercial rather than governmental is automatic data processing. The subcategories under it, like the official title of the Brooks Act, paint a picture of computing in the 1960s: "batch processing, time-sharing," "programming and systems analysis," "key punching, data entry, transmission, and teleprocessing services," and so on. It's easy to see why keypunching didn't rate as an inherently governmental function back in the sixties and seventies. It still wouldn't.

There was no reason government couldn't acquire the equipment and expertise to do automatic data processing on its own. But the perception—often justified—was that, without the dynamics of marketplace competition in play, government would become slow, expensive, and bad at what it did. It had happened before. In 1921, for instance, concerned about high prices for steel amid war-driven demand, the US government embarked on an effort to make its own. It did eventually build a plant, but the steel it produced was half as good as what was commercially available and cost three times as much.[6] Commodities like steel are best left to the market. It followed that the same would be true of automatic data processing. Both A-76 and the Brooks Act sought to make sure that the new tools of computing didn't meet the fate of government steel. They would be things government bought, not made.

Outsourcing the work of federal government to the private sector grew steadily in the subsequent decades. Vice President Al Gore's "reinventing government" initiative, known more formally as the National Performance Review, would shrink the government workforce by about 420,000 jobs.[7] In 1994, a democratically controlled Congress also passed the Federal Workforce Restructuring Act, which required the executive branch to get rid of 273,000 jobs. The following year, as those job cuts were ongoing, Republicans gained control of the House for the first time in forty years and proceeded to give the legislative branch a shearing to match the one the executive branch had just gotten. Congress's workforce—lawyers, economists, and investigators who worked on congressional committees, as well as auditors, analysts, and subject-matter experts in offices like the Congressional Research Service—was cut by a third. The Office of Technology Assessment, which focused on how to respond to technological advances in society, got the axe entirely.[8]

In theory, as computers increased the productivity of administrative and information workers, fewer people might genuinely be needed to retain the same competencies and capacities. But that didn't seem to be the logic of these reductions. Rather, the cuts were intended to prove that the Republicans could walk the talk of smaller government, modeling the behavior they hoped to see more broadly. Congressional staff who studied the effects of the many government programs and offices built in response to an increasingly complex world tended to defend them, frequently putting themselves at odds with Republicans who wanted the programs crippled or gone. Getting rid of the staff who cared about them—including, in part, staff who knew the world of digital technology—was a good first step.

Technology was not central to these outsourcing debates, but the result was a dramatic loss in the core capacity of government at perhaps just the wrong time. Steel has not changed that much over the decades, but computing has. In 1966, the year of the A-76 memo, Russia landed Luna 9 on the moon and Lawrence G. Roberts published a paper about connecting computers to one another over dial-up, which would lead to ARPANET, the predecessor of the internet. By 1994, when the Federal Workforce Restructuring Act passed, we had the first commercial search engines, the first online e-commerce, and the first streaming radio station. The world was hurtling into a digital future—and investing heavily in it—while government was busy handing out pink slips.

Since then, with a few exceptions, government has thought of digital technology much like the pens and paper clips that GSA buys for government offices: something government would be crazy to produce for itself. And indeed, the hardware and software to handle common tasks were increasingly available for purchase, and it *was* crazy when government tried to build custom software to meet commodity needs. But government had another need by the 1990s: to understand the seismic shifts the internet was causing, and how our institutions should respond to the changing needs of the public. No procurement could meet that need: by A-76's own definition, it was "inherently governmental," requiring "value judgments" from people knowledgeable in this new digital world. Meeting this need required developing new internal competencies.

But these internal competencies in digital became necessary just as we were jettisoning internal competencies of all sorts, not developing them. Instead of digital competency, government has developed extensive processes and procedures for *procurement* of digital work, and the ins and outs of procurements sometimes seem more complex and technical than the latest programming languages.

That's not to say that there aren't competent and even expert digital leaders within government. When I was coming to DC, a friend introduced me to one of them: Mike Byrne, who had also come from California, moving to the nation's capital a few years ahead of me to work for the Federal Communications Commission. Mike is one of those people who make digital work in government—incredibly well, actually, within the esoteric system those pink slips helped create. He gets the job done. But the outsourcing imperatives make it an uphill struggle.

...

MIKE HAD BEEN in a big hurry when he came to DC. He drove all the way from Sacramento in four days, arriving on a Friday night in time to crash on a friend's couch. On Saturday morning he showed up at an office park tucked between the Smithsonian Castle and the Thomas Jefferson Memorial, just east of the Tidal Basin, and found his way to the Federal Communications Commission's "war room."

Mike's first sight when he opened the door was of garbage, leftover food, and stacks of paper. There were almost a dozen people in the room, and it was clear some of them had been sleeping there. They welcomed him and tossed him some pages. "Grab a pen," one said. "We need help editing." It was late February 2010, a year after Congress had passed the American Recovery and Reinvestment Act. Among many other provisions, the law required that the FCC draft "a detailed strategy for achieving affordability and maximizing use of broadband to advance consumer welfare, civic participation, public safety and homeland security, community development, health care delivery, energy independence and efficiency, education, employee training, private-sector investment, entrepreneurial activity, job creation and economic growth, and other national purposes." It was a tall order. The team sleeping on the couches was responsible for writing that plan.

Mike loved the feeling in the war room. He loved the camaraderie, the focus, and the intellectual challenge. Mostly, though, he loved being around people whose common goal was to help others. He'd gotten hooked on public service right out of college, joining the state of California as a geographic information systems specialist, then doing stints in transportation and public health before getting a master's and taking a tech leadership job with the state. Now he was part of the team responsible for making broadband internet access available to everyone in the US. To him and many of his colleagues, it was this century's version of rural electrification, a chance to connect the nearly one hundred million Americans who did not have broadband at home with all the opportunities that come with being online. And it was a chance to keep the US globally competitive. On that Saturday in the war room, when the FCC chairman and the head of the National Broadband Plan came in to discuss the edits, Mike could tell that this wasn't the first off-hours meeting, nor would it be the last.

Mike is a good writer, but he hadn't been hired for his writing skills. When the team wrapped up its edits and published the official National Broadband Plan document, it was only the beginning of the work. No one really knew what kind of internet services were available to consumers and at what cost. Policymakers didn't know what parts of the country even had the opportunity to get broadband, so they didn't know who was left the farthest behind. That's what Mike had been brought in to figure out: what access was available to every census block in America. To do that, he was going to need to take in twenty to thirty million rows of data a day from fifteen hundred different providers of broadband data across fifty-six states and territories and display them in one very large and complex map. What this next job needed was not the writers and analysts who'd been holed up in that trash-strewn room but programmers, designers, and data wranglers. The problem was that Mike didn't have any.

To get them, he would need to write contracts. "That's how

this works," he told me. "All of the staff—the core civil servants—they manage, but they don't implement. One hundred percent of the implementation is contractors." He soon got a taste of what that would mean. A manager asked him to join a meeting that included some of the vendors currently under contract for other projects, on the theory that they might also bid to work on the map. Mike walked in and said something benign like "Good morning, it's nice to meet you." The contractor's response was curt. "I don't say a word until there's a COTR in the room." A COTR is a contracting officer technical representative—that is, someone with formal authority over the contract. "Well, all right," Mike thought to himself. "This is going to be fun."

Mike had no staff, but he did have a congressionally mandated deadline, which was why he'd been in such a hurry. The map was due just shy of one year from the day Mike had arrived in DC. That deadline became his mantra. Where his nameplate should have been on his desk, Mike instead stuck a Post-it note with the date: February 17, 2011. Congress had initially appropriated money for the project to the National Telecommunications and Information Administration, so for Mike to hire his contractors he needed to write a plan that the NTIA could use to reallocate the funds to the FCC. He wasted no time getting started. The clock was ticking.

In the meantime, Mike laid out three lines of work. First was the map's infrastructure, the backend data assemblage. Next was the user interface, which would present all that data in usable formats. And last, a quality control effort, which would provide independent verification and validation. Each of these areas would need to be a different contracting vehicle.

When his plan finally made its way through NTIA approvals, it was already mid-April. Two months down out of his year. Mike's next job was to make a prototype and load it up with sample data to validate the approach, at which point he got the go-ahead to write the three contracts he would need to award. Now he'd been there for almost four months, and the clock was still ticking.

Contracts take time. There were some very competent (and friendlier) contractors who'd been working on other jobs when Mike arrived, with whom he developed a great rapport, but they would need to compete alongside every other vendor who chose to bid in an open competition. By the time his contracts had been through the necessary reviews—sped through, by government standards—it was July. Then there were five weeks "on the street," the time the contractor community has to review and prepare their bids. So it was mid-August when the bid evaluation process could start, to be undertaken by independent review panels that Mike had to assemble and get approval for. Everything had to be exactly right, in part because these contracts had to achieve what few do: avoid being protested. Most government procurement rules allow for any of the vendors who aren't selected for a given contract to file an official protest, which triggers a formal and often lengthy review of the process that led up to that selection.

Mike couldn't afford delays like this. The money from the NTIA was what's called "one-year money." The way it was appropriated by Congress, that is, it had to be spent in the fiscal year it was granted, which would end on September 30. If it wasn't formally awarded to vendors by then, the money would disappear in a cloud of administrative smoke. And it was now late August.

The independent review panels did their jobs, the procurement officers pushed as hard as they could, and Mike kept checking off the boxes, all the while watching the clock. As it turned out, even without any protests they were down to the wire: the normal delays and hiccups added a day here and a day there, until finally it was September 29, and the first of Mike's three contracts got awarded. On September 30, the final possible day before the money went away, Mike sat next to the procurement officer throughout the evening as the second contract took the final steps across the finish line. There was no time to celebrate; they ordered takeout and hunkered down for the final stretch. Together, they got the third and last one out the door a few minutes before midnight.

Mike had hounded the contract paperwork for months, but he's quick to give credit and slow to blame. "People hear stories like this and they think it's like Marge's sisters from *The Simpsons* working at the DMV," he tells me. "That's just wrong. This got done because that procurement officer was a tireless, dedicated professional, and so was pretty much everyone I worked with there." Still, the next day was the first day of October. Mike would now have a staff—that is, as soon as he got the contractors through the clearance process, badged, onboarded, and oriented. But the year he'd had to build the map was down to four months.

Mike got lucky. Although it wasn't his decision, the contractor who'd declined to speak without a COTR in the room didn't get chosen for the project. The contractors Mike thought could do the job did. And he took inspiration from what he'd seen that first week in the war room, where the leadership was right there with the analysts, building a sense of common purpose and making it easy to bounce ideas around. From a diverse set of outsiders, he built a real team. The software developers, too, wound up jammed together in messy rooms through long days, nights, and weekends. And in the end, they lived up to the sticky note where Mike's nameplate should have been. Against all odds, they shipped the National Broadband Map on February 17, 2011, the day it was due to Congress.

These days, the tech industry has moved away from its stereotype of successive all-nighters in trash-strewn rooms. Today's hottest tech employers promise work-life balance and flexible schedules. Ironically, it's the public sector, with its "Marge Simpson's sisters" image problem, where these kinds of unsustainable heroics are necessary. The complexities of appropriations and procurement rules bump up against the inflexibility of congressionally mandated deadlines to create these conditions. At least Mike had a deadline in his pocket to help him jump the line in backed-up bureaucratic processes. The late nights were draining, but they were better (in his eyes, at least) than the alternative, which would have been taking so long to ship the map that it was useless to policymakers. But Mike's biggest problem wasn't the deadline or the procurement rules themselves—it was the prevailing operating model that says that government staff manage but they don't implement. Especially not when it comes to digital. They rely on contractors for that.

· · ·

IF IT HAS become conventional wisdom that government is bad at tech and shouldn't be trusted with it, that's partly because of a view that government is bad at, and shouldn't be trusted with, most things. But when it comes to outsourcing tech, government was also following the example of private-sector companies, and one in particular.

In 1989, a few years before the wave of pink slips in DC, Eastman Kodak struck a deal with IBM to outsource Kodak's IT department at a scale that other corporations had never considered. Hundreds of Kodak staffers suddenly became employees of IBM, essentially doing the same jobs they'd been doing but now for another company. A trend started in the corporate world, with CIOs bragging about the size of their outsourcing contracts. The CIO of Procter & Gamble signed a ten-thousand-page contract to outsource the company's IT to Hewlett-Packard—the paperwork was so voluminous he had to sign it standing up.[9] Federal, state, and even local governments followed suit.

Perhaps it was not a wise model to follow. Kodak had dominated photography for most of the twentieth century, and in fact produced the first digital camera prototype in 1975, taking an early lead in the digital revolution. But by 2003 its share of the digital camera market was only 15 percent, and by 2010 it was half that. In 2012, Kodak filed for bankruptcy. There were many reasons for its decline besides its decision to outsource IT, of course, but it's fair to ask how Kodak's future might have been different if the company had been less extreme about outsourcing. "It's conceivable that IT's views could have saved the company, had the culture been different and had executive management been willing to listen," writes Robert Plant in the *Harvard Business Review*. "Imagine if someone had asked, 'When we process a negative, why don't we capture images as digital files, store them in our system, and allow them to be viewed via a third-party service? After all, we have a great deal of skill with file transfer protocols.' But any insights IT might have had were filtered out and lost."[10]

It is impossible to say whether Kodak's future would have been drastically different had it kept more of its IT workforce in-house. But if Kodak regretted its choice, it was not the only company to feel that way. By the late 1990s the outsourcing trend began to wane; businesses started to make more careful decisions about which functions were important to retain internally for strategic reasons. Yet while the private sector generally moved away from such outsourcing megacontracts, government went in the opposite direction.

Government procurement expert Mark Hopson calls our overreliance on outsourcing everything digital the Kodak Curse. But the comparison understates the matter. Even Kodak's extreme outsourcing strategy kept the development of technology products in-house: IBM was charged with maintaining the software and hardware needed to run the business, but it was Kodak's own engineers and product managers who came up with the new digital cameras, printers, and other products they would take to market. That product development work may have involved partnerships with other companies, licensing of outside technologies, or hiring of strategy consultants. But throughout Kodak's long journey from photographic film to digital products, completely handing over the development of its products to others was never even considered. Government, on the other hand, didn't stop at hiring out the creation and maintenance of internal systems needed to run its offices. As expectation grew that it would serve its customers through digital means, it often lumped that need into the same bucket and outsourced it too.

When I arrived in DC in 2013, I heard a lot of talk about "building a government fit for the twenty-first century," as if we were not well into that century already. A big reason for the lag is that our government spent the first several decades of the digital revolution treating tech systems like steel—as a commodity to be bought, not a capability to be developed. Instead, the capability that government has developed well, perhaps too well, is that of procurement. Our modern-day Grace Hoppers and Alphonse Chapanises are spending their days on paperwork instead of programming and design. Many of them find themselves having to follow Hopper's advice to ask forgiveness instead of permission. We've been training our public servants to master procurement rules so complex and processes so drawn out that the technology they buy is outdated or irrelevant by the time it gets delivered.

Herman Hollerith, that pioneer of data processing and former Census Bureau employee, turned his tabulating machines into a business that eventually grew into today's IBM. He was smart to strike out on his own: it's companies like his, not government agencies, that we invest in. But at what cost?

. . .

THE LACK OF technological know-how within government doesn't only make it hard to get projects started, as Mike Byrne found with his broadband map. It can also be devastating farther down the road.

Consider the agents of the US Border Patrol processing people detained while trying to cross the country's southern border. For years, the agents used a computer program that directed them to choose one of three categories: "unaccompanied minor," "individual adult," or "adult with children." Each case was assigned an "A number" (for "alien"); for an adult with children, the entire family shared the same A number. That's how the process worked until, in 2018, the Trump administration ordered the Border Patrol to start separating detained children from their parents. The cruelty of the new policy provoked a storm of controversy, but while the debate raged, the agents were left to sort out the practical consequences of the sudden change. Reprocessing every child as an "unaccompanied minor" generated a new A number for each one. Previously, the only children to have their own A numbers had been those old enough to have made it across the border on their own, but now agents found themselves sticking Post-it notes with A numbers on infants' onesies. Worse, the system had no provision for recording a link between two separate A numbers. Some border agents tried to keep notes connecting the A numbers of parents and children, but in the chaos of the rapid transition these were easily lost.[11]

A few months later, a federal court ordered the Border Patrol to reunite the migrant families. When the agents largely failed to do so, many people assumed they were deliberately dropping the ball because they disagreed with the court's ruling. There is certainly some truth to that. But we also now know that many public servants fought against the policy and did whatever they could to try to mitigate its worst effects but were stymied by the technology limitations.[12] There was simply no official record of which kids belonged to which parents. And adding this functionality to the software would have involved jumping through the same hoops that Mike had had to deal with. Requirements would need to be gathered, requests for proposals developed, a budget allocated, project plans put in place. The vendor that had originally built the software would presumably get hired to make the change, but the project would probably need to be bid out more broadly to comply with competition requirements. Procuring an update like this—making it possible to record a connection between A numbers—could easily take three to five years.

Treating software as just another commodity overlooks the fact that mission-critical software cannot simply be bought the way you buy a truck or even a building. It's an integral part of the service you provide, and that service and the environment in which it operates are dynamic. There is plenty to be said about the inhumanity of family separations, but let's pretend for a minute that this was just a policy change like any other. They happen frequently. And they can happen quite suddenly, both for terrible reasons and for entirely understandable ones. The point is that keeping track of people in ways that are consistent with current policy (and, one would hope, consistent with some semblance of decency) is the job of the Customs and Border Control. It is, in part, what the agency exists to do. An agency that can't update its software quickly enough to adapt to a new policy—or at least implement some creative but reasonably consistent and effective hack in the meantime—can't do its job. It happens that the impact of this particular failure was horrific treatment of vulnerable children and their parents. But what it says about government's capacity to fulfill its mission more broadly is also frightening.

Government can, and should, buy commodity software products from companies to handle its basic internal needs, which are not all that different from the needs of the private sector:

communication tools, HR and payroll systems, and so on. Indeed, government procurement teams have a terrible habit of contracting for bespoke software when they could buy commercial products—partly because we tell these teams to collect every possible requirement they can think of, which encourages and even calcifies arcane practices within the departments they serve. Those practices might feel like they have the force of law, but a closer look will often reveal them as mere clutter. An accounting department within the Department of Defense, for instance, requires custom software to follow intricate DoD bookkeeping guidance. The need would be much better served by having the DoD simplify its bookkeeping practices to work with standard accounting software instead.[13] But as we saw at the EDD, procurement and technology are both so far downstream of policy that the idea is nearly unimaginable.

Though government should buy commodity products for commodity functions, when it's not accounting or payroll but your agency's mission, the technology needs to be your product. It can't just be a project that was contracted for, developed, tested, and declared "done." You need to own the code, and you need to be able to change it to meet your needs. This doesn't mean that you can't use contractors at all—in government, you will almost certainly use them. It means that you must have the core competencies to support a living, ever-adapting system. Government knows how to acquire technology. What we need to acquire are capabilities.

OPERATIONAL IN NATURE

For a long time, I thought of our government's lack of digital competence as an unhappy mishap, a mistake to be corrected. Tech leaders like Mike Byrne, who had learned to wrest victory from the jaws of procurement, seemed to see it the same way. But I eventually realized that many others inside the Beltway regarded it more as the natural order of things—inevitable and immutable. Even in the middle of the healthcare.gov website crisis, when I told people that I had come to the White House to improve government's strength in digital, they looked at me as if I'd just told them I was setting up a zebra farm on the South Lawn. "But government outsources that work," they would say, as if I had been missing a critical piece of information when I got on the plane. As if that was the only conceivable way for things to be.

This unquestioning belief about what is and isn't proper government work has been shaped not only by the logic that favors outsourcing. It's also intimately connected to elite beliefs about what really matters. "The website is not what we do," I have heard many times from government leaders. Sometimes they are technically accurate, in the sense that the agency's website doesn't do much at all—it's just a mess of headshots of deputy assistant secretaries and outdated press releases, not a place where things get done.[1] But sometimes what government leaders mean is that the core of their work is policy. In the case of, say, unemployment insurance, they're busy establishing the myriad rules governing the benefit: who gets it, how much, under what circumstances, with what limitations. The systems needed to actually pay out the benefit are merely a detail of implementation.

The obvious problem is that although the website and the plumbing behind it are "just how you get your check"—or your health insurance, or your construction permit, or the custody of your child—they are too often why you *don't* get your check (or insurance, or permit, or child). You don't get it when the website is broken and won't let you start your application at all, or when you start the application process and run into a wall of incomprehensible questions, or when you get through the process but your application winds up stuck in an enormous backlog. To the laid-off worker waiting months for unemployment benefits, the argument that those are merely delivery hiccups and not "inherently governmental" work is meaningless. But that kind of thinking has been around for a long time.

• • •

ALMOST THIRTY YEARS after the Brooks Act and Circular A-76 consigned digital to the purview of contracting, two members of Congress thought it appropriate to revisit computing's status as a purely commercial function. It was 1995, and the world was being introduced to DVDs, MP3s, Windows 95, and the Pentium Pro processor. Jeff Bezos was launching Amazon, Larry Page and Sergey Brin were developing the technology that would soon power Google, and Microsoft and Netscape were engaged in a battle to own the browser. In that context, Representative

William Clinger of Pennsylvania and Senator William Cohen of
Maine started wondering whether digital strategy for the federal
government really belonged exclusively with "America's buyer,"
GSA. The result would be the Information Technology Management Reform Act of 1996, also known as the Clinger Cohen
Act—the legislation that kicked off the creation of the Federal
Enterprise Architecture and the CIO Council, ultimately resulting
in the ESB imperative that doomed Weaver's work on GPS satellites. That unfortunate unintended consequence aside, Clinger
and Cohen were asking an important and timely question: Was
there perhaps something more important about the world of
computers and the internet than a price negotiation?

One provision of the legislation they introduced charged the
White House Office of Management and Budget with developing strategy for digital technology in the federal government.
OMB is part of the executive branch; it oversees the performance
of federal agencies, administers the federal budget, and reports to
the president. It has real power and authority. At the time, GSA's
procurement work—getting the best price for data processing
services or even for the computers that government increasingly
bought and operated itself—might have been valuable to taxpayers, but it wasn't sufficient to lead government into the dawn-
ing digital age.[2] Clinger and Cohen wanted to elevate ownership
of the digital agenda to an institution with the power to make
something of it, to respond meaningfully to a foundational shift
in our society.

Except that OMB wanted nothing to do with it. In hearings
debating the proposed legislation, OMB was represented by John
Koskinen, the deputy director for management. (Twenty years
later, he would be the IRS commissioner reminding members
of Congress that they were the ones who had made the tax code
so mind-bogglingly complex.) Koskinen had similarly concluded
that the Brooks Act needed updating, and he had pulled together

a cross-government task force to make recommendations about what to do about the increasing number of government tech failures. The task force saw how agencies were needlessly building bespoke software at great cost even as vendors offered off-the-shelf products that could meet their needs, so they concluded that buying really was the skill they needed to develop. Koskinen supported most of what became the Clinger Cohen Act, and became a powerful advocate for government IT reform, but he argued against the provisions in the bill that would have given OMB more power or responsibility over the federal government's acquisition and use of technology. Among his reasons was that the "contemplated responsibilities are operational in nature and do not fit with the institution's policy role."[3]

In other words, while it no longer made sense to funnel all technology purchases through GSA, because agencies needed to learn to buy their own systems (they did), neither did it make sense to burden OMB with details of implementation. Policy people tend to see those who implement the policy decisions they make as being far below them in the pecking order, perhaps even at the bottom of it. OMB was the pinnacle of that pecking order. In other words, No, thank you, that's lowbrow stuff. That's not the kind of thing we do in powerful places in government.

Koskinen got dressed down for that statement by Senator Cohen, who wondered aloud why OMB had an M in its name if it had no management capability.[4] And technically, he lost the battle. The Clinger Cohen Act, as passed in 1996, states that "the Director of OMB shall promote and be responsible for improving the acquisition, use, and disposal of information technology by the Federal government." But OMB did succeed in eliminating some of the provisions it liked the least, such as a proposed mandate for the office to hire an overarching CIO for the federal government. (That's why the Federal Enterprise Architecture wound up being assembled by a council of thirty-odd CIOs from individual federal agencies instead.) The office also succeeded as far as actual practice was concerned. Under Koskinen's tenure and that of later leaders, OMB basically ignored the law. A history of federal IT procurement calls the stretch from 1996 through 2008 "the lost years" and accuses OMB of a "failure to lead."[5]

This way of thinking has deep roots. The British civil service traditionally divided the work of government into two categories: the intellectual and the mechanical.[6] Although Koskinen wouldn't have used those terms, it would have been easy to mistake the field of digital technology in 1995 for just the latest evolution of mechanical work. It didn't belong in OMB or anywhere else in the White House, where intellectuals were engaged in important, strategic work. It belonged wherever mechanicals bought things that carried out those strategies. So even as computers and the internet began reshaping society as we knew it, government leaders simply handed off anything digital to purchasing officers. They had more important things to think about. They did policy.

The federal CIO post finally came into existence in 2009, with newly elected President Barack Obama appointing Vivek Kundra as the first person to hold the position.[7] Obama inherited a country in economic tatters, the subprime mortgage crisis having just devastated global markets. Vivek inherited, in his words, "$27 billion in IT projects that were years behind schedule and over budget." Trying to make up for lost time, he issued at least ten separate directives aimed at modernizing the federal government's technology infrastructure and practices. The directives were very sensible, but the federal agencies largely ignored them, and Vivek left after less than three years.

His successor, Steve VanRoekel, tried to carry on Vivek's vision, but he too was hamstrung in critical ways. For one, the CIO's key lever for control is a process called Capital Planning and Investment Control, which is supposed to review every single IT investment made by the agencies. But this investment review is entirely disconnected from the actual budgeting process that federal agencies go through with the budget side of OMB.

For another thing, the federal CIO is set up to report to OMB's deputy director for management, who reports to the director of OMB, who reports to the president (though often goes through the chief of staff). Three steps away from the president might seem extremely close to the center of power. But for a position meant to be the top tech job in all of US government, it's quite far from it. Think of how many other positions are at that same level. Within OMB alone it is dozens, and within the whole of federal government it is hundreds, maybe thousands. By contrast, the top tech job in a private sector company will typically report either directly to the CEO or to one of the CEO's direct reports. The distance between tech leaders and real power speaks volumes about how little government culture values the work of implementation, technology included.

■ ■ ■

I GOT TO experience these dynamics firsthand when Todd Park, Obama's second US chief technology officer, asked me to work for him at the White House. (While the federal CIO focuses on the government's internal tech systems, the CTO typically acts more as a tech evangelist and adviser, serving within the White House's Office of Science and Technology Policy.) Todd wanted me to do for the federal government what Code for America had been doing for state and local governments. With a fledgling nonprofit to run and a nine-year-old daughter to raise, both in California, I declined at first, but Todd carried on as if I were joining, convinced I would come around. When he treated my daughter to the largest ice cream sundae she'd ever seen, in the dining room in the basement of the West Wing, it was clear my resistance was futile. In June 2013, I showed up for my first day at the CTO's office in the Eisenhower Executive Office Building.

The EEOB is a massive edifice in florid French Second Empire style, located in the White House complex across a glorified driveway from the West Wing. It was originally built in the late 1800s for the Departments of State, War, and the Navy. By the Obama administration, it also housed several components of the Executive Office of the President, including many people in OMB. Its hallways, tiled in black-and-white checkerboard, seem to stretch off into infinite distance; the marble stair treads of its ornate spiral staircases are worn down from centuries of White House staffers running up and down.

I did a lot of my own running that year, mostly down to the office of OMB's deputy director for management, on the high-ceilinged second floor. The office of the deputy director was the size of a small ballroom, meticulously painted in half a dozen earthy pastel tones to accentuate the intricately carved moldings and appointed with lush if somewhat worn period-appropriate furniture. Waiting in the foyer meant sitting on an upholstered settee, and meetings were held at massive wooden conference tables that one could imagine William Taft's functionaries drafting memos on. When the enormous velvet curtains were pulled back, the view was of the North Lawn and the flag waving over the White House.

When I finished a meeting at OMB, I would run up the stairs to the fourth floor, home of the Office of Science and Technology Policy. The hallways were still beautiful, but the ceilings were lower and it felt a bit like ascending to the servant quarters. The twenty or so of us at the CTO's office—including Todd himself—were squeezed into three small offices; mine had four desks in a space meant for one. In contrast to the elegant furnishings of the second floor, those desks looked like they had been found in the sale section of an Office Depot, with chipboard showing beneath the dinged fake-wood laminate. There wasn't much of a view; to look out our small dormer windows required

standing on a chair. Still, the close quarters made up in camaraderie what they lacked in luxury, and we took a distinct pride in
our modest and often chaotic surroundings.

We also took pride in being the biggest computer nerds in the
building. But except for me and my few close colleagues, even
the nerds at the CTO's office were supposed to work on technology policy, not on digital delivery of government's promises.
Among other things, this meant that Todd had been kept at arm's
length during the development of healthcare.gov, the website that
was to administer the health insurance exchanges mandated by
the Affordable Care Act. Like most government software projects, development of the site had been contracted out, in this case
through sixty separate contracts going to thirty-four different vendors.[8] The lead company on the project was a firm called CGI
Federal.[9] It was known at the time mostly for enterprise resource
planning software—a category of back-office software you don't
need to understand, other than to recognize that asking CGI to
make a website that practically a third of the entire country would
use made about as much sense as asking the military to build
Instagram.

Few people at the Centers for Medicare and Medicaid Services (CMS), the agency responsible for the health insurance
exchanges, seemed too concerned about the mismatch in skills
and experience. Even if they had been, they wouldn't have had
much choice anyway. The agency already had CGI Federal available through a contract known as "indefinite delivery/indefinite
quantity,"[10] a kind of retainer for a wide range of things, in this
case tech related. Drafting new contract solicitations for healthcare
.gov, getting them approved, and reviewing bids would easily
have taken a year—and much longer if any vendor that wasn't
chosen had protested. The bigger the contract, the more likely a
protest, and the budget here was in the hundreds of millions of
dollars. But the Affordable Care Act, signed into law in March

2010, required that uninsured Americans be able to enroll in health insurance plans by October 1, 2013. If the agency didn't use an existing contract, it risked spending that entire three and a half years on hiring the vendor, leaving no time for development.

Given this and other constraints imposed upon the agency, it's remarkable that healthcare.gov went live on its due date at all, even if it promptly buckled under the load. Its launch shouldn't have been the day's biggest headline, since it was also the day when the federal government shut down for the first time in almost twenty years. The House had been facing off with Senate Republicans over budget negotiations, and when the new fiscal year arrived with no resolution, agencies shuttered by default. With almost the entire federal government out of commission, it seemed a bit unfair that so much attention was focused just on the sputtering healthcare.gov.

There was a reason for all that attention. If the site failed, Obama's signature policy would likely go down with it. With this threat looming, suddenly the most important policy of the administration would live or die by its implementation. It was the first time the highest priority of the White House was the performance of a website.

. . .

AS SOON AS the stakes became clear, Todd was abruptly declared indispensable, pushed into the center of the maelstrom. Most of the rest of us on his team were not. Along with every other "non-essential" government employee, we were furloughed. We weren't even allowed to use our government-issued laptops or phones or talk to our colleagues about anything work related, at the risk of violating the Antideficiency Act, which "prohibits federal agencies from obligating . . . federal funds in advance or in excess of an appropriation, and from accepting voluntary services." If we were not getting paid, we could not legally work.

The irony of the furlough was bitter. Our project was being put on ice right when the need for nerds who could help—technologists the White House could trust—was the most apparent. The Affordable Care Act, which had survived so many hostile attacks, was in the process of imploding of its own accord, a victim not of hardball politics but of the very thing I had come to DC to help fix.

I saw a silver lining. Eventually, the shutdown would be over and my colleagues and I would return to work. Surely the people who'd thought we were crazy for trying to hire tech talent into the very center of government would now see the light. Surely they'd recognize that implementation capacity belongs in the most powerful parts of government, because without it we risk losing the policies we most treasure. I was certain we would be on a glide path.

There was a precedent for an office of tech nerds within central government. In 2011, the United Kingdom had established the Government Digital Service (GDS), whose director of digital had extraordinary authority for technology spending and strategy across ministerial departments and reported directly to the minister for the Cabinet Office. The GDS was shaking things up in London, questioning government's reliance on enormous contracts with a small number of vendors and launching streamlined, easy-to-use services to take the place of clunky, overwrought ones. Unlike Kevin at the VA, this team had plenty of opinions on business requirements and preferred lightweight, simple construction over the bulkiness and inflexibility of Kevin's concrete boats. While the UK government would still, of course, use outside vendors, the GDS insisted that there were certain functions that could not be contracted out and that having digital expertise inside government was critical to getting good results from contracting. To outsource everything was to abdicate responsibility for the very things the public relied on most.

When Todd first asked me to come to the White House, I happened to be visiting the GDS in London, and what I saw there broadened my sense of what was possible and left me eager to bring what I was learning home to the United States. In the UK, the GDS had made a difference precisely because it was in the Cabinet Office, so as my discussions with Todd continued I assumed that the office we were standing up would be part of the White House. But the plan instead was to build a unit at GSA, the same agency that had been charged with buying "automatic data processing" since the 1965 Brooks Act. The head of GSA, Dan Tangherlini, was as excited as I was, and had already decided that his administration's mission of providing federal agencies with the services they needed had to include digital. GSA could already get them pencils, fleets of vehicles, and real estate, but what many of them needed most were websites that worked.

When I arrived, I was introduced to a White House staffer named Haley Van Dyck, who had already been leading the development of this project with a small team. She and I quickly joined forces, and one thing we found we had in common was that, while we loved the idea of GSA's new unit, we wondered what would be missing. A digital unit at GSA would work by being a sort of internal consultancy available to other agencies, who could decide whether they wanted to make use of it or not. The advantage of such a setup is that it's always easier to collaborate when the other party chooses to, and this is often an effective strategy for wider change. GSA was also chartered to make investments that could be leveraged across agencies— building tools and teams for common use was what they did. But a unit at GSA wouldn't be able to do some of the things that the Government Digital Service did across the pond, especially if agencies *weren't* asking for a new approach. Would a GSA unit have the authority and flexibility to help in a crisis? Would it be able to shake things up the way the Brits had done?

We'd been furloughed on October 1, the day that healthcare .gov launched and crashed. When we returned on October 17, with the site still sputtering, Haley and I assumed those questions that had been nagging at us would now be burning for everyone. But the tone that John Koskinen had set two decades earlier lingered. Digital was still "operational in nature." It did not fit, we were told in so many words, with the policy role of the White House's OMB. "You tech people think tech can solve all problems," one leader told us when we brought it up. No, Haley and I said to each other, we don't think that. But a lack of tech skills sure was *causing* some problems.

Meanwhile, Todd had disappeared from the fourth floor of the EEOB, moving in with CMS to help with healthcare.gov. He had a straightforward two-step plan. Step one was to recruit a small team of technologists with relevant experiences and skills. Through a trusted network, he reached out to a set of remarkable individuals who signed up to jump into the fire with him. Step two was to win the trust of CMS—an agency that, like all other agencies, really, was highly skeptical of people from outside and resistant to their interference. The situation was tense, but Todd made it clear that he and everyone who came with him were not there to assign blame. They were there to help.

The result was the opposite of the usual response to failure. Instead of the hardening that tends to come with increased oversight—of the kind Weaver would later experience working on satellite software, further limiting what he could do—the CMS team suddenly found themselves with something they hadn't realized they needed: a group of smart nerds they could trust. Like most other agencies, they knew how to acquire technology and technology services; after all, they'd issued those sixty separate contracts for healthcare.gov alone. But now they had people on their team who could look at the code, not the contract terms. That, it turned out, made all the difference.

Thinking back on it, I suspect the people who were so dismissive of having a White House office full of nerds never thought that Todd's rescue effort would succeed. Between the original CMS team and the various vendors, healthcare.gov already had thousands of staff. How could a few dozen more make any difference? As Mike Bracken, who ran the Government Digital Service in the UK, said in an interview a few weeks after the launch, "Government constructs its self-image in terms of size. It thinks of itself as huge. The harsh truth for governments all over the world is that many digital public services could be developed at a fraction of the size by very small teams."[11]

Small teams work, if they have the right mindset and the right skills. And the reality was that many of the thousands of people from the thirty-four outside vendors did not have the skills. One of Todd's recruits told me about finding a flaw in the code and asking one of the contractors to log in and make a change. The contractor was a member of the technical team, but this recruit had an uneasy feeling about him, so he wrote out exactly the change the contractor was to make in the code. The next day, the error had not gone away, so Todd's group asked to look at the codebase. There was the change, just as directed—but it was preceded by two forward slashes. Two slashes before a line designated a comment, essentially a note programmers leave for the next programmer who'll come along. The slashes told the computer not to read that line as code but to ignore it.

Why did the contractor do that? "I saw other lines had these slashes so I thought I should put them in too," he explained. This supposedly technical staff member had never written a line of code. Just as government's core competency has been in contracting with vendors, some vendors' core competency has been in getting those contracts. They may have lots of people who do account management and project management, but they don't always have the people who can make the websites work.

Todd's team had the skills, and it had the right approach, both to the software and to the agency. Together with hundreds of dedicated CMS staff members, they made things work. The Affordable Care Act would stand.

There was another victory ahead. Some of the naysayers came around to the idea of a tech team in the White House, in part because now they could see what we meant. They could see that having tech expertise was a matter not of taking over from an agency team but of supporting it. They could see that despite CMS's remarkable strength in acquisition (it's a lot of work to issue sixty contracts), the agency hadn't acquired key competencies. They could see that a White House tech team taking the right approach worked.

We named the unit the US Digital Service, in homage to the Government Digital Service in the UK. It would not work quite the way the GDS had been designed—legally, the White House can't tell an agency which vendor to hire or fire or what tools to use, the way that the Cabinet Office in the UK could. But it would shake things up. When people like Weaver and Mary Ann went to work in government, they would still have a struggle ahead of them, but the USDS would be their beachhead.

The GSA team got to launch a digital unit of its own to shake things up too. The team named it 18F, after the location of its offices on the corner of 18th and F Streets. In the end, we got the best of both worlds.

The shake-up, though, I now realize, had really started when President Obama decided to appoint a federal CIO and CTO in the first place—not because they were mandated but because he wanted them. By inviting digital expertise into the White House, he set the stage for the change that was about to happen. If Todd hadn't been there, trusted by the president and able to build trust with CMS, and if he hadn't had the exact skills and network that were needed, we wouldn't have gotten proof that Clinger and Cohen had been right all along. When Cohen pushed for a CIO in the White House back in 1995, his motive (so I imagine) was not for OMB to provide tech services to all government agencies—that was GSA's role, or at least it would become so with the advent of 18F. He wanted, I believe, for people with tech expertise to have a voice in how we govern. I don't imagine he cared about tech for its own sake or thought that "tech solves all problems," as Haley and I were accused of thinking. But he cared about the very policy work that the naysayers thought they were protecting. Or rather, he cared that our government's policies have the impact they intended. He cared that they make a difference to the American people.

■ ■ ■

THE SHAKE-UP OF government's approach to tech continues. The USDS and 18F have played important roles, and so have people in agencies like Mike Byrne at the FCC. Many cities and states are seeing a similar shake-up, and a dozen or so have started units modeled after the USDS or 18F. But the divide that became obvious in 1995 is not fully bridged. Culture runs deep.

One of the first to respond to Todd's call for help with the health care website was Mikey Dickerson, who would later help us clear the backlog of unemployment insurance claims at the EDD. He left his job as a Google site reliability engineer on a day's notice, immediately plunging into sixteen-hour workdays with no end in sight. Credit for the site's rally of course belongs to hundreds of people, including career public servants, some of the vendors, and the rest of Todd's team. But it was Todd, Mikey, and a handful of others who ended up on the cover of *Time* magazine, hailed as heroes.

You'd think Mikey might have relished the triumph. Not only was the nation impressed with what he'd accomplished, he was just about Obama's favorite person. With the leaders of the most powerful tech companies gathered in the Roosevelt Room one day in December 2013, the president didn't want to start the meeting until Mikey got there. In Mikey's previous life, he had been one in a vast army of engineers those executives presided over. Today, he would be the center of attention. As it happened, a burst water pipe had shut down traffic a few blocks north of the White House, and Mikey had to run the last twelve blocks. He arrived late, sweaty, out of breath, and even more uncomfortable than normal in his only suit. But the president visibly relaxed when he showed up and teased Mikey affectionately. It would not be the last time Obama thanked him for saving the Affordable Care Act.

But the attention of the leader of the free world could not make up for Mikey's fundamental unease with the culture of government. "It was only when they were desperate that they turned to us," he told Steven Brill in the *Time* cover story. "They have no use for someone who looks and dresses like me."

Government did, in fact, have a use for Mikey, though I never saw him in that suit again—he went back to his T-shirts and cargo shorts. And it also had a use for Haley, who'd been ignored and sidelined for years as she'd tried to bring digital competency into this institution she cared so much about. The two of them would lead the USDS in its first years. It wasn't easy: Haley faced plenty more skepticism, even hostility, and Mikey never got over his alienation. Every week, it seemed, someone questioned whether the USDS should exist or came up with a plan to shutter it. But by the time Donald Trump won the presidency in 2016, the USDS was a couple of hundred people strong and known for far more than having helped save healthcare.gov. It had also helped seven agencies develop their own digital teams, some of them so strong, like the team at the VA, that they no longer needed the outside help. Today, the USDS is still thriving under a third president, a third OMB leadership.

Still, Mikey hit a nerve with that comment in the *Time* story. Brill, having spent several weeks observing Todd's team, agreed with him. The way the administration managed the program, he said, looked "almost as if they thought that actual governing, the nuts and bolts of governing, is for peons. And they are policy people." Intellectuals versus mechanicals. Policy people versus operational peons. You can almost hear Koskinen reminding Congress that the digital world was "operational in nature" and didn't fit with OMB's policy role.

Eighteen years earlier, Clinger and Cohen had asked the White House to develop a strategy for digital technology, but OMB hadn't wanted to let the mechanicals in the building. That decision came back to haunt them with healthcare.gov. The need for basic digital competency cannot be unclear now. But as they say, culture eats strategy for breakfast. The culture still has a ways to go.

7

STUCK IN PEANUT BUTTER

The lawmakers who voted to cut the federal workforce in the 1990s, just as digital technology was starting to truly reshape our lives, wanted smaller government. But starving government of know-how, digital or otherwise, hasn't made it shrink. It has ballooned it. Sure, there are fewer public servants, but we spend billions of dollars on satellite software that never goes to space, we pay vendors hundreds of thousands of dollars for basic web forms that don't work, and we make applying for government services feel like the Inquisition. That's the funny thing about small government: the things we do to get it—to limit government's intrusion into our lives—have a habit of accomplishing the opposite.

Take, for example, an application for food stamps that requires answering 212 separate questions. That's what Jake Solomon at Code for America discovered when he tried to find out why so few Californians in need enrolled in the state's Supplemental Nutrition Assistance Program, or SNAP. Many of the questions were confusing, while others were oddly specific and seemed to assume the person applying was a criminal. "Have you or any member of your household ever been found guilty of trading SNAP benefits for drugs after September 22, 1996? Have you or any member of your household ever been found guilty of trading SNAP benefits for guns, ammunition, or explosives after September 22, 1996?" It would often take up to an hour for people to fill out the entire form. They couldn't apply on a mobile phone; the application form, called MyBenefits CalWIN, didn't work on mobile. Lots of the people Jake observed tried to complete the form on computers at the public library instead, but the library computers kicked you off after half an hour. You had to wait for your turn to come again and pick up where you left off.

SNAP is a federal program that states are responsible for administering. In theory, the smaller the jurisdiction in charge, the more likely that the program will be attuned to local needs and values. California, along with nine other states, has chosen to further devolve administration to its individual counties, putting the burden of managing client data on fifty-eight separate entities.[1] To handle that burden, the counties (with the exception of Los Angeles) formed two consortia that pooled IT resources. When it became clear that clients should be able to apply online, each consortium then contracted for a single online application form to save money. It turned out to be quite expensive anyway: MyBenefits CalWIN, the form Jake studied, cost several million dollars to build. But at least that got divided across the eighteen counties in the consortium.[2]

What those several million dollars had gotten them was another question. Jake and his Code for America colleagues published a "teardown" of the website, over a hundred screenshots of it in action, with each page marked up to highlight the parts that confused and frustrated the people trying to use it.[3] (To be fair, the teardown also highlighted elements that were helpful to users; there were just far fewer of them.) The teardown was a powerful critique. It was noticed by anti-poverty advocates and the press alike, and the ways in which the counties were failing their clients started to get a lot of attention. Jake should not have been popular with the people responsible for MyBenefits CalWIN. Which was why he was surprised when HP, the vendor managing the website, invited him to a meeting of the consortium to present his work.

The meeting brought representatives from each of the counties to a business hotel in downtown Sacramento. It was only after Jake finished showing them his observations that he realized why he'd been invited. The HP representative at the meeting presented a variety of options for how the consortium might use its resources over the coming year, and then the county representatives began engaging in that hallmark of democracy: voting. One of the questions up for a vote was whether to engage some of HP's contracted time to make MyBenefits CalWIN usable on a mobile phone. Fresh off Jake's critique, that priority got the votes it needed to proceed. Jake had done the job he'd been invited to do without even knowing what it was.

What struck Jake about the process was not his success in convincing the county representatives. It was not that different from what Mary Ann had achieved when her recording of Dominic convinced the deputy secretary of the VA to let her team fix the health care application. The HP rep was interested in bringing to life for the county reps the burdens that applicants experienced. Jake was very good at doing that, and the rep had been smart to use him.

What Jake did find remarkable was the decision-making process. To him, it was clear how to decide the kinds of questions the group discussed that day. SNAP applicants were by definition low-income, and most low-income people use the web through their phones. So at Code for America, when Jake developed applications for safety-net benefits, he built them to work on mobile phones from the start. And when he and his team were trying to figure out the best way to phrase something, they came up with a few options that sounded simple and clear, and tested these options with program applicants. If lots of people stopped at some point when they filled out the form, it was a sign that that version of the instructions was confusing them. If some wording resulted in more applications being denied because the applicant misunderstood the question, that was another sign. Almost every design choice was, in effect, made by the users.

The counties, on the other hand, made those same choices by committee. Because each of the eighteen counties administers the SNAP program separately, the focus was on accommodating the unique business processes of each separate county and the many local welfare offices within the counties. It wasn't that the county reps didn't care about the experience of their users—their vote to start making MyBenefits CalWIN work on mobile phones was proof of that. But the process the consortium followed was not constructed to identify and address the needs of users. It had been set up to adjudicate between the needs of the counties. The result had been, for years, an experience for clients that was practically intolerable.

Ever since the founding of the United States, a core value for many has been restricting the concentration of government power. The colonists were, after all, rebelling against a monarchy. When power is concentrated in the hands of one person or one regime, the reasoning goes, we lose our liberty. We need to have some government, so we'll have to trust some people to make some decisions, but best to make it hard for any one person to do anything significant, lest that person begin to act like a king. Best to make sure that any decisions require lots of different people to weigh in.

But as Jake saw, the way you get 212 questions on a form for food assistance is not concentrated power, it's diffuse power. And diffuse power is not just an artifact of the complexities federalism can bring, with decisions delegated down to local government and then aggregated back up through mechanisms like the county consortia. The fear of having exercised too much power, and being criticized for it, is ever present for many public servants. The result is a compulsion to consult every imaginable stakeholder, except the ones who matter most: the people who will use the service.

A tech leader who made the transition from a consumer internet company to public service recently called me in frustration. He'd been trying to clarify roles on a new government project and had explained to multiple departments how important it would be to have a product manager, someone empowered to direct and absorb user research, understand both external and internal needs, and integrate all of it. The departments had all enthusiastically agreed. But when it came time to choose that person, each department presented my friend with a different name, sometimes several. There were more than a dozen in all.

He thought perhaps he was supposed to choose the product manager from among these names. But the department representatives explained that all these people would need to *share* the role of product manager, since each department had some stake in the product. Decisions about the product would be made by what was essentially a committee, something like the federal CIO Council that resulted in the ESB imperative. Members would be able to insist on what they believed their different departments needed, and no one would have the power to say no to anyone. Even without the complications of federalism, the project would still be doomed to exactly the kind of bloat that MyBenefits Cal-WIN suffered from.

This kind of cultural tendency toward power sharing makes sense. It is akin to saying this project will have no king, no arbitrary authority who might act imperiously. But the result is bloat, and using a bloated service feels intrusive and onerous. It's easy to start seeing government as overreaching if every interaction goes into needless detail and demands countless hours.

Highly diffuse decision-making frameworks can make it very hard to build good digital services for the public. But they are rooted in laws that go back to long before the digital era.

. . .

WHEN MARY ANN Brody and Emily Tavoulareas met with Dominic, the veteran who had written to the president about VA health care, they weren't just having a friendly chat with him. As they recorded him struggling with the online form, Mary Ann was careful about what she said and didn't say. She was not guiding him through the application, nor was she asking him whether he liked it or disliked it. She was observing how he interacted with it on his own, what assumptions he made on each screen about what to do next, and where he got stuck. She and Emily were practicing user research, a discipline critical to making consumer internet products. User research is not limited to observation: it can be both qualitative and quantitative, including interviews, surveys, and analysis of aggregate usage data. It is likely that almost every software product you use today, especially those that don't require formal training for you to use, was crafted based on the results of extensive and ongoing user research. And yet conducting user research has long been considered all but illegal within federal government.

If you hang around government long enough, you'll eventually encounter one of the laws that can be spoken of only when preceded by the phrase "comically misnamed." Perhaps the most prominent of these is the comically misnamed Paperwork Reduction Act of 1980, which created the White House Office of Information and Regulatory Affairs (OIRA) and charged it with measuring how long it takes to fill out any public government form. The law also required federal agencies to get permission from OIRA before collecting any information from the public. That's why at the top of every passport application, tax return, and so on you'll see something like "OMB No. 1545–0074." The number tells you that OIRA, which is part of OMB, has reviewed the form and approved it.

The intention of the Paperwork Reduction Act was to limit the administrative burden imposed on the American public by mandatory paperwork, such as filing taxes. But it has been interpreted to cover any time anyone in a federal agency wants to ask any member of the public any kind of question. And that interpretation has effectively functioned as a ban on user research. Getting OIRA approval typically takes six to nine months, includes several rounds of formally soliciting public comment through the government's official daily journal, the *Federal Register*, and requires a researcher to submit in advance every single question that will be asked. Imagine Mary Ann having to go through this process before she could interview Dominic. As tech veteran Erie Meyer points out, "Setting aside the daunting prospect of nine months of wait time and White House sign-off for one round of testing, knowing every single exact question [a developer] will ask in advance of a usability test is impossible— it's a conversation."[4]

To the law's credit, the fine print of the Paperwork Reduction Act excludes much of what counts as user research from its purview, including "facts or opinions obtained through direct observation by an employee."[5] But many federal officials choose the "better safe than sorry" route and require OIRA approval anyway—the norms are more powerful than the intent, and even the words, of the law. The justification is that approval "minimizes risk," though what they mean is that it minimizes the official's personal risk while increasing the risk to the project. By the time the approval comes, if it ever does come, the work that the research was supposed to inform will inevitably have moved on. Digital services will have been built or amended in a vacuum, lacking a basic understanding of the challenges their users face. Making user research impossible is particularly ironic because digital professionals typically use it to *reduce* the burden of their applications—it is the very practice that holds the key to more streamlined, easy-to-use services. Today, Americans spend 10.5 billion hours a year—about forty-two hours per adult—on paperwork just for the federal government.[6] That doesn't count time spent on forms from state and local government, which can add up quickly.

The Obama, Trump, and Biden administrations have all worked to clarify policy to allow this much-needed practice.[7] But the norms of risk aversion continue to defeat even official guidance from the White House. The Consumer Finance Protection Bureau, for instance, recently asked OIRA for permission to continue some research it was already doing to improve its financial education programs—the kinds of interviews that Mary Ann had done with Dominic, plus a few lightweight surveys. OIRA responded by posting the request to the *Federal Register* for two months of public comment.[8] In other words, it sought feedback from the public on the CFPB's plan to seek feedback from the public. In the meantime, no research would be allowed.

• • •

WHILE THE PAPERWORK Reduction Act has functioned to severely limit the input that designers of government services can get, another decades-old law *requires* such input—but in such a way that it, too, makes it very hard to properly implement digital services. The Administrative Procedures Act (APA) was written explicitly to be a check on the power of government, particularly the administrative agencies. Before agencies can enact new rules or regulations, the APA requires that they publish their drafts in the *Federal Register*, allow the public to comment on them, and demonstrate that they've taken the public comment into consideration before issuing the final rule. As long as the public gets a voice, the logic seems to go, government won't be able to do too much damage. All this sounds eminently reasonable in terms of a government of the people, by the people. But, as with the Paperwork Reduction Act, it's important to consider how it has worked out in practice.

The origins of the APA go back to debates surrounding the New Deal. To help the nation recover from the Great Depression, President Roosevelt created new federal agencies like the Social Security Administration, the Works Progress Administration, and the Federal Deposit Insurance Corporation. The people in these agencies needed to make a lot of decisions about how to implement laws like the Social Security Act, and because there existed no comprehensive standards that governed agency action, Congress didn't have much control over how that was done. Some of Roosevelt's team seemed to rub the fact in. When Congress asked the head of the Federal Emergency Relief Administration to explain how he had decided to allocate the agency's funds, for instance, he refused to answer.[9] Republicans, who were already opposed to all this federal activism, sought ways to curb the power of the new agencies. Democrats acknowledged the need for clearer standards for agency action but also wanted administrative agencies to be able to exercise their own judgment and to move more quickly than the legislative process allowed for, especially given the urgency of the moment.

A bill governing agency procedures made it through Congress in 1938 but Roosevelt vetoed it. Another attempt was made in 1941 but failed as the country entered World War II: it's hard to justify slowing down decision-making when the country is at war. But in 1946, with the war over and Roosevelt dead, the issue resurfaced. This time, the Democrats no longer had such strong majorities in Congress, and they worried that the Republicans, if they took control, would undo much of the New Deal. Procedural restraints on agency action suddenly looked pretty appealing when the other guys might be in charge. The APA passed both houses of Congress in early 1946, and President Truman signed it into law later that year.

Like so many other laws that were written long before the internet, the APA seems antiquated. In a world where participation in public dialogue happens everywhere, publishing notices in the *Federal Register* is like requiring name changes to be printed in the local town paper. (Though at least the *Federal Register* is now available online, and some agencies allow electronic submissions of public comments as well.) But the bigger problem is that, while the APA dates from the mid-twentieth century, it is hamstrung by thinking from even earlier eras. As law professor Edward Rubin puts it, the APA is grounded in a "pre-administrative approach to governance."[10]

"In the Middle Ages, government was regarded as an essentially judicial function and all its officials, including the king, were viewed as magistrates," writes Rubin. Earlier in American history, administrative agencies in the federal government, though not medieval, were weighted toward judicial functions as well. Before the New Deal, the number and scope of things the federal government did was much smaller, and Congress could make far more of the rules that were needed. The agencies were therefore called on mostly to interpret and enforce federal laws when there was a conflict between parties. Their roles were more reactive and more incremental, with officials weighing in on the nuances over which the conflict had arisen.

But by 1946, when the APA became law, a lot had changed, including, as Rubin says, "the advent of the administrative state itself." The federal government was starting to resemble the larger and more ambitious institution we have today. The New Deal required spending massive amounts of money on programs to

STUCK IN PEANUT BUTTER

save farms, provide work for the unemployed, and protect the poor and the elderly. Agencies old and new were crafting the rules, processes, and forms that would establish and administer these new programs. They were increasingly in the business not only of adjudication but also of rulemaking and the delivery of services. And of course the enormous administrative effort of World War II had required far more than merely interpreting federal laws and resolving disputes between parties. All these functions required "priority setting, resource allocation, research, planning, targeting, guidance, and strategic enforcement."[11]

None of those administrative competencies are enabled by subjecting every decision to the equivalent of a jury trial. But the APA, stuck in its outdated notion of government as primarily judicial, doesn't really offer anything else. As Rubin points out, the APA-mandated official notice, public comments, and formal accounting of how those comments are used "replicate . . . the due process requirements of notice, a hearing, and an impartial decision maker for adjudicatory decisions." These are all "requirements that are largely judicial in nature." Agencies today are supposed to implement our laws, turning high-level direction from Congress into the practicalities of functioning government. But they're made to do that while operating like they're constantly in court.

The result is that very procedure-heavy, cumbersome, and lengthy decision-making processes—which are necessary and appropriate for high-level decisions—bleed into determining the details of implementation. There absolutely *should* be a lot of debate, due process, and formal rules governing the commitment to provide food assistance to the needy nationwide. But precisely how to word the questions on the application for that food assistance might benefit from less debate and more informed research.

Is the APA just the cost of a representative democracy that relies on checks and balances? Rubin says no, instead charging

both the law itself and the way it continues to be applied with
something akin to myopia or laziness. "Courts expand the adjudicatory implications of the statute because of their own familiarity with the adjudicatory process," he writes. "The judicial model
persists because of its familiarity, combined with the unfamiliar-
ity of more modern administrative alternatives. In its persistence,
however, it smuggles incremental . . . adversarial approaches into
a comprehensive law-creating context, where they encumber the
process"—without improving the outcome.

Before the New Deal, government implemented less, so questions like how to format a benefits application just didn't come up
as often. Today, we have not only far more such questions but also
new problems—like how to let people apply on mobile phones
and, more generally, how to keep up with rapidly changing tools
and expectations. Essentially, the APA used nineteenth-century
(or perhaps medieval) thinking to try to solve a twentieth-century
problem, which has snowballed in the twenty-first century.

• • •

THE JUDICIAL FRAMEWORK for decision-making is such a bad fit
that much of what the APA stipulates is largely ignored today.
For instance, the law defines both formal and informal rulemaking. When you hear about the many months or years it takes for
an agency to get through an APA process, you might assume it
was governed by the formal rulemaking provisions. In fact, today
everything goes through the informal option. The formal process
requires that agencies provide private parties potentially affected
by a new rule with an oral hearing in which they can present their
witnesses and cross-examine opposing ones, taking the judicial
metaphor entirely literally.

The United States Department of Agriculture tried this when
it was about to issue a rule regarding the minimum peanut content
in peanut butter. Advocates wanted it to be at least 90 percent

peanuts, manufacturers wanted to require only 87 percent peanuts, and adjudicating that 3 percent difference under the formal rulemaking process took the Food and Drug Administration twelve years of the 1960s and 1970s. The case went almost all the way to the Supreme Court, and the oral hearing alone took twenty weeks and produced a 7,736-page transcript.[12] (The advocates ultimately prevailed.) Since then, when Congress writes laws, it usually avoids the words "on the record" when it comes to rulemaking, leaving agencies the option to choose the informal "notice and comment" process. Unsurprisingly, it's chosen every time. Peanut butter killed formal rulemaking.

If you want to limit the power of government, making a small decision about a food product take twelve years and hundreds of thousands of hours of staff time might sound attractive, because it would limit the number of issues that agencies could take on. A lack of oversight in some areas might initially feel like smaller government. But as genuine needs inevitably arise (What do you do about a bad batch of a common over-the-counter drug? A salmonella outbreak? A deadly bacterium found in a baby formula plant?), the heavyweight procedural requirements result in government that is literally big—since agencies must grow to handle those needs—and very slow. Even the informal rulemaking process is bogged down with far too much "judicialization." The original team on healthcare.gov would likely agree: the full set of rules governing the program they were supposed to administer wasn't finalized until the site was due to launch.

Judges do not seem to care about speed, whether in the courtroom or in administrative agencies. As one analysis puts it, they want agencies to practice "intensive, multipolar forms of deliberative rulemaking," and they tend to punish them if they deliberate too little or consult too few stakeholders.[13] And it's only getting worse. A recent court decision regarding a hedge fund manager found by the Securities and Exchange Commission to have defrauded his clients is a good example.[14] The fraud had originally been determined at an administrative hearing within the SEC, and the defendant sued the agency in response. The case made its way through the courts for ten years (speaking of speed), until in 2022 the US Court of Appeals for the Fifth Circuit ruled that the SEC's normal procedure was unconstitutional because it did not involve a jury trial. Public policy professor Donald Moynihan calls the ruling "a major break from almost a century of precedent that accepted that the SEC could employ administrative hearings and administrative law judges," noting that "from an administrative capacity perspective, the decision makes it extraordinarily difficult for the SEC to regulate industry."[15] It likely causes the same difficulty for a wide range of other agencies, from the Environmental Protection Agency to the Federal Trade Commission. If the ruling stands (cases on the same topic are currently pending before the Supreme Court), it will inevitably make their actions even slower. The peanut butter is back.

Today, when digital professionals come into government ready to build services for the American people, they are shocked at how hard it is to build anything at all. It's not only because the government policies they are attempting to digitize are enormously, needlessly complex. It's not only because they have to spend so much of their time on procurement, since the actual code writing and interface design must all be outsourced. It's not only because seemingly arbitrary aspects of their work have been wildly overspecified by distant rule makers with little understanding of the problems at hand. And it's not only because we put the people who build vital government technology at the bottom of the hierarchy, where they have little voice or power. It's also because the administrative agencies many of them work for were designed—on purpose—to be unable to make the kinds of decisions that good software development requires. A lot of people still don't want them to. But that desire makes the agencies into the very thing those people fear.

The next time you're struggling with a government form or process that makes you feel like some nameless, faceless bureaucrat is trying to torture you, remember that no one public servant has that power. That form or process was the result of committees, comment periods, and countless opportunities to object, influence, overturn, and relitigate. If someone had been given the power to understand your needs and make decisions in your interest, you might be having a very different experience. But our fear of concentrated power has made that incredibly difficult. In our attempts to keep government small, it's not the disease that has hurt us, it's the cure.

THE PROCEDURE FETISH

There's an old joke I used to love when I started working in software. It goes like this:

> A man flying in a hot air balloon realizes he is lost. He spots someone below and descends to him. "Excuse me," he shouts, "can you tell me where I am?" "Yes," the man below replies. "You're in a hot-air balloon, hovering thirty feet above this field. You are between 42 and 44 degrees north latitude, and between 88 and 90 degrees west longitude." "You must be an engineer," says the balloonist. "I am," the man replies. "How did you know?" "Well," says the balloonist. "Everything you told me was technically correct, but it's entirely unhelpful. And I am still lost."

Over the course of my career, I've met my share of engineers who fit this stereotype. But when I went into government, it was the engineers and other digital team members who were more often on the receiving end of comments that were "technically correct but entirely unhelpful." And it wasn't other coders they were getting them from. It was bureaucrats invoking the law.

While the government-limiting tactics that have largely backfired are mostly associated with conservatives, when it comes to burdening government, liberals deserve their fair share of the blame. The *New York Times* columnist Ezra Klein notes that the environmental movement in particular has spawned what he calls "an entire branch of liberalism . . . dedicated to criticizing and then suing and restraining government." We may think of the 1960s and 1970s campaigns to clean the air, preserve wildlife habitats, and stop chemical pollutants from being dumped in waterways as being anticorporate, and indeed it was corporations committing these atrocities. But overwhelmingly, it was not companies that the activists sued but the government agencies that gave the green light for the companies' projects.[1] Klein credits the movement with critically important successes but also urges us to recognize the long-term impact of both the laws the movement fought for and the antigovernment instincts it produced, which the left continues to exercise with a sort of automatic muscle memory. Laws that made new construction projects much harder, for instance, are today huge impediments to mitigating both the housing crisis and the climate crisis, blocking not only affordable housing but also critical renewable energy infrastructure like solar and wind farms. The environmental movement got really good at stopping bad things from happening but less adept at enabling, and speeding up, good things. Now the habit of suing has itself become a great threat to our environment.

And it's not just an overreliance on blocking that the left is guilty of but too much legalistic thinking. To be sure, our government has always been dominated by lawyers. Alexis de Tocqueville remarked on this back in the 1830s, when he wrote that "the aristocracy of America is on the bench and at the bar." More recent commentators like Nicholas Bagley blame the profusion of lawyers for what he describes as government's "procedure fetish": "If all you've got is a lawyer, everything looks like a procedural problem."[2] But while lawyers are found throughout US politics, the left seems especially fond of them. All the recent Democratic presidents and vice presidents, dating back to the Bill Clinton administration, have gone to law school, and all but Al Gore hold law degrees. Neither Bush presidents did—both were business-men, the younger the only American president to hold an MBA. And Trump is the opposite of a lawyer, flagrantly dismissive and even hostile to the law. Klein reads more into this than simply a party preference, describing liberals as "legal institutionalists." "As they captured the heights of the legal profession," he says, "it captured them. Their thinking became defensive. Their thinking became small and cramped, professional."[3]

Klein's diagnosis is not specifically about implementation. He's describing a problem with how liberals approach policy in general—overly technocratic expertise substituting for a larger sense of purpose. But his analysis captures the need for an approach that is more democratic (in the small-d sense of the word), more open to popular interpretation, than our current bureaucratic culture allows for. Such an approach would recognize that fussy, technically accurate readings of law and policy can be entirely unhelpful when it comes to creating services that make sense to people.

. . .

NATALIE KATES HAS run up against the technically-correct-but-entirely-unhelpful approach to law many times. As a member of the US Digital Service, she was assigned to help the Centers for Medicare and Medicaid Services with the implementation of the 2015 law designed to bring value-based care to Medi-care. The legislation, known as the Medicare Access and CHIP

Reauthorization Act, or MACRA, was designed to make Medicare pay doctors more for better patient care and better outcomes. So a website had to be built, one that would let doctors submit the data that CMS would need to determine the quality of care they had provided. CMS had just been pummeled by the failures of healthcare.gov and was eager not to repeat the experience. This time, the website needed to work.

Having the site work wasn't just a matter of uptime and throughput. The program the website administered had to make sense to the doctors who were supposed to use it. Natalie's first task was to put up some informational pages—not the site that would allow the doctors to file their claims and submit their data, just something that explained the new program and its new rules. It should have been a simple task. But she immediately hit a barrier, the first of many.

A doctor could participate in the new Medicare program either as a sole practitioner or as part of a group. There were lots of places in the regulations that CMS was drafting that said what groups could or couldn't do. But as Natalie and her colleagues gathered what they needed so she could write plain-language copy for the website, they found that the various policy teams working on the regulation defined "a group" differently. In fact, there were nine different definitions. And none of them were simple. Doctors might qualify as part of a group when they were trying to do X, but not if they were trying to do Y, and maybe yes again if they were trying to do Z. Doctors who take Medicare were already angry about what they saw as bureaucratic hell. This, and other complications like it, was going to alienate them further.

It was also going to make the website CMS would eventually build, the one that would let doctors submit their quality data, inordinately complicated and fragile. Coding, debugging, and quality-checking software that accounted for nine different

definitions of a group would take a very long time, time the team
didn't have. Like Mike Byrne with his broadband map, they had
a congressionally mandated deadline.

Natalie and a CMS colleague who understood the problem in
depth went to the policy lead, who saw their point. They agreed
to get everyone together to discuss the issues, which was itself a
challenging task. Representatives from each of the policy subteams gathered, along with half a dozen people from MITRE,
a large nonprofit government advisory organization that CMS
had hired to work on the policy. As the head of policy began
explaining the problem, the staff from MITRE began explaining
why there absolutely had to be nine different definitions.

The MITRE team wasn't trying to be difficult. They were trying to be accurate. And technically, they were right. To start
with, the new program brought together a few existing programs
that CMS had been running for several years. Those original
programs had been created by separate policy teams at separate
times, and the teams hadn't talked to one another. Each of those
programs had already established distinct definitions of a group.
Adding to the confusion, each health care provider in the United
States has at least two unique identifiers: a tax ID number from
the IRS, which has been around for a long time, and a national
provider identifier, which CMS started issuing in 1996. Each of
these designations also distinguishes between individual providers (largely sole practitioners) and groups. Doctors have lots of
options for how they set up their medical practices and there's
a whole industry of consultants that help doctors optimize this
setup for tax advantages. So there was a legitimate basis for the
nine different definitions.

But there was also a lot in common among the definitions,
and Natalie was convinced that the differences—which were
small and fairly technical—could be negotiated, so that all the
policy teams would agree on one definition that met most of

their needs. A doctor should be able to file as an individual or a group consistently across the program, and it should be reasonably easy to understand which designation a doctor had qualified for. At Natalie's urging, the policy lead asked the team to go back and keep trying. "I understand that it's complicated," she told the MITRE team. "But it needs to make sense to a person."

Making sense to a person is something that often gets lost along the way. One of Natalie's peers at the USDS, for example, was helping the Small Business Administration with a form that business owners had to fill out to qualify as a minority-owned business. This user experience designer watched proprietors stop and squint in confusion at questions such as "Does someone receive greater compensation than the highest officer or individual upon whom eligibility is based?" In one session, one of the business owners looked up and said, "Why don't you just ask if I'm the highest-paid employee at my firm?" "Bingo," she thought. The SBA team confirmed that that wording would work just fine. There's a lot less squinting at this form these days.

The CMS team kept boiling the pieces down too. The MITRE staff objected to every simplification, but the policy teams kept reconvening to negotiate, and in the end they resolved most of the conflicts among the various definitions and got down to two definitions of a group that could take the place of the previous nine. Natalie wanted to keep going: she was certain that they could get down to just one and that it would make for a better program, with greater clarity, lower administrative burden, and better outcomes. But the MITRE advisers, and a few of the CMS staff, were already operating outside their comfort zones. To them, simplicity came at the expense of what was technically accurate according to the law, and accuracy was their job. Two definitions was as far as they could go. It wasn't the outcome Natalie wanted, but she took her partial win and moved on.

Based on her experience working in government, she knew there were dozens more battles like this ahead.

• • •

EZRA KLEIN'S CHARACTERIZATION of overlegalized thinking as "small and cramped, professional" will resonate with anyone who's had to fight the sort of fight the team at CMS did. And that kind of thinking can be literally fatal. In January 2020, before there were any known cases of COVID transmission on US shores, Seattle researchers who had been collecting nasal swabs for a flu study realized that they could use those swabs to find out whether the virus was circulating in their area. But federal and state officials repeatedly rejected their requests for permission to do so. The subjects hadn't consented to any use of their samples other than for the flu study, so the officials were certainly technically correct. After weeks of trying, out of desperation, one of the researchers tested the swabs anyway. She found COVID present in swabs from people with no recent travel history, meaning that the virus had been circulating undetected in the United States for well over a month.[4] By the time shelter-in-place orders were finally announced, it was exploding all around the country. Applying the rules without reasonable interpretation had been more than unhelpful. The delays it caused contributed to an untold number of deaths.

"Professional" isn't often meant to be derogatory. But it's an expert with specialized knowledge who will insist on nine different definitions of a group. Sometimes it's lawyers who do this, but other experts in niche subjects are just as likely to. Their identity—and the measure of their value—can become deeply tied to the specialized knowledge they possess. And that knowledge, which ought to serve the goals of the program, instead begins to serve its own, often conflicting goals. It becomes master of the people who wield it.

When a service designer like Natalie says, "I understand it's complicated, but it has to make sense to a person," she is rejecting elite, professionalized authority in favor of something more accessible, practical, and commonsense. She is also invoking a historically deeply rooted notion that we, the people, are allowed to interpret the law in ways that make sense to us.

It is only recently that we have given over the ultimate power to interpret law to such professionalized authorities. Law scholar Larry Kramer, describing what he calls "popular constitutionalism," explains that courts were never considered the final say on interpretation of the Constitution until the late twentieth century.[5] The system was originally designed to have play between the views of the different branches of government and ultimately to allow the public to choose the winning interpretation. A system so conceived would, one hopes, increase the chances that the winning interpretation would take into account what Klein says liberals are too often missing or too timid to claim: a vision of what the law is for. MACRA was for making health care better, and Natalie's interpretation put that goal first. Kramer would cheer her for it.

Liberals' penchant for suing to enforce regulations contributes to the cramped professional thinking that loses sight of the big picture. As scholars have demonstrated, litigation changes agencies over time.[6] To begin with, the more they are sued, the more legal staff they must invest in. But more importantly, courts tend to hold agencies accountable not for their outcomes but rather for their fidelity to procedures, compounding the accountability trap the bureaucracy is already stuck in. The more an agency is exposed to the courts, the more everyone there, not just the legal staff, must care about, pay attention to, and layer on procedures when they are required to make any decisions—in other words, the more everyone starts to think like a lawyer, and a defensive one at that. This is a rational response: extensive documentation

of administrative procedures and the technical and legal information that supported every choice not only helps in the event
of litigation but tends to ward off lawsuits in the first place. And
litigation is expensive.

Of course, conservatives are famous in their own right for
suing government to stop it from doing things. They're so good
at it, and recently so good at capturing the courts, that they may
be in the process of stopping federal agencies from doing much
at all. The Supreme Court's 2022 ruling in *West Virginia v. EPA*,
for example, gutted the agency's authority to do its job in ways
that could have implications for many other federal agencies and
could trickle down to states and municipalities. But this alarming
court decision and others don't rely on slowing agencies down in
order to reduce government's influence; they simply strip them of
their powers. It's not so much hobbling government as cutting it
off at the knees. That may end up being more dangerous than the
slow death-by-a-thousand-legal-definitions, but the gradual hobbling of government set the stage for what has now come to pass.

As often as not, people file lawsuits against government because
they believe they are fighting for a righteous cause. And lawsuits
serve many purposes in a complex and sometimes bizarre ecosystem of stakeholders. I've been politely asked more than once by
savvy public servants if I would be willing to sue the agency they
worked for, because they agreed with technological or administrative changes I was suggesting but didn't feel they had the
mandate to push them through without a lawsuit as a catalyst. (I
declined.) But however just the cause, every lawsuit over process
and procedure has an undeniable impact not only on the culture
of the agency it targets but on the zeitgeist of government. Each
one is a cautionary tale for another agency or another jurisdiction. Each one makes government less tolerant of risk. Each one
makes the bureaucracy more technically correct but entirely less
helpful. Perhaps the fact that none of that caution and diligence

did anything to keep a conservative Supreme Court from attacking agencies' power will change that, but I doubt it. Culture changes slowly, even in times of great upheaval.

. . .

LITIGATION IS EXPENSIVE, which is why agencies try so hard to avoid it. But when defensive legalistic thinking pervades government agencies, that is expensive too, and not only because it increases the complexity of their work and slows down decision-making. Many of the costs are borne by the public, who must slog through confusing, time-consuming processes when they need to interact with government.

There is an indelicate term for digital services that take complicated policies and rules and just plop them—all of them—directly into forms. I once asked a designer who was trying to speed up the bureaucracy of immigration applications why the process took so long and was so hard both for the petitioners and for the workers who handled their cases. Her first answer (there were other reasons too) was that the agency had "vomited the policy into the forms." She meant not that the policy stank, necessarily, but that it had been left as an essentially undigested mess. There'd been little to no attempt to transform the policy into a usable service—no design that tried to present what is understandably a complex process via an interface that made it easier on both client and bureaucrat. The operating logic had apparently been little more than "Well, we're going to need the following information to process their application, so let's make one form that asks for all of it." There'd been little thought given, for instance, to which questions were easy or hard to answer and when they might be asked. Do we really need the exact dates and locations of every out-of-country trip the applicant took in the past ten years at the very beginning of the process?

Of course, much of the information needed could come from

sources other than the applicant. If you have a green card, for instance, and you're applying for citizenship, the immigration agency has a lot of information about you already. Administrators often want to borrow data from other parts of government to streamline applications and reduce errors. I long ago stopped counting the number of times agencies have put forth visions of "prefilled applications" or "single sign-on services" that leverage the information an agency already has about its customers. But the number of agencies that have delivered on those visions is small, for the kinds of reasons I've already discussed, including lack of internal digital capacity, arcane and lengthy procurement processes, the many restrictive procedural requirements set forth in laws like the Computer Matching and Privacy Protection Act of 1988, and policy complexity that leads to thousands of formal requirements and doomed megaprojects.[7] Whatever the reasons, though, for the people who must use these services the outcome is the same: they must wade through policy vomit.

The decision to allow someone to immigrate or naturalize is high stakes for both parties. It is never going to be reduced to a handful of questions followed by a simple yes or no. But even a necessarily detailed process can be made easier through thoughtful service design, including the kind of policy simplifications Natalie championed at CMS. Conversely, even what seems like a very simple interaction can become burdensome when legal and policy thinking trump service design.

Imagine if a government agency decided to make its own car service available to its employees and designed the interface taking the usual government approach. A project manager interviewed lawyers and policy leads to collect the official requirements, which then got handed off to developers at a contractor. Testing consisted only of making sure that the developers did what the requirements said.

You are an employee of that office, and you need a car to take you to the airport one morning. The online form tells you to type in your name, department, division, office branch, email address, and phone number. Then it asks for your employee ID number, which alone would have allowed it to fill in all the info that came before. It requires your office address, your mailing address, your home address, and then separately the addresses where you want to be picked up and dropped off. To enter each address, there are separate fields for house number, street name, and street type. That last one is a drop-down menu that requires you to scroll through dozens of different options: *alley, arcade, boulevard, causeway, circle, court, crossing, drive,* and so on. *Street* is buried near the bottom, between *station* and *summit*. What's more, the form requires the exact address of your destination, and you've never thought of the airport as having a street address. You find something plausible sounding online and hope that it will do. When you hit "submit," the form tells you that you've made an error somewhere and makes you start the process all over again. None of the information has been saved.

When you come across services like this, you may assume that they've been poorly designed. The reality is often that they haven't been designed at all. The developers have essentially just taken the official terms of service—which even in an easy-to-use app like Lyft are often dozens of pages of legalese—and made that the interface to the user. Because the agency's overriding goal was not to design a service but to avoid being sued. If it makes you miss your flight, so be it.

■ ■ ■

CONSERVATIVE EFFORTS TO limit government by slowing it down have given us a government that is indeed slow and cautious but that is still big, at least for now. Liberals, ostensibly pro-government, have done their own share of damage by cultivating a fussy, technocratic culture and by relying too much on the law as the lever for social change. There's a final irony here, one that both the left and the right can agree is painful. The pledge of "a government of laws, not men" promises to protect us from the biases of flawed human beings and to ensure equal treatment for everyone.[8] But when pervasive legalistic thinking turns our government services into policy vomit, the burden that it creates undermines both those values. The point of the law is fairness, but when law gets applied without a thoughtful delivery framework it is rarely fair.

For example, consider the regulations implementing MACRA, the Medicare law where Natalie encountered the nine definitions of a group. A program that spends $605 billion of taxpayers' money a year—15 percent of the entire federal budget—is going to get some attention, especially from the large health care systems that receive the bulk of that money. But when CMS published a draft version of the regulations in the *Federal Register*, the volume of comments surprised the team. There were about four times as many as previous payment rules had received, and many were quite angry about a specific part of the draft: Table 64. MACRA was designed to pay doctors more for high-quality care, so the law directed CMS to change some of the ways that it would calculate payments to doctors. Table 64 attempted to estimate the effect of those changes. If the new rules went into effect as per the draft proposal, what would be the impact on clinicians?

Each row in the table offered the estimate for a particular size of medical practice, starting with solo practitioners and going up all the way to practices with a hundred or more clinicians. There were eleven columns of data, but the two that got most people's attention were labeled "Percent Eligible Clinicians with Negative Adjustment" and "Percent Eligible Clinicians with Positive Adjustment." The table estimated that 87 percent of solo practitioners would have a negative adjustment on their payments—that is, they would make less under the proposed new rules than under the old ones. Just 13 percent of solo practitioners would make more. For the practices with a hundred or more clinicians, the effect was reversed: 18 percent of these large practices would make less under the new rules, and 81 percent would make more. It was right there in black and white, in the *Federal Register*: if the draft rule went into effect, it was going to make more money for large health care systems. And it was going to hurt small medical practices.

There is no correlation between the size of the medical practice and the quality of care. You are just as likely to get great care from a doctor in a one- or two-person private practice as from a Kaiser or HCA Healthcare facility. Programs designed to pay more for better quality care, therefore, should reward independent doctors on average just as well as they reward large health systems. They don't. As a member of the policy team on MACRA told me, large health systems consistently benefit more from value-based medicine programs. It's not because they are delivering better quality care but because they are better at understanding program rules, choosing the right options, and reporting the right data. "We were not really measuring the quality of care doctors provide," he admitted. "We were measuring them on how well they do administrative tasks."

Large health care systems aren't naturally better at those tasks. They're better because they can hire expensive legal counsel, pay for specialized training, and allocate dedicated staff to master the ins and outs of the program. They have money and resources. Small practices don't, so they can't make these huge investments to get the most out of the program. MACRA, like many other government programs, wanted to promote meritocracy—to have the rewards go to the most deserving, the providers who contribute the most to the overall health of our society. But because evaluating merit involved such a big administrative burden, the program itself tilted the playing field. This puts Natalie's fight to reduce the number of definitions of a group in a new perspective. Choosing simple and clear over technically legally accurate wasn't just a matter of aesthetics or convenience. Greater burden also means less equity.

After the outcry over the draft rules, CMS found some creative ways to adjust the formulas so that in the final version only 5 percent of solo practitioners were projected to see their payments go down. Doctors were mostly satisfied. But the larger lesson is one we keep having to learn again and again. To administer programs or regulate industry, we must have some paperwork (or the digital equivalent). To administer them more equitably, we often need more data, which means more paperwork. But paperwork favors the powerful. And health care is far from the only field where this happens. For instance, scholars studying the impact of General Data Protection Regulation, an online privacy and security law covering the European Union, found that while large technology companies experienced a 4.6 percent drop in profits after it went into effect in 2018, small technology companies saw their profits drop by over 12 percent.[9]

Nor is this true only for businesses. A fifth of low-income families eligible for the earned income tax credit fail to claim it, while the wealthy have armies of lawyers and accountants looking for every opportunity to use the enormously complex tax code to their advantage.[10] This dynamic plays out within government administration itself. Procurement regulations are meant to make the process as fair as possible, but the very existence of those intricate, voluminous rules means that large government contractors—who have the resources to master them—have an advantage over smaller firms, as well as over firms that don't specialize in government clients.

I was once asked if Code for America might help with a project underway at the Department of Housing and Urban Development. Recognizing that large cities had more resources to apply for federal grants than smaller cities, and therefore got disproportionately more federal money, HUD wanted to create . . . a new program that small cities could apply for that would provide help with applying to other programs. Our suggestion that HUD instead simplify the grant applications for all cities was not well received. Paperwork is often a necessary evil, but when not managed thoughtfully to reduce administrative burdens, it can become the very problem it's trying to solve.

Fast-forward almost ten years, and the problem persists even as the stakes have grown higher. The Infrastructure Investment and Jobs Act, signed into law by President Biden in November 2021, provides over a trillion dollars, most of it in grants to state and local governments, but for local officials to access this capital they have to sort through almost four hundred separate grant application processes. Many are concerned that the communities that need these funds most will be the least likely to receive them. About $80 billion of the total is supposed to go to upgrading water systems, including drinking-water systems in places like Flint, Michigan, and Jackson, Mississippi, but a study of $25 billion granted for these purposes in the past decade found that small communities and communities with larger minority populations are less likely to receive assistance.[11]

It is sometimes the very efforts to ensure equity that contribute to the lack of it. The Biden administration set a laudable goal that 40 percent of the overall benefits of certain federal investments flow to "disadvantaged communities that are marginalized, underserved, and overburdened by pollution."[12] But when the additional data requirements for the program were imposed on one grant program at the USDA, staff noted a steep drop in applications. As with Medicare doctors, the more information you ask for, the more you reward administrative capacity, and the harder it is to help those who need it most.

■ ■ ■

ALL THIS STACKS the deck in favor of those who already hold the most cards, which is why this moment in the evolution of government is meaningful to so many. The digital world has made things easier in so many other aspects of our lives that its potential to help with public services is tantalizingly clear.

I remember the two times I've refinanced my home mortgage. The first time, the application process took weeks of collecting documents, filling out forms, waiting to hear back about my options, choosing among them, and waiting again. It culminated in a multihour meeting for which a closing agent came to my house and walked me through signing a mound of papers half a foot high. The second time, just a few years later, I got curious about interest rates one night when I should have been going to sleep. I popped open my laptop and went to my bank's website. I clicked here and there, and before I knew it I had submitted an application. Most of the screens I clicked through simply displayed what the bank already knew about me and my house (which was a lot) and asked me to confirm that the information was correct. Two weeks later, I signed some documents electronically and the deal was done.

It's tempting to assume that simple, easy-to-use services are just solving simpler problems. Sometimes that's true. But mortgages aren't simple. Lending is a highly regulated business and banks must be sure to comply with hundreds of laws. Behind the scenes, a digital team at my bank had worked hard to make a complicated process easy for me.[13] The internet made it possible to take various kinds of data input burdens off me, the user, and to present the choices I had to make in a way that was easy to understand. The bank also managed to do its part ethically, without hiding important information that I needed to know. Legal compliance was certainly an enormous part of that design process. But the lawyers would have played a supporting role. The competency that led the way was digital service design. In government, the roles are usually reversed. If a digital design competency even exists, it is too often in service of the lawyers, instead of the user.

It's not surprising that I had access to a streamlined process (and therefore a smaller mortgage payment): the benefits of digital transformation have largely gone to the middle and upper classes. And had I had to endure the longer, more complicated refinancing routine a second time, I probably would have persisted through it. But many people with less free time and more stress do not persist in getting past such hurdles, even when there's a benefit to them on the other end. The people most likely to pay the cost of outsize administrative burdens are often those who need help the most. Those who care about equity, then, must be all the more on guard against the kind of thinking that puts technical nuances of law ahead of what makes sense to a person.

PART III

User Needs, Not
Government Needs

THE FAX HACK

When I was starting Code for America, back in 2011, I got an email from the UK government asking if some officials could visit. It was an intimidating request. We had just launched and were still settling into the office space we were borrowing. A friend had worked at a startup that got absorbed into a big tech company, and we had somehow convinced that company to let us use the startup's empty office for a year. The first day our fellows arrived, they had had to assemble their own cheap Ikea chairs. The entrance to our only conference room was through a roll-up garage door. It was not the kind of place one imagined hosting British dignitaries.

The dignitaries turned out to be Francis Maude, the minister for the Cabinet Office, and Mike Bracken, who was standing up what would soon become the UK's Government Digital Service. They were both much less intimidating than I had feared. I had no way of knowing then that two years later I would go to the White House and lean heavily on Mike for inspiration and support. All I knew then was that a cabinet minister of the UK was in our grungy conference room, asking all sorts of questions about what we were doing and actually listening to the answers. This seemed highly unusual.

A few months later, the GDS published its first piece of doctrine, a set of design principles for government digital services. I clicked on the link with interest, wondering what those lovely British people had been up to. The first principle read "Start with needs." But there was an asterisk after "needs," so I scrolled down to see what it referred to. "User needs, not government needs," it said. Cheeky, these folks. But so on point. I'd spent a lot of time trying to explain to people what Code for America was for, what we were trying to do. The GDS had nailed it in five words.

• • •

WHEN JAKE SOLOMON put together his teardown of MyBenefits CalWIN, the food-assistance application form with 212 questions, he didn't stop there. He and two other graduating Code for America fellows, Dave Guarino and Alan Williams, wanted to get to the bottom of the question: Why was California, a mostly blue, pro-welfare state, tied with Wyoming for the worst food stamps participation rate in the country? About 43 percent of the people eligible for the Supplemental Nutrition Assistance Program in California weren't enrolled.[1]

To understand why people were having so much trouble signing up for SNAP, Jake, Dave, and Alan spent a lot of time at 1235 Mission Street, the main food stamp office in San Francisco. It happened to be around the corner from the Code for America offices, so most of us walked by it every day on our way to work. It was once a beautiful building, clad in ornate blue, green, and terracotta tile, with alternating onion domes and delicate minarets along the cornice. Today there are metal detectors at the entrance, and the floors are worn linoleum. Bulletproof glass separates the workers at their service counters from the clients in the waiting room. There is a table where clients can pick up a variety of paper forms, and Jake, Dave, and Alan hovered around that table. While clients waited for their number to be called over the speakers, one of the three would approach them and ask if they'd tried applying online. If the client was willing to give it a shot, they'd ask if it would be OK if they watched and took some notes.

Inevitably, Jake, Dave, and Alan would learn more about the client than just how that person experienced MyBenefits Cal-WIN. They'd hear about how the client had been enrolled in SNAP before but got kicked off, about the confusing notices that had come in the mail, about rumors that you have to answer such-and-such a question in such-and-such a way if you want to get approved. And they'd hear about past difficulties these clients had had with different parts of government. Genevieve Gaudet, a service designer, talks about the accumulated impact such difficulties can have:

> I often talk to people who find themselves in a government office, asking for help with some basic need. And when I ask them what brought them into that office, the story always starts far in the past. It starts with parents and children, military service, illness, moments of good news and moments of bad news, all leading up to what brought them here today. Over the course of those stories, which can represent generations, they've learned that help isn't always easy to find. We can't fix this until we understand that in government, we're not starting a new relationship, we're repairing a deeply broken one.[2]

The clients that Jake, Dave, and Alan met at 1235 Mission Street were no different.

These conversations were helpful. But even after all the interviews, they still felt they were missing a lot of understanding.

They wanted to know more about what it was like to actually be on the program. So Alan enrolled in SNAP himself.

When the three self-organized into a team at the end of their fellowship year, I was away in Washington, DC, helping to start up the US Digital Service. I tried to stay in touch as best as I could, but my job at the White House was all-consuming and I knew only that the three of them had decided to keep working on SNAP. When I came back, the first thing I noticed was that Alan—tall, thin, and fastidious when I left—was noticeably thinner. I was concerned. "It's hard to live on food stamps," he told me. In order to qualify for the program, he had declined his salary. Jake and Dave were helping to pay his rent.

By then, Alan had already been through the 212-question application. He had already tried and failed to enroll on his mobile phone and had tried again to enroll on the computer at the library. When that didn't work either, he gave up pretending that he didn't have a reasonably up-to-date MacBook and access to fast Wi-Fi and got through the application that way. By the time he finally received his EBT card—the electronic benefit transfer card that works like a debit card at grocery stores—Alan already had plenty of ideas about why California's enrollment rate was so low. Even for a conscientious student of social services and an expert in online interactions, the whole process was remarkably hard.

But it wasn't until he was grocery shopping for a date that Alan felt he finally got a real glimpse of what it can be like to depend on SNAP. He was at a store near his apartment, buying a few things he needed to cook dinner for a woman he'd recently met, when he suddenly realized that he didn't have the receipt from his last swipe with his EBT card. That receipt had his balance printed at the bottom; without it, he didn't know how much money was in his account. His items were on the conveyor belt at the checkout stand, his date was on the way to his apartment, and he was quickly approaching the moment of truth: the possibility that his EBT card didn't have sufficient funds. He'd have to take items off the belt and return them to the cashier, one by one, while angry customers he was holding up judged him.

It was the kind of thing you don't think much about, the awkwardness of checking your balance on an EBT card. In most states, there's a number on the card you can call, but the number goes to an automated phone system, and it can take a while to navigate it and find out how much money is left for groceries that day. (For people with prepaid, metered phone plans, the call also uses up valuable minutes.) There was no way Alan could find out his balance before he got to the front of the line. In the seconds before he would have to step up to the cash register, anticipating the groans of impatience that were sure to come from everyone behind him, Alan started to sweat. It no longer felt like "user research." His anxiety gave way to shame, followed by a flash of anger at being stuck in this position.

Alan knew he did not live in persistent poverty. He knew he couldn't really understand what it was like not to have a back-stop. But in that moment, he got a glimpse of what it can feel like to use a service that technically does what it is supposed to but ultimately has little regard for the people who use it. As Jake puts it, "Our services disdain those they are envisioned to help."[3]

●●●

ALAN'S MOMENT OF stress at the grocery store sparked the first of the team's many small experiments. They created a simple web tool that allows SNAP users to type in their EBT card number and get their current balance in a text message quickly enough to avoid being embarrassed at the checkout counter. Another experiment aimed to help SNAP outreach assisters who were working on clients' behalf. Many of them told Jake, Dave, and Alan about spending a lot of time on hold while calling other bureaucracies to follow up on client eligibility. So the team built a tool that would let the worker hang up, then get a call back when someone finally picked up on the other end of the line.

Beyond that, naturally, the team tackled the burden of the 212-question online application. They knew that not all those questions were needed for all clients. For example, if you said you'd never been convicted of a felony, there was no need to ask you seven clarifying questions about your history of trading SNAP benefits for guns, ammunition, or explosives. Moreover, getting SNAP required an interview anyway. As long as the client provided enough information to get to that interview stage, an eligibility worker was going to go over a lot of the details with the client on the phone.

So the team tried a hack, but a hack with a point. Over the past year, they'd built a good relationship with Leo O'Farrell, the CalFresh director for San Francisco County—CalFresh being the California branding for the state's SNAP program. As outsiders go, the team had a lot of trust with the folks inside the bureaucracy. They asked Leo if they could show him something they'd been working on, and Leo invited them to his office.

When they arrived, Dave took out his phone, opened the browser, typed in *GetCalFresh.org*, and handed the phone to Leo. On the screen was the most bare-bones version of a SNAP application you could imagine, just four questions and a signature. At the bottom was a big button containing two words: APPLY NOW. "Try it," Dave said, and Leo quickly filled it out. When he hit the button, the three team members held their breath, waiting for a sound. Soon they heard it: the hum of the office fax machine starting up. They walked over to it to find a SNAP application for Leo O'Farrell slowly emerging. According to regulations set by the Food and Nutrition Service in Washington, DC, this blurry fax with its basic information represented a valid application for food assistance. Had it been a real client, Leo's office would have been obligated to follow up with the client and schedule an interview.

The team had fretted that their hacked-together web-to-fax system might not work, but they were more worried that Leo would be annoyed by the shenanigans. He wasn't. He was delighted, immediately calling in another colleague to try it out. He wanted to launch it right away, but he also knew it was more of a stunt than a real solution. He had faith that Jake, Dave, and Alan had more up their sleeves—and he was right. For starters, there was no need to fax anything. With Leo's support, they worked out how to get data from the GetCalFresh form directly into the backend system that his office used. At that point the workers could process it like any other application that came in through existing digital channels.

Another key improvement had to do with appointments for the phone interview. One of the biggest reasons clients ended up not getting their benefits was that they missed their interview call. They were supposed to look for a letter in the mail telling them when the call would come in, but sometimes that letter arrived after the date of the interview. Jake, Dave, and Alan made sure their GetCalFresh form recorded clients' cell phone numbers. (The MyBenefits CalWIN application had several fields for phone numbers, but few clients had realized the benefits of including their cell among them.) Then they set up a system that would text clients to let them know about their interview and tell them how to reschedule it if they missed it. This fix helped more people make it all the way through.

The interview itself was an additional hindrance to getting benefits, but it mitigated a worse problem: in the official application, the questions about income and assets were so detailed, wide-ranging, and confusing that it was very difficult to answer them accurately without help from someone who knew what they meant. Indeed, the biggest predictor of success for eligible applicants wasn't whether they had answered all 212 questions. It was whether they had uploaded pay stubs, bank statements, and other documentation so that the interviewer could properly fill in the income and assets information on their behalf.

But the existing MyBenefits CalWIN online form only asked for those documents at the very end. Even if you got to the end and uploaded those documents, the system frequently lost them anyway. (Clients who submitted their application without the documents would get a letter asking to send them in by mail. That was easier for some people, but those mailed documents had to make it into the person's file before the process could continue, adding a lot of time, and physical documents get lost even more often than digital ones.) Uploading documents was the step that clients most needed to work, but it was the one that worked worst.

So when Jake, Dave, and Alan built their site, they made it easy to upload the pay stubs and other documents near the beginning of the process. They also worked with frontline eligibility workers to understand which other questions were most important to ask first, and they added those too. Bit by bit, the bare-bones page that sent a fax to Leo's office that day became more robust. But because the team used branching logic to make sure no clients were asked questions irrelevant to them, the entire application could still be completed in about seven minutes. And unlike MyBenefits CalWIN, it was mobile-friendly from the start.

Once GetCalFresh became a real product, the Code for America team started approaching counties one by one, asking if they'd like to give their clients the option of applying through it. Some declined, but many county welfare directors welcomed it. After a few years, the state SNAP director, noticing that participation rates were going up in the counties that were using it, expanded GetCalFresh to all California counties. MyBenefits CalWIN still exists. For the time being, you can still work your way through its 212 questions to apply. But most applications for SNAP in the state now come in through GetCalFresh. And California's SNAP participation rate has gone up.

It's not hard to understand what the team building the UK's Government Digital Service meant by government needs. The official specifications for government software—compulsory ESBs that turn a simple software component into a Rube Goldberg contraption, mandated versions of outdated browsers and file formats, complicated rules about docking someone's benefits because the person was too sick to look for work one day—those are all government needs. So are the voluminous documents that teams must write to satisfy internal stakeholders, oversight bodies, and all manner of compliance offices. So are the approval processes for plans to solicit feedback, which themselves get held up while feedback is solicited on the feedback-soliciting plans. When you need to attend to all these things and more, it's no wonder you don't get out of the office and talk to people struggling to obtain health care coverage or food assistance. You don't have the time.

Government needs suffocate not only the people building systems, but those operating in them. A researcher in the UK studied one low-income family's interaction with seventy-three different government entities, including social services, educational supports, and interventions from law enforcement, the costs of which the government had calculated topped one million pounds annually. Though these services and programs theoretically existed to support this family and keep them safe, only 14 percent of the time public servants spent on this family involved any actual interaction with them, the rest of it being spent on tasks like reporting, data entry, and interfacing with other parts of the bureaucracy. Of that small fraction spent face-to-face with family members, most of that was spent collecting the data that would then be put into government systems and reports. In other words, even when they were with the family, public servants were still meeting government needs.[4] The family members, unsurprisingly, experienced all of this supposed "support" as surveillance and control. Far from improving their lives, the effect of the million pounds a year was further conflict and poverty.

We don't lack for examples of government needs, but it can be harder to grasp what the GDS meant by user needs. Defenders of the waterfall process will tell you that gathering requirements, the first stage of waterfall project management, is when the team understands the needs of the users. But software requirements are not user needs. Writing down everything everyone thinks the system might need to do per official policy and per multiple conflicting compliance regimens does not help you understand your users. It doesn't even really help you understand the bureaucracy. It just gives you a list of elements that you'll need to check off to call your job done. Actually understanding user needs often doesn't look anything like what we think of as software development in the first place. It looks like building empathy.

...

WHEN YOU TALK about understanding and meeting user needs, adherents of the waterfall approach will also remind you about testing and say that's another phase where you make sure the software works for its users. It's right there at the end of the process, after requirements gathering, analysis, design, and coding, and right before deployment. But being the last stage before deployment means that most of the money and time allotted to the project have already been used up; when budgets and schedules slip, testing is the only thing left to cut. (What looks like a rocky launch is often simply a project that wound up doing its testing *after* deployment; just ask the healthcare.gov team.) Even when there's plenty of time for testing at the end, it doesn't do much good at that point. If software has been designed without an understanding of the needs of its users from the start, it is very hard to fix its deficiencies in testing, because the team has fundamentally built the wrong thing.

Take benefit screeners, for example. Many of the people applying for benefits such as food assistance are eligible for other safety-net programs as well. But while these various programs generally target people of the same approximate income level, each is available only for people with certain characteristics. Some require you to be eighteen or older, some twenty-five or older; some are only for people with children or for pregnant women. For some you must be a homeowner, for some you must rent your home, for yet others you must be in subsidized housing. Some are available only for veterans, students, or the disabled. Some are available only to documented US citizens; others don't have this restriction. And each program has its own set of qualifiers and disqualifiers, like the questions in the MyBenefits CalWIN application about having traded benefits for drugs, guns, ammunition, or explosives. Figuring out if someone is eligible for any one of these programs can be a lot of work.

All that work is why there is a constant cry in the social services world for online "screeners," web forms that ask prospective clients some questions and match them up with the relevant benefits programs. If only someone could program a perfectly accurate screener, we would be able to tell people in need of support exactly which programs they should apply for. That would involve programming in all the very specific rules for as many programs as one could identify. But the same observations that helped the GetCalFresh team make a better online SNAP application—one that got food benefits to far more people—also suggest that in-depth screeners are a mistake.

Dave Guarino, one of the three creators of GetCalFresh, says that technocrats' desire for a comprehensive screener is a misunderstanding of client needs. The way he recommends screening clients instead is very simple: "Made less than $X last month? You may be eligible."[5] As he explains, "Oftentimes people have an acute need that triggers them to go get *that* specific need met— like food. People just want to know if it's worth their time to apply." Given that the burden of applying for even one safety-net program, like SNAP, is often quite high, it defeats the purpose to have clients start with a process that will ask them even more questions in the hope of referring them to other programs they probably wouldn't have the bandwidth to apply for anyway.

In theory, very accurate and comprehensive screeners could increase the number of safety-net programs an individual or family could benefit from. But in practice, it often doesn't. "You know what high-precision accuracy requires?" Dave asks. "A really high-burden, complex form that starts to resemble a full application." Much of the time, it's not even the eligibility that keeps a client from getting the benefit—it's the need to persist through all the forms, interviews, documentation, and phone calls. Putting another long, complicated form at the front end of the process would just increase that burden. Why add to clients' stress and possibly scare them off before they've even started applying?

It's hard to convince the welfare agencies that administer these programs to screen clients Dave's way. You will inevitably end up with some (small) number of people who've been told they're likely eligible but aren't. The mere notion that the screening process might not be completely accurate can create a chilling effect. As Natalie Kates saw at CMS, being 100 percent thorough and technically accurate is always safer, even if it's worse for the people the service is supposed to help. But to Dave the tradeoff is worth it. The upside is a better experience for the vast majority of clients, which ultimately results in higher enrollment. A detailed, heavyweight screener may meet an agency's requirements, but it doesn't meet the users' needs.

The skill of understanding and meeting those needs is something that professional service designers learn and hone over years. But developing empathy for users of government services is a great starting place, and any of us can begin doing that. There are opportunities for doing it in our daily lives, but many of us have to be more intentional about it than you might think. Take taxes, for example. Almost everyone has to submit a tax return, but the majority of Americans use a tax preparer. I'd filed my own 1040EZ forms in my twenties, but once my taxes got more complicated I turned to an accountant. Years later, when my daughter had to file for the first time, I tried to help her. The IRS by then had retired the 1040EZ; I found the new form inscrutable and the online version unusable. Her taxes were almost as simple as they could be, but for three painful evenings we struggled to figure out what the various instructions meant and why the form kept giving us errors when we tried to submit. I still don't know if we did it right.

At the time, Code for America had a project to help low-income families claim their earned income tax credit, and I knew from our research that many families struggle to file accurate returns and claim the money they are owed. But I had let the frustrations they experience remain abstract. Now, suffering through my daughter's taxes, I could hear Jake, Dave, and Alan in my head, telling me again that there's no substitute for actually using the service. People with means can avoid the pain of many government interactions, but when we do, we are missing a chance to build empathy for those who can't.

User needs aren't necessarily all that complicated. Some of them become apparent through observation. After spending the day in a school vaccination clinic, a colleague of mine quipped: "Every time you add a question to a form, I want you to imagine the user filling it out with one hand while using the other to break up a brawl between toddlers."[6] Applications for government benefits might be completed under similarly chaotic circumstances. Users who have a lot else going on in their lives need to be able to apply for the service without an undue burden of time, technology, and cognitive overhead. If they're asked for documentation, the documents need to be ones they have access to. If they need to correspond with the program, there has to be a way for them to do so even if they lack a stable mailing address. If they have family who are undocumented immigrants, they may need reassurance that applying for a program won't get them or their relatives in trouble.

Few of those needs will be mentioned in a policy document. Few of them will come up in a formal notice-and-comment process. They reveal themselves through the practice of user research, to those who are present, observant, and respectful. (Physical presence is usually the best kind, though much excellent user research is done over the internet.) They emerge when you get out of the office, knock on doors, and literally meet the users where they are. They reveal themselves when we set aside our assumptions about what would work based on our own experience and instead test and measure what works for others.

There is one need, however, that can be assumed across all government services: the need to be treated with dignity. When services respect our time, minimize intrusion, use language we understand, and don't make us feel stupid, that deeply broken relationship with government can start to mend.[7] There's a lot of mending needed—low trust in government erodes our ability to fight climate change, to respond to public health threats, and to maintain our national security and our democracy. There's never been a more important time to show the American people that their government can put their needs first.

10

BYRNE'S LAW

Dave Guarino and his colleagues had a creative service-design answer to the problem of screening benefit applicants for eligibility. They programmed a lightweight screener into the Get-CalFresh application itself. (A similar approach can be used for multibenefit applications, such as those that let people apply simultaneously for food benefits, housing support, and childcare assistance.)[1] As GetCalFresh evolved from its web-to-fax proof of concept to a real product, the team looked at which questions were the most likely to disqualify clients and put those at the front. Now, clients start filling out the application form and, if after the first few questions it seems like they won't qualify, they get a message letting them know they might not want to continue.[2] And for those who do seem likely to qualify, they've now answered those questions in the actual application rather than in some screener that will direct them to start a separate application from scratch. Dave didn't want to waste the time of those people who weren't going to be eligible, but he also didn't want to waste the time of the larger number of applicants who did meet the CalFresh criteria.

When the GetCalFresh team made these choices, they were practicing a discipline called *product management*. It is frequently confused (especially in government) with *project management*, but the two are distinct, and the difference between them is crucial. Project management is the art of getting things done. Product management is deciding what to do in the first place—and also, as in the case of the benefit screeners, deciding what not to do. If you collect hundreds of formal requirements and just start building software for all of them, you've generated a whole lot of work for skilled and dedicated project managers, but you haven't made any real choices. That's how you end up with a 212-question SNAP application, or a website that works only on computers in your building, or a system so complex it takes seventeen years to learn.

Project managers are all over government. Their sheer numbers became clear to me when I was working at the White House in the months after the launch of healthcare.gov. I found myself in touch with a lot of federal IT managers, and I noticed that most of them had something after their name in the email signature: PMP. I'd spent fifteen years in the consumer technology world but I had never seen that abbreviation before, so I looked it up. It stands for project management professional, and you can put those letters after your name only if you've completed an accredited course of study (traditionally on waterfall principles) and passed a certification exam. In the civil service, many promotions and raises rely on getting this certification. It can be hard to climb the career ladder without it. No wonder there are so many PMPs.

On the other hand, product managers in government software development have been essentially nonexistent. Between 2015 and 2020, in a federal workforce some two million strong, only seven people had "product manager" or "product management" in their job title.[3] There are lots of people like Natalie trying to do what product managers do, but they are frequently seen as rocking the boat. It's not what their job is supposed to be. They do it through sheer force of will.

I met one IT project manager in state government who was acting quite a bit like a product manager, fighting the same kinds of fights that Natalie had. She had gone through the PMP training but hadn't bothered to take the certification test. She didn't find the coursework very useful. "It's all about the planning, mostly at the beginning of the project," she said. "And then tracking the requirements." What about skills like reducing the requirements, the way Natalie had managed to get nine definitions of a group condensed into two? "Oh, no. They don't teach that," she told me.

■ ■ ■

IN THE AFTERMATH of the healthcare.gov disaster, armchair quarterbacks from all corners offered their reasons for the failure. Some thought the Centers for Medicare and Medicaid Services had spent its budget too slowly. Others said the problem was that CMS had tried to be its own "systems integrator" and should have charged CGI Federal with pulling all the pieces together. Still others thought that CGI and the dozens of other vendors involved were the real problem. (Indeed, the absence of truly basic functionality like site monitoring software suggests some serious deficiencies on their part.) A report by the Office of Inspector General offers ten key reasons for the disaster, spanning everything from lack of clear leadership and an overly bureaucratic culture to failures of integration, communication, execution, and oversight.[4] The report is thorough, but that's a broad diagnosis. If I had to pick just one thing that maybe, just maybe, would have made a difference, it would be this: the site had a lot of project managers but no product manager.

With all the dysfunction cataloged by the inspector general swirling around, what could a product manager have done for healthcare.gov? In a word, *less*. Healthcare.gov was a truly massive undertaking. It didn't just let people shop for and choose insurance plans. It had to communicate with dozens of other government databases to verify the person's income, Social Security number, citizenship status, and whether the person was enrolled in any other health care programs; it had to make sure the enrollee was charged the right amount for coverage; and it had to transmit enrollee data to hundreds of different insurers. Not only did the site need to scale to handle enormous traffic but dozens of connections had to work just right for any given transaction to go through.

In any service like this, you will find a core of users whose circumstances are the most common and a long tail of increasingly rare "edge cases." For instance, the Affordable Care Act generally extends coverage only to applicants who are US citizens. But there are seventeen unique immigration statuses that are exceptions to that rule, and the people those exceptions cover represent a tiny fraction of users. Programming in the logic and database connections to automatically verify all seventeen exceptions makes the software orders of magnitude more complex than what would be required to support the most common type of user. The people with edge cases could have initially been helped through other channels, including call centers and various agents and assisters who could meet clients in person. Mike Byrne, the guy who built the broadband map for the FCC, estimates that most government tech projects could cost 10 percent of what they do and still provide 85 percent of the functionality.[5] I hereby dub this "Byrne's Law."

It's not that that final 15 percent of the functionality shouldn't ever be built—the software can and should eventually support edge cases. It's just that trying to have it all done by launch, before you've had the chance to work out the kinks with the core workings of the project, will often tank the operation of the other 85 percent. Mike's modern-day estimate resonates with a

1975 observation known as Gall's Law, named for pediatrician and systems design theorist John Gall. "A complex system that works is invariably found to have evolved from a simple system that worked," Gall wrote. "A complex system designed from scratch never works and cannot be patched up to make it work. You have to start over with a working simple system."[6] Because CMS tried to build something very complex that worked for everyone right from launch, healthcare.gov worked for no one. Everyone swamped the call center and the in-person assisters. Those high-touch channels should have been reserved primarily for the people with unusual cases, those without internet access, and others who needed extra help, but instead they were jammed up with the cases that software could have easily handled.

Theoretically, CMS could have heeded Gall's Law: limited the functionality of the site for launch, planned for call-center support for people whose circumstances the site couldn't handle, and, as resources allowed, incrementally added online support for the edge cases after launch. In practice, however, Congress had ordered a fully functioning website, so a fully functioning website was what CMS had to deliver. Project managers had all their requirements to check off. The idea that some choices could be made, and in fact would very much need to be made, was unspeakable, perhaps unthinkable. Many considered anything but the whole nine yards illegal. Clay Shirky describes being at the Harvard Kennedy School, one of the country's top public policy institutions, a month after healthcare.gov launched and being told that the site simply could not have been built and tested iteratively over time because that's not how government works. "It is hard for policy people to imagine that HealthCare .gov could have had a phased rollout, *even while it is having one*," he wrote at the time.[7] Incremental fixes is exactly what the agency got, just in the worst possible way.

(Equity policies can also make it hard to choose a phased-rollout

approach. Government services are not supposed to treat different groups differently, and pilot programs designed to start small
before launching big are often scuttled on those grounds. As we
saw with the EDD, these well-intentioned policies can result in
harm to the very people the policy is supposed to protect.)

Even during the all-out effort to rescue the site after its launch,
leadership remained in denial about the need to prioritize. Mina
Hsiang, a member of Todd Park's tech surge, was assigned the
task of representing the team on a nightly call with the key vendors and a handful of senior CMS staff, including Marilyn Tavenner, who as CMS administrator was nominally responsible for
the success of the site. On one such call, Tavenner brought up
the Spanish version of the website, which had been in the original requirements. It would meet an obvious need for millions of
Spanish-speaking Americans. But with healthcare.gov working
for almost no one even weeks after launch, the Spanish site had
taken a back seat. Now Tavenner wanted to know where the team
was with it and when it would be ready.

Mina spoke up first. She was afraid the contractors would try
to placate the administrator, making promises that would further
distract from the core work of fixing the site, and she wanted to
get out ahead of them. Language access should have been a high
priority from the start, and to make it happen other features,
like handling the various immigration edge cases, should have
been deprioritized. But those choices had not been made, and
now the top priority needed to be fixing the main site. "You can
have either one site in English that works or two sites that don't,"
Mina told the CMS administrator. Tavenner apparently didn't
like the answer. She hung up in the middle of the call.

Product management as an official discipline is rare in government, but it's not just that there's no job classification for it. In
the most extreme cases, it feels like it simply cannot exist here:
not only are implementers not empowered to make choices but

the people above them aren't even willing to consider the option. When there are too few resources and not enough time to fulfill all the requirements that have been handed down, the only response our political class seems to have is to throw money at the problem—massive amounts of it.[8] That generally works out just about as well as it did with the hiring spree at California's backlogged EDD, which is to say, it makes the problem worse. At no point do our leaders seem to ask whether the requirements—which they have themselves helped set—might be the problem.

Despite all that, healthcare.gov didn't stay broken. By the end of the first open enrollment period, six months after the site's launch, more people had gotten health care than had even been projected before the launch fiasco. The inspector general's report praises Todd's surge team and the tech fixes they brought, starting with installing monitoring software to even know if the site was working or not. But it was not tech know-how that made the difference. Monitoring software can't fix a culture where the leader hangs up on you when you deliver bad news. But ignoring leadership's outbursts and staying focused on priorities can help, and that's what both the surge team and the career civil servants wound up doing. Together, they took the initiative to make tradeoffs and set priorities based on user needs. They hadn't started out with a product manager, but they did the best they could to make up for that.

■ ■ ■

IN 2015, WHEN Natalie found herself fighting over the nine definitions of a group, she was part of what many at CMS thought of as a do-over, a chance for the agency staff to redeem themselves after the beating they'd taken for healthcare.gov. Congress had dropped MACRA, the value-based Medicare overhaul, in their lap, and they were again staring down the barrel of a deadline to implement complicated health care policy through technology.

The people at CMS had learned a lot, and learned it the hard way. They didn't want to make the same mistakes, which may be why so many of them were fighting alongside Natalie to simplify those nine definitions. But when it came to deciding what to do—and, sometimes more importantly, what not to do—the team still faced challenges.

It was a few months into the MACRA work when Natalie first heard about the other website that needed to be built, the one for virtual groups. Natalie didn't understand. There were a lot of moving parts on this project, an insanely complex set of rules still to be clarified and made usable if this policy was going to succeed, and a limited number of months left to do it all. But somehow there was another whole website that needed to be built? What did they mean?

The team explained. MACRA was designed to pay doctors more for better quality care, but doctors in larger practices have the advantage of aggregating quality measures across a larger number of patients. Thus, the law gave smaller practices the option of filing together with other small practices (as a group, of course, which now had only two definitions) in order to have that advantage as well. In the text of the law, this is referred to as "election of practices to be a virtual group." Somehow, that provision had turned into a mandate to not only allow doctors to file together but give doctors who didn't know one another a way to *find* one another, read about one another, and message one another to link up and become a virtual group. They'd started calling it Facebook for Doctors, though Tinder for Doctors sounded to me like a more accurate metaphor.

The CMS policy team, in fact, had not written this requirement. The same contractor team who'd insisted on the nine definitions of a group had. But it had become hard to overrule. There was one doctor posting in the public comments about the need for this feature, and the Office of the General Counsel at CMS had noticed him, so they flagged the idea as something that needed to happen. Natalie and her CMS colleagues were alarmed. They knew how messy and complicated it is to build and maintain social sites. Perhaps a Facebook for Doctors would be smaller and less complex than actual Facebook, but this was still an enormous undertaking—and a classic concrete boat. CMS was assigning forty people to the project—forty people who should have been working on making it easy for doctors to file claims, getting them their feedback quickly, and all the other urgent needs the team had been hearing about in its research. Natalie and others appealed up the chain not to require this extra website. But the lawyers had spoken. "We have to do this. It's the law."

Natalie could not believe that members of Congress wanted CMS to make a Facebook for Doctors. And even if they did want it, there's no way they would have insisted if they understood that trying to build it would jeopardize the entire rest of the project. It just wasn't important to achieving the overall goals of the law. So Natalie decided to go to the source. She called up the people in Congress who had written MACRA: not the members of Congress themselves but the Office of House Legislative Counsel, a permanent bipartisan fixture in Congress that works with the members and their staffs to help laws get written. Surely they would be able to put a stop to this nonsense. She asked them what had been their intent.

The author Michael Lewis once said, "You never know what book you've written until people start to read it."[9] The same appears to be true for laws. "We thought it should be easier for small-town doctors and other smaller practices to report together, if that's useful to them," was the gist of the legislative counsel's response. What about a way for the doctors to find one another, a Facebook for Doctors? Natalie asked. We have no idea what you're talking about, they said.

Natalie came back to the team. Congress doesn't want a

Facebook for Doctors, she was pleased to share. And other than the one gadfly who was ranting about it in the public comments, no doctors appeared to want it either. The user research team asked doctors about it during their interviews. Would they want to get into a legal business agreement with another provider that they didn't know and didn't work with? Would they peruse a Facebook for Doctors looking for potential partners? To a one, they had said, No, I would never do that.

It didn't matter. The lawyers were adamant. The regulations would require Facebook for Doctors.

...

I HAD SEEN this desire to overdeliver to Congress before. I was working at the White House in 2014, trying to draft the foundational documents for what would become the US Digital Service. The federal CIO had assigned me a partner, pointing out that, while my ideas about how to build digital services might be good, I didn't really know how things worked in government. (This was true, even after a few years working with local government and ten months in the White House.) I needed someone by my side who could "governmentize" what I had written. My partner, whom I'll call Henry, had been in government for twelve years and was now in OMB's Office of E-Government. He was a clean-cut, well-meaning, eager guy who routinely suggested 7 a.m. meetings: it was the only time free on his calendar.

Several weeks into our partnership, we were getting nowhere. I had written the first draft of a "playbook" for what would become the USDS, essentially a set of principles by which it would operate. I'd been inspired by the precepts of the UK's Government Digital Service, which were clear, concise, and bold, and I wanted the USDS's to have those same qualities. The first draft was three pages, and I thought it was much too long. I passed it over to Henry, asking him to help me simplify it. He sent it back a few days later. It was full of very specific guidance and many very long words. It was seventy pages.

I sent him back something that was five pages, as a concession. He sent back eighty-three. (He'd thought of more things we needed to include in the meantime.) We met at 7 a.m. again. We talked but did not communicate. I was running out of time; my leave of absence was going to be up and I would have to leave the White House having not finished even the most basic thing I had come to do. At the end of my rope, I went to see a friend and mentor in the White House who understood what I was trying to do. "Go back to first principles," he told me. "Your partner doesn't understand why simple and clear matters to you so much. Tell him what you learned from working with local government, about how all this complexity trickles down to real people and makes their lives harder."

I emailed Henry and asked him to clear an afternoon for me. It was important that we spend some real time together and talk this through. I invited him to meet me at GSA, where the nascent 18F team, the partner group to the USDS, had populated the open-floor office with whiteboards and journey maps and all the artifacts of user-centered, iterative service delivery. And I planned out what I would say. I would tell him the story of the burial plot.

As I'd learned from the GetCalFresh team, when people apply for food stamps, they have to fill out an application form. Different states have different forms, some longer than others, but they were all much longer than they needed to be, which meant a lot of people who were eligible for the benefit never got through the application. Michigan's took up forty pages. What made them so long? Well, for example, many states asked if applicants owned a burial plot. How could owning a burial plot be relevant to whether the state should give you assistance with food? The level of detail was unnecessary, it was insulting, and it was a hindrance to the aims of the program, which was to raise people out of poverty.

I was ready with this story and a few others that would illustrate why simplicity and clarity in the USDS playbook would set the stage for simplicity and clarity in the services we would help government build. Eventually, as our discussion went around and around again, my opportunity arose. I channeled my mentor and asked Henry to consider why this was so important to me. I passionately delivered my speech, ending with "Why *on earth* does government want to know about a burial plot?"

He listened politely and said, "Yes, I know about the burial plots. I wrote those regs."

Had I been a bit more savvy or a bit more diligent, I would have noticed the five years at the Food and Nutrition Service on his LinkedIn profile. I could have chosen a different example of benefit applicants being treated heartlessly by government bureaucrats than one he had personally drafted. Instead, I was an hour and half into what I'd planned to be a four-hour meeting, our meeting to end all meetings, in which we would hash out all our differences and not leave the room until we were perfectly aligned, and I'd just ground whatever scrap of congenial relationship we had left into the floor. There was nowhere to go, no way to pretend, so I just went forward. "But why?" I asked.

"Congress said to assess their assets," he said. "A burial plot is an asset."

That was it. That was his explanation. For once, he was compellingly clear and simple. As he stared at me in silence, with no malice or even discomfort in his eyes, I believed him. In my head, a thousand food policy advocates screamed at me that these barriers are politically motivated, intentionally added to keep poor people from getting benefits. Perhaps they were right, but in that moment I thought about his 7 a.m. meetings and his eighty-three pages and I saw Henry as that kid in class who did the long

division out to twenty-five decimal places and completed every
extra-credit assignment early. Henry's superpower was that he
was thorough. Now Congress was the teacher—a distant, harsh
teacher. And Henry was determined to get an A. No, an A+.

...

NATALIE BELIEVES HER policy colleagues at CMS wanted a good
grade from Congress too. They also wanted to avoid being sent
to the principal (imagine an inspector general's report on why
doctors couldn't link up!) and genuinely wanted to do right by
the program. But while they continued to insist that the extra
website had to be built, Natalie didn't give up. She recalled that
the legislative counsel team had mentioned that a few companies
had advocated for the "election of practices to be a virtual group"
provision, so she asked to talk to them.

One of those companies was athenahealth, which provides
cloud-based electronic health care records. Natalie got on the phone
with its lobbyist. "You lobbied for this, right?" she asked. "What
were you trying to do? What was your intention?" "Oh, well, we
work with a lot of individual providers and we want to be able
to report on their behalf," the athenahealth rep told her. "But we
can see from our data that they would make more money if they
reported as a group. So we want to be able to offer them a service
that connects them with the right practices to partner with so
they can make more money."

What CMS was proposing to do by building Facebook for
Doctors was exactly what the company that had lobbied for the
provision *didn't* want them to do. The company intended to do
the matchmaking itself; it just needed to make sure the partnerships would be allowed. So Congress didn't want the site, and the
lobbying companies wanted the opposite. The policy team was at
the joke end of a big game of telephone.

Natalie and a colleague on the CMS policy team eventually

found a different lawyer in the Office of the General Counsel who agreed to take a fresh look at the language in the statute. This lawyer came up with a different interpretation. In his view, MACRA mandated the option of virtual groups, but he saw much more flexibility around how to facilitate them. There was no legal need for Facebook for Doctors.

Indeed, as it turned out, there was no practical need for Facebook for Doctors either. Armed with the new guidance, the team included a few lines of text on the website explaining how doctors could tell CMS if they wanted to report as a virtual group. In the first year of the program, no more than a handful of doctors even asked about that option. It was easy enough to support those few without any technology at all.

Private-sector companies make this kind of mistake all the time. Teams building new products usually worry about the quality of their design and engineering, the size of the marketing budget, the strength of the sales force, and so on. They forget to worry about something much more important: whether anyone wants the product at all. Entrepreneur and author Eric Ries has founded a whole movement based on his experience finding out the hard way that no one wanted his company's initial product.[10] After months of work to launch a product no one had the slightest interest in using—a social network built around instant messaging—he realized he could have just bought a few hundred dollars' worth of Google ads promoting the service and discovered that no one clicked on them. Or he could have put together a barebones mock-up of the product in a couple of weeks and tested it with a few potential users—they would have told him the same thing.

Ries's tale is widely known in Silicon Valley, but the consumer tech world keeps making this mistake. Remember Bodega, the AI-powered vending machine that was going to replace corner stores? Turns out people like their corner stores. The startup took

$45 million in funding before going under.[11] With an internal team of forty and an additional budget to outsource development, Facebook for Doctors could eventually have spent a similar sum. The difference, though, is that it might never have been shuttered, even if hardly any doctors used it. Once a program is established in government, its value is rarely measured by usage or utility. (In fact, low usage is often welcomed because it doesn't create scaling problems. Recall all the people at the VA agitating to go back to the online form that made it so hard for veterans to apply for health care—*because* so few people used it.) When the private sector makes mistakes like these, at least the market sooner or later corrects most of them. When the public sector makes them, bureaucrats tend to wait for further orders from lawmakers. But the lawmakers have usually moved on.

■ ■ ■

WITHIN BUREAUCRACIES, DEFERENCE to Congress (and other lawmaking bodies at the state and local levels) is natural. In Washington, DC, in particular, Congress is the ultimate boss; it makes the law of the land in a town dedicated to the interpretation and implementation of its words. Waterfall development isn't just an arbitrary choice of methodology in this context. Hierarchical, one-directional, top-down communication is built into the structure of the entire country. It's everywhere you look, from the organization of federal agencies to federalism itself. But even the people issuing the orders are getting fed up with the outcomes of this dysfunctional waterfall. It doesn't serve them either. It serves no one.

I am encouraged by the increasing number of product managers being hired into government today, but it can still be hard to practice their discipline inside government bureaucracies. The mindset of "find all the requirements, fulfill all the requirements" is engrained in IT teams, policy teams, legal teams, compliance teams, contracting teams, purchasing teams, oversight bodies, and agency leadership. Even the press that cover government waste, fraud, and abuse beats measure projects by this yardstick. Having people on the digital team with "product manager" on their business cards doesn't change any of that. Product managers have to be willing and able to make unpopular decisions. And they have to have an environment that will allow them to do the job. That goes beyond their not getting hung up on when they deliver bad news. Making room for product management, and the iterative, user-centric practices that come with it, is long, hard work.

We live in a time when the idea that administrative agencies should make any decisions at all is in question. The notion that a member of some digital team buried deep within an obscure bureaucracy could make critical choices about how to fulfill the intent of a law doesn't sit well with many people. The right is deeply skeptical of the bureaucracy on principle. The left sometimes is too and may see the empowerment necessary for product management as fundamentally undemocratic. Staged rollouts that don't try to serve all users equally from day one can be seen as inconsistent with values of equity and inclusion, even if they serve everyone better in practice. On the flip side, diffuse authority and consensus-based decision frameworks appear to promote inclusion; in fact, they are thought of by people of all political persuasions as hedges against abuse of power.

But I would argue that good product management, or whatever other name you want to give it, is not only helpful but necessary to honor the core values of American government. It is not an excuse to go rogue; it is a path to getting the outcomes the democratic process has agreed upon. When done well, it appeals to the better angels of both the left and the right. It's not just that it allows for more streamlined government programs that cost less, deliver more, and treat users with dignity and respect. It's that we are supposed to be a government of the people, for the people, and by the people. Fundamentally, a product manager is someone who hears everyone—this compliance issue here, that niche concern there—but puts that panoply of interests into the proper context. A good product manager never forgets whom government is supposed to serve.

Product management is an active, not passive, take on fundamental questions of representation and voice. It doesn't rely on simply issuing an open invitation to whoever wants to participate in the discussion. It starts from the recognition that most of the people who need to be heard won't show up—their relationship to government went sour long ago, sometimes generations ago, as Genevieve Gaudet observed. It is government's job to figure out who they are and go knock on their doors, literally and figuratively. They shouldn't need to read the *Federal Register* or to craft a meticulous lawyerly argument in response. They shouldn't even need to be as charming and articulate as Dominic. In their interactions with government, we've been overburdening people, and product management thinks it's time we did some of the work for them. The mechanisms we've built for public input have inadvertently allowed for colossal capture by government needs, special interests, and even well-meaning but often misguided advocates. Product management done right is an anti-capture mechanism.

Just as it doesn't take orders from above literally, product management doesn't take user feedback literally either. You don't gather a list of what your users say they want and check off that whole list, any more than you should gather a list of internal requirements and fulfill all of those. The art of product management is finding elegant ways to give users what they really need, even if they can't necessarily articulate their needs themselves. As Henry Ford is credited with saying, "If I had asked people what they wanted, they would have said faster horses."

When no one decides what a program should do and not do, the result is the digital equivalent of mounds and mounds of paperwork. And as I've said before, paperwork favors the powerful. Product management promises a counterweight to that power imbalance. We are long overdue to reimagine representation and voice so as to honor the values our government is supposed to be founded on, however poorly we may have upheld those values before. We should use the tools of today to help.

11

THE INSIDERS

Today, the Centers for Medicare and Medicaid Services does have product managers. In fact, some of the best product managers coming into government want to work at CMS. Specifically, they want to work for Yadira Sánchez.* And though newcomers to government like Natalie Kates may serve as catalysts of much-needed change, it is longtime public servants like Yadira who ultimately make that change stick.

In her over twenty years at CMS, Yadira has held quite a few titles but has most often been called a project manager. She came to CMS by accident. An air force brat from Puerto Rico, she was helping out her father's junior ROTC class by showing them how to introduce themselves to employers at a job fair. She had never heard of CMS and had no idea what it did, but when she play-acted her job search at the CMS booth, she ended up with a job offer. CMS hired her under an outstanding scholars program, though she's the kind of person who quickly corrects

* Yadira spoke to me for this book in her personal capacity. Her views do not reflect that of the federal government.

the record when I call her a straight-A student. "I tried a litera-
ture class in Spanish to see if I could do it. Let's just say it was a
mistake." She was wary of CMS, but the agency offered to pay all
her moving expenses. She got on a plane to Maryland.

"CMS does a really poor job of teaching people about Medicare and Medicaid," Yadira told me about her first months.
"When I first joined, they would give you a binder several inches
thick you were supposed to read. It was overwhelming and dry
and boring, and it doesn't help you understand how to actually
support the programs." She found she was expected to implement technology projects but not to understand how the technology was to be used. "My biggest complaint about IT at CMS
is that they focus on the technology and forget the importance of
the programs that they're supporting," she says today.

That never sat well with Yadira. "I hated working in a silo
and wanted to know what the users were actually interested in."
When she ran staff training sessions, she treated them as opportunities to talk to people and observe them using the tools she was
implementing. She wanted to see how they interacted with the
tech, to learn what made sense to them, which parts they didn't
get or would never use, and where they got frustrated. She was
good at her job and got opportunities to work in more and more
parts of CMS. As she jumped around the agency, watching and
listening, she learned more and more about her colleagues' roles
and the challenges they faced. Thirteen years in, she could have
rewritten that new-employee binder. And she learned that she
cared deeply about what CMS does.

When healthcare.gov launched and faltered, Yadira was a natural choice to help fix it. She was pulled into first one and then
another emergency project, quickly becoming indispensable. She
was calm under pressure, had great instincts for problem solving,
and, unlike many of those brought in to help, including Todd
Park's tech surge recruits, she knew how the agency worked. But

her role in the rescue also offered her the opportunity to see how her agency might change.

Eventually she and her boss were put on a doozy of a problem. People signing up for health insurance through the Affordable Care Act were supposed to get a tax credit, but that didn't seem to be triggered consistently. Reconciling health insurance enrollment with tax credits meant changing the data in the system, frequently and at large scale. But the way the production environment had been set up, she was supposed to make those changes without a safety net.

The way Yadira had always worked, you didn't make changes to any website directly, much less one that millions of people were using. First, you'd make a change within the development environment, which is basically where coders are trying out new things. Then, if it worked there, you'd make that same change in a replica of the code called the test environment, and then, if the change worked there too, you'd make it in a version of the code that connected to other elements of the project, called the integration environment. Only after integration testing would you make the change in the production environment, otherwise known as the live website. If at any of these points along the way something bad happened, you would roll back the change in each environment you'd touched and start over again in the development environment. It's a safe, if very time-consuming, way to reduce the likelihood of taking the whole site down with a programming or data change.

But for reasons Yadira still doesn't understand, that's not how the healthcare.gov team had set things up. None of those layers of safeguards existed. Her team was supposed to make live updates to the site without the benefit of development, test, and integration environments to ensure they had gotten things right.

"It was the scariest thing I'd ever had to do," she told me. Yadira had always taken pains to understand the impact of what she did on real people trying to use the technology she worked on, but never had so much been at stake and never had she had so little assurance she wasn't causing harm. She started by adding just one layer of safety net, a copy of the system that her team could test in before they pushed changes live. There was no time to re-create the four layers she was used to; the site needed to be fixed yesterday, and this would have to do. She and her colleagues developed processes to reduce the likelihood of disasters and got every single team member on a fifteen-minute call every morning to go over what needed to happen and to get on the same page.

She was surprised to find that it worked—they could make do with just the one test environment. Over time, she began to prefer this streamlined process and the speed it offered. "The way we always did things before, we would create a contract just to gather requirements, and that would take a whole year, and then one contractor would hand off to another and it was always a terrible handoff because of course the requirements were no longer valid. Everything took so long it was always so outdated by the time you started development." Now they had thrown all those time-consuming steps out the window and were just figuring out how to make the site work with what they had on hand. "All of a sudden we were doing things day by day, changing the schedule and making updates on the fly to adjust. It really pushed the agency. We had never run this way before." Maybe it was for all the wrong reasons—making changes directly to the live site was still a terrible idea—but change had come to CMS. And Yadira liked it.

The team was making updates on the fly out of necessity, and amid hair-raising chaos. But Yadira discovered that there was a way of developing software that intentionally expected changes along the way, moved quicker, and still provided effective safety nets. Todd's tech surge team offered a language and a framework for how Yadira had begun accidentally operating. "That's when I first learned that agile was a thing," she recalls. Even before the healthcare.gov crisis, Yadira had been frustrated with CMS's waterfall practices and culture, but she had never known there was a well-established, highly respected, and commonly accepted alternative.

Mikey Dickerson and Todd would be on the cover of *Time* magazine, but Yadira—like many other CMS employees—was a hero of the healthcare.gov rescue in ways that went unnoticed and unappreciated in the press. She doesn't seem to care. Not everything had gone smoothly in the collaboration with the tech surge team: there had been some tensions, and sometimes even Yadira didn't appreciate the way these outsiders disrupted the agency's own progress. Sometimes they seemed to think they knew better than everyone else. But she was learning a lot. The change that was emerging was, in her view, long overdue.

A year later, Yadira was asked to work on MACRA. She would be working alongside some of the same people from the tech surge, except now they were part of the US Digital Service. And now, Yadira wouldn't be coming in to clean up someone else's mess. She was on the project almost from its start, responsible for making sure that the website for medical providers didn't just technically meet requirements but could be used by them with some ease. She wanted the effort to succeed, to show the world that CMS was more than the disaster it had become known for. And she wanted to go beyond just being aware of agile development, user research, and product management as things that some people did. She wanted to master those disciplines.

More than anything, Yadira relished the chance to institutionalize practices that could, in her words, massively transform the agency she cared so much about.

・・・

ON HEALTHCARE.GOV, SOME of the biggest problems stemmed from the left hand's not knowing what the right hand was doing.

MACRA couldn't afford that but it, too, involved staffers from various specialties within CMS, including policy and tech; members of the USDS, such as Mina Hsiang and Natalie Kates; people from other parts of government; and, of course, external vendors. To improve communication, it was decided to bring them physically together: wherever their home base might be, they were all expected to spend three days a week in an office just outside the giant walled complex that housed CMS in Baltimore.

Even so, divisions emerged within the group. And the biggest divide was not between the CMS staff and the USDS staff—it was between policy and digital. "Initially, the tech side tried to implement the policy as it was written and the policy team continued to write the next version of the policy," Yadira recalls. "But the policy team was not taking into consideration how difficult it was to implement the words that they were writing." What's more, with over two hundred people working on the project, divided into many subteams, there were communication gaps between those units as well.

These communication gaps threatened to create even more burden for doctors. In one of the rules, one policy team had written that medical practices would need to choose by January of each year which track within the program they were going to participate in. To make that choice, those practices would need to look at analysis of the previous year's data from the government. But a separate policy team, writing a separate part of the regulations, had set a date to deliver that analysis to doctors in March. So the policy as drafted required doctors to make a decision before they had the information they needed to make it.

When Natalie noticed this inconsistency, she took over an empty conference room and divided its walls into twelve sections, one for each month. She asked all of the policy people to write on Post-it notes each action medical practices were supposed to take. Each communication doctors would receive went on a different-colored note. Natalie then asked the team to put each one on the wall in the month when it was planned to happen. Then they drew lines between the sticky notes to show where one action was dependent on another. It turned out that the problem Natalie had caught was not unique. When you put all these complex pieces together, there were multiple inconsistencies in the timeline. Fortunately, the policy team had time to fix them.

Another time, in a long hallway that had been painted with whiteboard paint, a member of the USDS team grabbed some dry-erase markers and started making a chart. "Here are the ten different options providers are starting with," he explained, "and here are the ten different options that stem from each of those ten options." The policy team began to gather in the hallway as he continued to draw and explain. "From there, each of those hundred options has ten more options, which makes a thousand. It continues exponentially."

Yadira recalls vividly how the policy people watched the wall fill until there was no more room for branches. It was like she could see light bulbs going off in their heads. They had wanted to provide as many options for providers as possible, to make providers feel like they could customize the program for their needs. With the best of intentions, though, they had created an unmanageable tangle. "After that, I saw a change in how they went about writing the policy and merging it with the actual implementation of the work," Yadira told me. "It was absolutely phenomenal. But it wasn't until that moment in front of that whiteboard that they realized how complicated the policy was becoming."

Many people assume the tools of the digital trade are bits and bytes. But walls, markers, flip charts, and sticky notes often play a more important role in digital work than screens and keyboards. Not only do these tools provide insight into the user experience and expose the inconsistencies that can doom a project if caught too late but they also provide a bridge between factions that believe they lack a common language. Policy people can be secretly intimidated by digital teams, worried that they'll look stupid when technical topics come up, and the reverse can be just as true. But there's something about little slips of colored paper—maybe because they remind us of kindergarten—that puts everyone on the same level. Working with the MACRA team, Yadira saw how they can break down those toxic barriers.

■ ■ ■

YADIRA WOULD NEED those tools. The more she thought about the program from the perspective of the users, especially the sole practitioners and small practices that didn't have a professional staff dedicated to dealing with government regulation, the more she found the CMS IT team at odds with the policy team and their sometimes unhelpfully conscientious interpretations of the law.

One skirmish emerged over practices that were meant to be exempt from the entire new program. The authors of MACRA recognized that participating in value-based care would be a big burden for practices that saw only a few Medicare patients, so they had allowed for those practices to opt out. This was great news. Many doctors were complaining about the hassle the new law was going to create for them, but this provision let a chunk of them entirely off the hook. Yadira and her colleagues found themselves champing at the bit to let those providers know.

But they couldn't. When Congress passes a law like MACRA, it will generally direct an agency like CMS to write regulations, specific rules that help implement the law on a practical basis. The law as written by Congress stated that practices that billed Medicare under a certain amount per year were exempt. But how was the exemption to be established? The policy team decided that a practice would need to collect its data for a year, submit it to the government, and show that it was under the threshold. Effectively, that meant that these providers would need to do everything all the others had to do: read and understand the program options, make their selections, and update their electronic health care record systems to collect and report all the required information. All that trouble and expense, only to be told at the end of the year that none of that difficult work had been necessary, because they were exempt. "It sounds like the right thing to do if you're trying to get the absolutely most accurate program enrollment," Yadira said. "But if you look at it through the eyes of the providers, it is the worst possible experience."

A slightly less accurate but far less burdensome option would be simply to look at the data from the previous year, which CMS already had, and determine who was in or out based on that. But when she and a colleague proposed this, the policy team gave the same answer they had given Natalie when she was arguing against Facebook for Doctors: "Sorry, Congress says we have to." Like Natalie, Yadira was told over and over that the proposal was simply not compliant with the law.

In the past, Yadira might have accepted that the call wasn't hers to make. It was the policy team's job to write the regulations and her job to implement them. But Yadira found it hard to believe that Congress wanted to give thousands of small medical practices even more reason to stop seeing Medicare patients. And she had not only the tools she'd seen the USDS team use but something that Natalie didn't: deep, long-standing relationships in the building. She may have been outside her lane, telling policy folks how to do their job, but she wasn't from outside the agency. Her long tenure in so many different parts of CMS gave her credibility, and she used it.

Eventually, Yadira won her fight too. And when the leadership finally agreed to exempt medical practices based on the prior year's data, they didn't just save hundreds of thousands of Medicare patients from losing the doctors who'd been caring for them for years. They also gave the tech team an opportunity to build its first product: a simple web page that let providers enter their Medicare identification number and find out whether they were exempt from MACRA. This is a best practice in the broader tech industry: teams have a better chance of shipping big, complex software projects if they first ship small, simple ones. As Yadira exercised her muscles breaking down the barriers between IT and policy, she was also making room for the team to exercise its delivery muscles.

The website that implemented MACRA's value-based medicine regulations—now branded the Quality Payment Program—launched on schedule on January 1, 2018. CMS leadership, once bitten, twice shy, prepared for the worst. They needn't have. It was the most successful launch in CMS history. It was on time and dramatically under budget. It met all the legal requirements (yes, even without Facebook for Doctors). The call center had braced for a flood of calls from users needing support; instead, those who did call were more likely to be confused because they had been expecting the kind of difficulties they'd encountered in the past. "This is almost too easy—it's scary!" one caller said.[1] A doctor who'd said that he was considering leaving the profession because of Medicare's burdens alluded to the trust that still needed to be built, but for now he was back on board. "Think of the Quality Payment Program as the beginning of a journey," he wrote. "I'm willing to pilot some of these programs and see how it goes. CMS is listening and I thank them for it."[2] The hundreds of public servants who turned this program around deserve enormous praise, not just from the doctors but from all of us. If, like me, you have family members who rely on Medicare, you too owe them thanks.

CMS had a goal: improving health outcomes. There was no

lack of support for the goal, but a deep dissatisfaction with the burdens that came with it. As we look to implement even more ambitious policy goals today, the lessons of MACRA can help. The Infrastructure Investment and Jobs Act wants to turn $1.2 trillion into not only better roads, bridges, railways, power grids, and broadband access but also millions of jobs that pay middle-class wages. The CHIPS and Science Act wants to bring semiconductor manufacturing back to the United States and spur regional economic growth. And the Inflation Reduction Act, a document longer than the book you are reading, wants to lower the prices of prescription drugs, convert every American household to solar energy and heat pumps (while also creating good jobs), build new nuclear plants, modernize the IRS, and keep global warming below 1.5 degrees, among other things. There is broad (though not universal) support for most of these goals, but just as MACRA's success depended on tens of thousands of health care providers' willingness to engage with government, fulfilling today's critical policy ambitions will depend on millions of companies' and consumers' willingness to do the same. It even depends on the willingness of other governments, particularly states and counties, to engage with the federal government and with each other—don't think for a moment that people in bureaucracies aren't stymied by the burdens imposed by other bureaucracies.

As they apply for permits, claim rebates, and demonstrate compliance, will the people critical to the success of these new laws feel the way doctors felt about Medicare before MACRA, ready to throw up their hands? Or could we imagine them saying "This is almost too easy!" and eagerly taking on the next project? So much hangs on that question.

Perhaps there will be websites that help make each of these tasks easy, but as Natalie discovered, you can't make a good website for a bad program. And you can't make a good program if the people in government agencies just take orders, and take them literally.

■ ■ ■

PUSHING BACK ON what appear to be official policy requirements is not easy for anyone. Today, though, Yadira doesn't seem to have much trouble with it. For example, Congress recently passed legislation that requires CMS to release claims data to prescription drug plan providers. The rule specified that CMS should release the data on a quarterly basis. But Yadira knew there was a better way. What Congress said it wanted was standardized data extracts, but what it intended was that these providers should have access to claims information so they could improve health outcomes. The best way to do that would be to build an application programming interface (API) that would let providers pull data from CMS systems directly. They'd have immediate and ongoing access, instead of getting extracts of claims data that were months out of date. And while the API would cost a bit more up front to develop, it would be cheaper and more reliable in the long run. Yadira didn't want her team to build an inferior product just because "Congress said to."

So she showed up at a town hall meeting with the providers. She explained that if they did exactly what the law said to do, the claims information would be significantly delayed. Indeed, getting the data packaged up into quarterly extracts would be so time-consuming that the first files they'd receive after the law went into effect on January 1 would come only that fall—nine months later. Then she pitched her alternative: the API. The providers loved it, so she told her team to run with it.

When Natalie averted the Facebook for Doctors disaster, she had to pit her interpretation of the law against that of agency lawyers and policymakers. But she wasn't arguing that they should ignore Congress's explicit directions. Yadira isn't arguing anything either; she's just getting the job done. "We're not following the letter of the law," she admits. "But we're producing the results that we know Congress intended." That's a level of product management—of taking charge and deciding what to do—that even the USDS, with its power as a White House unit, would find daunting. "I'm not worried," she told me, "because we've proven time and time again we get the right results."

This kind of leadership amounts to a quiet but genuine repudiation of the waterfall. Oftentimes, when government leaders hear that private-sector companies get good results from something called agile development, they simply order the bureaucracy below them to switch to that way of doing things, without really understanding what it means. Unsurprisingly, this doesn't work. Sometimes the tech teams adopt some of the trappings of agile, like having daily stand-up meetings or dividing the work into two-week sprints, and then wait for their next orders. Everyone still has requirements to check off, and it is still no one's job to figure out the right thing to build. In other cases, teams just make PowerPoints with the word *agile* on them and continue operating entirely as they were. (As Eric Schoonover found when he used the same trick to get around ESB requirements, it really does satisfy the higher-ups most of the time.) Nothing changes, and then the leaders get even more upset with the tech teams.

The problem is that issuing orders, especially from a place of disdain or disrespect, only reinforces blind obedience to the hierarchy. You cannot get the benefits of product management and agile development in a top-down culture—these practices require that "mechanicals" working on details of implementation be able to exercise meaningful judgment, and even to weigh in on issues out of their lane. Product managers can't always go back up the chain for permission on every minor decision. Sometimes they just need to do the thing that will get the agreed-upon outcome.

Success shifts from the number of orders you faithfully executed to the results you delivered.

Yadira's success also suggests that the policy class has less desire to be taken literally than many in the bureaucracy assume. Although government workers often feel that they can't do what's right lest they be fired or sued, leaders like Yadira assume the right to reinterpret law and policy when the outcome is at stake—to do what is needed rather than what was ordered. She is the kind of fighter General McChrystal would praise for following the orders he would have given if he'd known what she knows. She's the kind of public servant Ezra Klein would celebrate for escaping the small, cramped, narrowly professional mode of thinking and claiming an interpretation of the law that makes sense to a person. If Congress were paying attention, it'd thank her for doing what it intended, not exactly what it had asked for. Indeed, Congress and the multitude of oversight bodies that hover over tech projects would do well to spend more time identifying and celebrating people like Yadira and less time harping on tech's failures.

It is always a bit risky to take the kinds of liberties Yadira did. Even if the alternate solution works better, things can go wrong. An overzealous oversight staffer can take issue with it on principle or politics can come into play, and someone may be looking for reasons to charge the agency with wrongdoing. But Yadira has earned her confidence. Instead of the downward cycle of poor performance, erosion of trust, and ossification of the chain of command, exercising her judgment has produced results that earn her more trust and give her more leeway to exercise her judgment next time. It has also made her a magnet for talent. Experienced product managers want to work for her, because under her they can do the job they're trained to do and make services that work for people. The more people like Yadira normalize product management in government, the less everyone else has to fight to be able to do it.

Today, CMS is far from perfect. Yadira wishes that more of the agency would make the kinds of changes she's embraced. She estimates that about 15–25 percent of tech development at CMS currently follows agile, user-centered product management practices, but it's hard to say for sure, in part because the word *agile* is so often used on projects that are anything but. Every time a team adopts "fake agile" and it doesn't work, defenders of the status quo gain proof points. "Using the words [of agile] but not taking the actions destroys our progress," says Yadira.

Still, the agency is a very different place from what it was before the failure of healthcare.gov and the success of MACRA. "The biggest takeaway I have from those years," she says in retrospect, "is that government can make change—huge sweeping change—for the better. It is painful. It is controversial. But there's more of a commitment from staff, and from leadership. It's an exciting time to be at CMS."

Yadira points to the healthcare.gov crisis—and her treasured colleagues—as the reason for the improvements. But if you ask Natalie why CMS has gotten better, she'll point to Yadira. (This makes Yadira deeply uncomfortable. She is quick to deflect praise and shift credit to others, reminding me constantly of her teammates she sees as more deserving than her.) I've talked with dozens of people like Natalie who work in catalyst roles around state, local, and federal government, and they all have their own Yadiras—the career public servants who not only enable change when the opportunity arises but keep it going after the tech surges, task forces, and angry politicians leave. Like Yadira, they often seize the initiative, quietly assuming the responsibility of honoring lawmakers' intent rather than their words. And though Yadira learned agile development from newcomers like the USDS team, her practice of it is in some ways truest to the original manifesto, one principle of which is: "Agile processes promote sustainable development. The sponsors, developers, and users should be able to maintain a constant pace indefinitely."[3] Tech work is hard, and many people burn out. But twenty-two years after Yadira got on that plane from Puerto Rico, she is still at CMS, still discovering what people need to make health care in this country better.

The media hardly noticed that MACRA was the agency's do-over from healthcare.gov. This is partly because it wasn't a president's signature policy initiative, partly because it was mostly doctors rather than the general public who interacted with it, and partly because things working well seldom make the news. But doctors noticed, and so did thousands of people around CMS. Perhaps if this keeps up, the rest of us will notice too.

If journalists *had* noticed, you can imagine how they might have told the story. CMS had had second-rate programmers on healthcare.gov, they could have said, and Todd's tech surge had given them access to better ones now. Government technology has become such a convenient punching bag, and the trope of the outside tech geniuses has become familiar. It's unlikely journalists would have written about the hallway markered over with exponentially branching options, the conference rooms covered in sticky notes with lines between them like a conspiracy-theory wall. It's unlikely they would have understood how much the normal waterfall from Congress to regulators to digital teams had been disrupted. But the most unlikely angle would have been pointing to a twenty-year veteran of the IT department who'd used the biggest disaster her agency had ever seen to spur a dramatic transformation.

They'd be missing the story, and so would we. We miss it every time we count on policy change alone to cure what ails the nation, every time we indulge in the fantasy of the silver bullet, and every time we honor change agents from the outside without recognizing people like Yadira, and the many thousands like her, who fight to make our government work for us every day—and win. They are the key to meaningful, lasting change. We neglect them at our own peril.

12

UP THE WATERFALL

The policymakers upstream from the tech teams, or at least some of them, are starting to see the possibilities of a different relationship with the people responsible for digital implementation. Dialogue gets better outcomes than directives get, and to have that dialogue—and avoid unforced errors that can tank the project—you need to include the implementers much earlier in the process. You need to give them a voice on matters that were previously considered out of their lane. You need to find tools (like sticky notes!) that let everyone speak a common language. The dialogue goes both ways, of course. Everyone benefits when policymakers can explain to programmers what they intended, instead of leaving them to make their best guess. And the more digital teams understand the policy domain, the more opportunities arise for creative solutions.

But policymakers and programmers alike are the target of directives that come from legislators above both groups. When Natalie Kates won her fight about the nine definitions of a group or about Facebook for Doctors, it was because she and the policymakers managed to agree that her preferred solution would still honor Congress's intent. But what about when the problem isn't with the interpretation of the law by policymakers in agencies but with the law itself? Can the shift from directive to dialogue reach all the way back upstream to the people and processes that create the laws of our land? If you ask Cristine Soto DeBerry, it has to.

・・・

CRISTINE'S PROBLEM WAS not Table 64 but Proposition 64, California's Adult Use of Marijuana Act. As the chief of staff to San Francisco's district attorney, Cristine was responsible for making sure her office did its part to implement the new law. There was a whole host of new regulations related to all the companies that were springing up to sell pot legally. Cristine wanted to know about the people who weren't part of those new businesses, the ones who were still walking around with felony convictions.

"We'll be fine," she was told. "We already have a calendar for expungement, so anyone who applies will simply go to that court. We just need to state our policy that we won't oppose any petitions for clearance under the new law, and we'll be done." District attorneys, victims, and victims' families are those who would normally oppose an expungement. But Cristine's boss, District Attorney George Gascón, had already taken a decriminalization stance on marijuana; even before Prop 64, his office had stopped actively prosecuting those cases. And marijuana offenses aren't like theft; there's no victim who could show up and make the case that the conviction should stand. It was a given that no one would oppose, which made Cristine wonder: Why make people petition at all?

Cristine knew what an enormous hassle the petition process was. She knew that many of the people who managed to complete it were the ones who needed it least, often because they could afford to hire a private lawyer to do all the paperwork and jump through all the hoops. And there were a lot of hoops. It wasn't just gathering the records from across multiple siloed government agencies, filling out forms, filing motions, and paying fees. It was also the waiting, the responding to notices, following up, and showing up in court. And if a petitioner is lucky enough to get a determination to have a record sealed, the court doesn't disseminate that order. It's on the petitioner to send copies of it to the state police, DAs, arresting agencies, municipal courts, and other relevant organizations who held the criminal record in the first place. Then, assuming all the right offices have been hit, the petitioner has to hope that the courts, the DAs, and state and local law enforcement pay attention to the paperwork and actually update their databases. Individually.

Cristine knew about the petition process because she'd been on the other side. Her first job after graduating from UC Berkeley's law school was as a public defender in Los Angeles, where she'd grown up. It's a noble job defending those who can't otherwise afford legal representation, but it's grueling work, and Cristine often felt frustrated. "Public defenders have to work client by client," she told me. "The reason I became a prosecutor is because I realized in a situation like marijuana legalization, I could make a whole file cabinet disappear just by making the right policy decision."

Petitioning was fundamentally flawed, but that's what the law allowed for, so that's what San Francisco and every other county in California were doing: waiting for those petitions to come in. And waiting is exactly what they would do. Cristine's office was averaging fewer than two petitions a month. She couldn't let the problem go, even if others could. "It felt to me just principally unfair that we would create more hurdles and obstacles to people accessing a right they're entitled to," Cristine told me later. "And obviously very inefficient. This was just going to be an exorbitant misuse of funds."

Normally the petitions would come from individuals, public defenders, or legal aid clinics, who had to work one by one with clients to get access to each individual's record of arrests and prosecutions—or RAP sheet—from the State Bureau of Investigation. It didn't have to be that way, Cristine thought. Her office had access to the database that held the RAP sheets, as well as to the county's court management system. It basically had the information needed to build a petition right there in its computer systems. Why couldn't the DA just file petitions on behalf of those who were eligible?

Not everyone liked Cristine's idea. To some, it seemed like borrowing trouble. This was pretty far outside the obligations a DA's office usually assumed. But Gascón loved it, and others got on board to figure out how to make it happen.

It started with the county's court management records, held in a mainframe computer system dating back to 1975. There were five distinct charges that Prop 64 had decriminalized, so Cristine's team asked the data folks for a list of everyone in the system with those charges. List in hand, they started to beg and borrow paralegals who could take a name from the list, look the person up in the RAP sheet database, and fill out the form on the person's behalf. It went slowly. Cristine had had to broker a deal with the courts to accept these petitions despite their unconventional origins, and the courts had agreed to process only a hundred of them a week. But the paralegals couldn't produce even that number. It took twenty or thirty minutes to find and download the right RAP sheet, more time to confirm that the person was eligible for expungement, and another twenty or thirty minutes to fill out the petition. A paralegal doing this job on a lunch hour could usually get only one done before having to go back to work.

Still, it was better than nothing. Gascón decided to tell the public what his office was doing, in the hopes of inspiring other DAs to do the same. "We in the criminal justice system have been part of the problem," he told reporters. "So I made the decision that we would do it on our own." Advocates who'd been hoping for "automatic expungement" of marijuana convictions gave Gascón's efforts that label. Had the tech startups scattered around the DA's office in San Francisco taken notice, they might have wondered how a labor-intensive process that took an hour per petition—as just the first step—could be touted as automatic. They didn't notice. But Jazmyn Latimer did.

· · ·

JAZMYN HAD COME to Code for America several years earlier to work with the police department in Vallejo, California. The daughter of a cop, she understood how to develop trust with police. This was in 2015, before movements to defund the police took the national stage, but her work building tools to influence how they patrolled the community was prescient. She spent months shadowing cops on the beat, observing 911 call centers in action, running workshops with residents at the local farmers markets, and facilitating hard conversations with city leaders. When the yearlong Vallejo project was over, she was hooked on working with government. Luckily, there was another project that Jazmyn was able to join. She and a colleague would name it Clear My Record.

The project had started before the passage of Prop 64, but its goal was exactly the kind of thing Cristine would try to do at the DA's office: make it easier to remove outdated criminal records. In 2014, another California referendum, Prop 47, had reclassified a slew of felonies like shoplifting and check forgery to misdemeanors, if the amounts involved were no more than $950. People previously convicted under the felony laws were now eligible to change their records. But for those with convictions, the effect of Prop 47 had been pretty much the same as that of Prop 64:

not much. People either didn't know they could get their record reclassified or they tried and got discouraged.

Jazmyn and her team built an online tool to help people start the expungement process—asking simple, clear questions that most petitioners knew the answers to, and connecting them with public defenders and pro bono attorneys. But that work was going slowly too. Two years into the Clear My Record experiment, the tool had helped about seven thousand people across the state begin the process. The team didn't know how many of them had gotten all the way through, but they suspected it was not many.

Jazmyn started with technology and design, working from the outside. Cristine started with paperwork, working from the inside. They both wanted to make a difference for the people affected, and both had the same problem: the math didn't add up. With Prop 47 and 64 each making hundreds of thousands of people eligible, neither filing a handful of petitions through paralegals every week nor assisting a few thousand people over two years was fast enough. In either case, it would take many years to clear all the eligible records. Meanwhile, people with outdated convictions would continue to fail background checks, continue to struggle with employment, and continue to be excluded from the economy. Nationally, as many as 1.9 million workers are estimated to be shut out of the labor market because of criminal histories, costing the US economy up to $87 billion each year in lost GDP.[1]

Was there a way to make things go faster? Observing petitioners and attorneys, Jazmyn saw that once people had their RAP sheet in hand, a big stumbling block was determining whether they were actually eligible. RAP sheets are written in code—not computer code, legal system code. They're essentially lists of numbers that map to particular sections of the California penal code that the person was convicted of violating. It takes training and knowledge to read one and determine whether the person is likely to be eligible for expungement. And there are not nearly enough people with that knowledge to help the people who need it.

Jazmyn noticed that people stumbled at this step, but she also noticed that most of them had something by their sides while they struggled: a smartphone. She knew what smartphones could do. She'd seen people depositing their checks using one. Most bank apps let you take a picture of the check, and optical character recognition reads the numbers on the bottom of the check and verifies the account number. Why couldn't a smartphone take a picture of the RAP sheet, read the codes there, and do the hard work of matching them up to the convictions that were eligible for expungement?

Jazmyn's team at Code for America had the technology, but there was one thing they didn't have. To truly determine eligibility, you need to know not just what the codes mean but also how they interact and how the district attorney is going to interpret them. For instance, if someone has only low-level nonviolent drug offenses, the person is very likely going to get a determination in their favor. But some people with nonviolent offenses have also been convicted of something else far more serious, and in that situation the DA will not clear the low-level convictions. And then there are cases in between; the law leaves DAs a lot of room for discretion. To write the logic engine that would tell you for sure whether a given conviction on a RAP sheet is eligible for expungement, you need the DA to make a bunch of decisions in advance, and you need to encode those decisions into the logic.

So when Gascón's office announced its scheme to actively initiate expungements under Prop 64, Jazmyn's team gave the office a call. And they found quite a lot to talk about. Cristine and her team needed a way to process the paperwork faster. Jazmyn and her team needed a way for their app to tell people whether they were eligible. But when you put the two problems together—paralegals laboriously pulling RAP sheets from the state database one by one and a logic engine trying to parse RAP sheet codes according to the DA's rulings on eligibility—something became immediately clear. If you built the logic engine, as Code for America had, and you had the authority to clear all the eligible criminal records in a given jurisdiction, as the San Francisco DA's office did, why scan each RAP sheet individually? Why not just write the computer code to go through all the records in the database at once, determine which ones had the legal codes that pointed to eligibility and didn't contain any disqualifying criteria, spit out a list of expungeable records, and auto-fill the petitions all at once?

Working together, that is exactly what they built. It helped that a new law mandated that all county DAs review and clear eligible convictions and that the California Department of Justice was now willing to provide the RAP sheet data.[2] A few months after that first phone call, the new software program, called Clear My Record Automatic, identified 8,132 San Franciscans whose records were eligible to be cleared. The DA's office filed a single petition for expungement with an attachment listing those 8,132 names as the petitioners, and the court agreed to render one judgment for all 8,132 based on the logic in the software. Instead of decades of work, the software program had taken about thirty seconds to run.

■ ■ ■

THE PRESS HAD a heyday with the notion that an algorithm was, for once, helping people get unstuck from the criminal legal system instead of stuck in it. We were automating justice, including racial justice: because Black people were hugely overrepresented in the population of those with pot convictions, they were also overrepresented in the population that received the record clearance. It was a huge victory for Cristine, for Jazmyn, and especially for everyone whose records had been expunged.

But there were still millions of records to clear across California, and Cristine and the team at Code for America were not about to rest on their laurels. "I could not believe how ridiculously we'd been operating in the system," Cristine said. "Nothing should be petition-based!" When the San Francisco DA's task was done, she set her sights on the rest of the state. She helped draft a bill that would automate the expungement of records that were already legally expungeable. The first attempt to pass it didn't go as planned: the legislature limited the bill so it applied only to future arrests and convictions. That, of course, misses the point of providing relief to people who are eligible and unfairly strapped with convictions that could be cleared. In 2020, Cristine tried again. Her new organization, the Prosecutors Alliance of California, reintroduced the bill to capture old convictions as well, going back to when electronic records started being collected.[3] This time the provisions became law. Cristine would get automatic expungements after all.

Or at least some of them. The marijuana convictions covered by Prop 64 were straightforward to automate, but the assorted convictions decriminalized under Prop 47 were not. For instance, under Prop 47, commercial burglary—stealing property from a store or other business—is no longer a felony if the property was valued at $950 or less. But there is no specific RAP sheet code just for burglaries under $950, or even just for commercial burglaries. You can run a report to give you every past burglary in San Francisco, but then for each one of them you'd have to look through paper files, sometimes handwritten ones, to answer questions like: Did this happen at a home or a business? What was actually stolen? Let's say it was a camera. OK, how much was the camera worth? For that, you need to know the make and model, which may or may not be in the police report. Even if they are, you then need to establish how much, say, a Canon PowerShot S80 was worth back in 2005 when the crime was committed. That's both hard to research and open to contention. A judge, or a victim, could dispute the value and argue that the expungement didn't meet the criteria.

Even if all the data needed to establish eligibility were in the police files, it wouldn't be easily accessible to a software program. It is theoretically possible to digitize old paper records, but it would require enormous human effort. It is theoretically possible to train a software program to read police officers' handwriting, but it's not as if there's a particular box on the pages of their reports for "make and model of object stolen" that you can point it to. The software would need to try to read the whole report and figure out which scrawled abbreviation referred to the item. This theoretical software would need to be quite sophisticated, and it would be quite error prone. Even if you could overcome all the other barriers, lawmakers and judges would be unlikely to trust the program's output (rightly so) and to approve bulk clearance on that basis. The only way to establish that any given conviction meets the criteria for expungement under Prop 47 is through laborious research performed by human beings. The way the law was written makes automated expungement impossible.

This reminds me of a comic by Randall Munroe from his much-loved series *xkcd*. In it, one stick figure is directing the work of another, presumably a programmer, who is sitting in front of a computer. "When a user takes a photo," the standing figure says, "the app should check whether they're in a national park." The programmer replies, "Sure, easy GIS lookup. Gimme a few hours." The other continues, "And check whether the photo is of a bird." "I'll need a research team and five years," the programmer replies.

Need all marijuana-related felonies? Give the team a few hours. Need "burglaries of property under $950"? Not even a research team and five years is likely to help.

The irony of Prop 47 is that the authors of an early draft of the law were none other than Cristine Soto DeBerry and George Gascón. "We have really learned from those mistakes," Cristine says today. "When you get in the weeds with Jazmyn's team and see how this actually works, you learn that you need to think about the technical implementation of a law when you write it." Otherwise, you've written a law that looks good on the books but doesn't accomplish much at all. If it relies on the petition process, it helps a tiny fraction of the people it was meant to help. People with petty crimes on their records are still treated as felons, still can't pass background checks, still can't contribute to the economy. It doesn't matter what the magic words of the law say if they don't make a difference for the people they're supposed to help.

For all her regrets about Prop 47, Cristine's bill mandating automatic expungement of marijuana convictions was still a huge accomplishment. The Code for America team, for their part, helped dozens of counties in California comply with the legislation, ultimately identifying 144,000 convictions eligible for expungement. Clear My Record Automatic did its magic wherever the county leadership would let it.

Four years later, there is still a lot of work to do. It's estimated that the number of Americans with some sort of criminal record is between 70 million and 100 million—as many as one person out of every three in the country. Legalizing marijuana is the clearest (though not the only) path to lowering that number. As of 2022, nineteen states and the District of Columbia have fully legalized it, and several others have decriminalized it to some extent.[4] Lawmakers and voters are changing these laws for numerous reasons—some because they see prosecuting pot possession as a waste of resources, some because they see the devastating consequences to racial equity, some on other grounds. Whatever the impetus, the people penning these laws imagine they will make a real difference in people's lives.

But that difference is far from ensured. The implementation challenges California experienced were not unique. Other states are now learning what Cristine learned, that you need to think about the technical implementation of a law when you write it. That means having people like Jazmyn at the table from the start—not figuring out how to make the best of a law after the fact but helping to design it. It means conversations with diverse voices, including technologists, policymakers, advocates, and people living with convictions. If the goal is to deliver on the promises of our policies, dialogue once again beats directives.

···

IT'S NOT NEW that policymakers need to think about how their magic words will get implemented. They've always had to. But the degree of government's reliance on the digital realm has grown steadily for decades, without a corresponding growth in digital literacy in the government workforce or leadership. In fact, since the mid-1990s, when Clinger and Cohen tried to establish a top tech job in the White House, what's grown is the complexity of already byzantine government processes, making getting things done in government an increasingly specialized skill. Today, you can go to a three-month boot camp and come out an employable coder. But to become functional as, say, a procurement officer or HR manager in government can take years.

As the tools of administration have moved from paper forms, phone calls, and in-person office visits to bits and bytes and websites, the realm of implementation has become less accessible and more distant from those whose medium is magic words. It used to be that a competent manager could weigh in on delivery challenges through astute analysis. Today, getting the data you need to perform that analysis involves querying a system that belongs to an entire other realm of specialized knowledge. Public servants of all stripes used to be exposed to service delivery in their daily routines and intimately connected to its development. Now the digital world tends to separate them from it. No wonder policy decisions so often seem to be made without sufficient thought to how they will be delivered. Policy and delivery breathe increasingly different air.

Getting those who write our laws and policies to engage with the art of the technologically possible can help. They don't necessarily need to limit themselves to what's easy. Perhaps they will sometimes still choose policy options that are very hard to automate, like decriminalizing burglaries of property under $950. But if they do, they should make their decisions understanding the consequences. If there's enough time and money for implementation—if there are people who can go through all those police files, for instance, and make the case for expungement under those criteria—then the consequences may be tolerable. Mostly, though, those resources are not available, and choosing harder-to-implement options introduces the real possibility that the policy simply fails. When there are important human and societal outcomes on the line, we can't afford to fail just because lawmakers didn't understand the difference between a provision that would take five hours to implement and one that would take five years.

There is no need to sign up members of Congress and their staffs for programming classes, although the tech in question is quite accessible. Much of what's most useful in government today is not part of this brave new world of machine learning and artificial intelligence that many of us are understandably wary about. If you recall if-then statements from your freshman-year comp sci class, you can understand the basics of what the Clear My Record algorithm does. Writing policy with these considerations in mind isn't a matter of staying on the cutting edge of computing, or even being able to question Mark Zuckerberg in a hearing without embarrassment. It's just a matter of inviting different voices into the conversation and finding a common language with them.

That common language is neither tech-speak nor legalese. It focuses on people—understanding their needs and testing our assumptions about them. Tom Loosemore, one of the founding members of the Government Digital Service in the UK, worked with a policymaker who'd compiled mountains of academic research and analysis in advance of a revision of a major social policy. He was sure he knew to an incredible level of detail what the new policy should do and how it should work when Tom started working with him. But Tom's work didn't start with academic analysis. It started with user research, talking to real people who would use the service and be affected by the new policy and understanding their circumstances, their resources, and, most of all, their needs. This approach was very different—and very eye-opening—for Tom's policy partner. A few weeks into working with the GDS team, he came to Tom with his inches-thick binder of documents and plopped it down on the table. "You know," he said, "I've come to the realization that what I'm holding is really six hundred pages of untested assumptions. I'm just going to set it aside for a while." Tom, who now works with the global transformation consultancy Public Digital, has now seen that realization occur many times. "Why," he asks, "is so much policy educated guesswork with a feedback loop measured in years?" It doesn't have to be.

I often hear that tech changes so fast it's difficult to keep up. But what government needs to keep up with is not tech but people. In part because of technology, people's behavior and expectations have changed. Simple apps that do a lot for us have made people less tolerant of complex, multistep paperwork processes. Our devices constantly steal our attention, making it harder to persist through administrative burden. Increased inequality has made the time and attention burden even more costly to those who are most likely to engage with government. We push people to online interactions, but they've learned to distrust them, often for good reason. All these things matter enormously to how government must now relate to the public.

Cristine, who became a prosecutor so she could "make a whole file cabinet disappear," wanted to make change at enormous scale, and she wasn't afraid to employ an algorithm to get there. As a champion of automatic records clearance, she succeeded in that. But the algorithm that runs through the database sucking up all the right legal codes was not, in the end, the most valuable contribution the Clear My Record team made to this effort. Rather, it was the team's proof, after a few years of watching petitioners fail, that even when we streamline the petition process it's too hard for most people to get through. The need to fix that, not some vague desire to use an algorithm, drove the development of the tech. Employing tech for its own sake is often as unhelpful, and sometimes as harmful, as staying stuck in a fully manual mode.

Cristine saw the benefit of this tech to the people she was hoping to help. There will be others in positions of authority who distrust algorithms categorically and disallow their use. Hopefully, people like Jazmyn will be there to help demystify the tech and turn what have been directives from the top into dialogues with a diversity of voices. But our dialogue with those who represent us shouldn't start—or even end—with technology. It has to start with what people need. In that sense, we should already have a common language.

WHAT WE BELIEVE MATTERS

In September 2017, Kenneth Glueck, a senior vice president at the technology megacompany Oracle, wrote a letter to Chris Liddell, a senior official at the White House. Liddell had been charged with carrying out Executive Order 13800, "Strengthening the Cybersecurity of Federal Networks and Critical Infrastructure," issued in May of that year by President Trump. While its name makes the order sound like it's about the security of federal systems, the word *cybersecurity* is often used in government to mean all things digital, and this particular order was really about the continued poor state of government technology systems. And although Trump purported to be a very different kind of president, the order did what most orders do when the problem is persistent and challenging: it called for a report. Part of the writing of that report involved soliciting feedback from outside government, and it was in response to that request for feedback that Glueck wrote.

At the time, the USDS and 18F were a couple of years old, and each was starting to build a reputation. The USDS was known for its role on healthcare.gov and other presidential priorities.

18F had its own slate of successes and was helping federal agencies with procurements, teaching them how to write RFPs that would give the agencies and their vendors a better chance at success. But that same year I gave a talk at a conference of tech professionals in DC and asked who in the audience had heard of the USDS or 18F. Of about three hundred people in the room, a dozen or so raised their hands. The two groups, and their distinct ways of operating, were far from mainstream.

Nonetheless, in his letter, Glueck expressed alarm at changes he and his colleagues perceived. He complained about "false narratives" that had taken the US government "off course." Among these was the notion that "in-house government IT development know-how is critical for IT modernization." The reality, Glueck wrote, was that "in-house government procurement and program management expertise is central to successful modernization efforts. Significant IT development expertise is not."[1]

The letter is at its core a call to keep people who understand technology out of government. Shortly after the letter was delivered, Oracle's lobbyists tried to sneak a provision into a bill that would have prohibited government employees from participating in procurements if they had been hired under certain hiring authorities. It so happens that most of the team at the USDS and 18F had been hired under those exact authorities. One of Trump's tech advisers, a champion of the USDS, caught the provision, and it was ultimately removed from the bill. But the incident made clear that Oracle doesn't want technologists like Matthew Weaver or Natalie Kates anywhere near decisions about technology in federal government. Oracle sees digital talent exercising judgment instead of blindly following process as a threat to its business.

Glueck got a few things right in his thirteen-page letter. He properly warns against government's unhelpful addiction to building custom software when a commercial solution would work

just fine: "The most important skill set of CIOs today is to critically compete and evaluate commercial alternatives." He touches
on the need for government to modernize processes as a precon-
dition to modernizing tech. But where he is most on target is that
the narrative matters. Addressing the gap between the promises
government makes and the reality of what it delivers to its people
requires changing the narrative. Just not in the direction Oracle
would like.

• • •

IF OUR GOAL was to maximize Oracle's profits from its public-
sector business, Glueck's advice would be helpful. But what we
want to do is enable our government to deliver on its promises
in a digital age. And on that score, the evidence is decidedly not
in his favor.

Glueck sounds on the defensive, and it's not only because of
high-profile cases that reveal the flaws in his narrative, like the
failure and resurrection of healthcare.gov. It's also because over
the past ten years government has been attracting and developing more leaders like Mike Byrne or Yadira Sánchez, and their
approach is beginning, very slowly, to sideline those who are
happy to build multibillion-dollar concrete boats. Concrete
boats are a lucrative and high-margin business. Their true cost
is the failure of policy goals and further erosion of the public's
trust—through broken promises to veterans, for example. But
the financial costs add up too, and digital leaders like Mike and
Yadira make government a better buyer. A mayor once begged
me for advice on negotiating with Oracle, desperate for a way out
of a deal that she felt was strangling her city. I called up a friend
who worked for a different city government, someone with a
deep knowledge of technology—not just tech procurement but
the tech itself. "I once had a negotiation with Oracle where their
opening bid was $17 million and mine was $1 million," he told

me. "Where did you end up?" I asked. "$1.5 million." Most cities don't have someone with that kind of substantive expertise to go toe-to-toe with tech vendors. So they pay closer to Oracle's opening offer.

Because it's good for their bottom line, Oracle and companies like it promote the narrative that government shouldn't have internal tech capacity. But for others the objections are ideological. A group called Citizens Against Government Waste, for example, which calls itself "the legacy of President Ronald Reagan's Private Sector Survey on Cost Control," has called for GSA to "scrap the 18F program and issue a request for proposal so a private-sector company can step in and provide these services more efficiently and at a lower cost."[2] Much of 18F's work is, in fact, helping agencies issue RFPs to private-sector companies. They help their agency partners define clear goals ("modernization" is not a meaningful objective), scope projects (will we just do everything everyone can think of or will we figure out the best way to achieve a defined goal?), structure teams for helpful feedback loops, and bid out the right work with appropriate development methodologies. The true measure of 18F's value is the success of the policy goals it helps implement, but along the way its work has been successful in getting private-sector companies to provide services to government "more efficiently and at a lower cost." Contrary to what Citizens Against Government Waste claims as its goal, it seems chiefly to object to the fact that government is not completely abdicating all responsibility to private vendors.

These "waste watchers," as they call themselves, align with Oracle's incentives. But what about the rest of the tech industry? Most tech firms are not in the business of government contracting, and one might think that tech industry leaders would see the need for digital competence within the institution that runs the country.[3] Some do, to be sure.[4] But Oracle's narrative has a strong hold even among the startups and big tech firms that have revolutionized how we use the internet. Few in Silicon Valley (by which I mean an industry and a mindset, not a geographic location) see building government capacity as worthwhile—or perhaps even possible—placing all their bets on what the private sector can achieve. Venture capitalist Marc Andreessen epitomizes their attitude. A year into the pandemic, he casually referred to the "chronic collapse of state capacity virtually everywhere in our time," saying that "the good news is that . . . the private sector can and does deliver even under considerable duress, and even when much of our political system is devoted to stifling it with regulatory handcuffs and damaging it with misguided policies."[5] In this view, the question of whether government should have digital capacity is moot, because no one with the skills to build digital products should waste their time working in government. When the pandemic spurred Andreessen to issue an inspiring call to the country to "build," he meant that entrepreneurs should build things that people need—masks, vaccines, housing, even educational institutions.[6] If he'd seen the way public servants like Yadira build things within government, he might have had more confidence in the public sector's ability to build as well.

Andreessen is not the only one to lack faith that government can build the capacity it needs. I have lost count of the number of tech entrepreneurs who have told me with complete certainty that government will never do tech well. The biggest reason they give is that salaries in the public sector don't match what they pay, so the best people will never do public service. I am told this mostly by people who claim to value data and evidence above all else. But the evidence doesn't support that statement.

For one thing, the pay disparities are not nearly as dramatic as one might imagine. An experienced technologist working at the USDS or 18F could make $172,500 a year.[7] That's less than most developers would get at a company like Google, but it's not that far off from what you might get in a mid-tier role at a tech startup. The big difference is that, at a startup, you are hoping for a life-changing windfall when your company is acquired or goes public. But three-quarters of venture-backed startups fail outright; only a tiny minority of startup workers benefit from an exit that leaves them with enormous wealth.[8] Most people who take a startup job will end up with their salary and no more.

In addition, government work versus private-sector employment is not an all-or-nothing proposition. Lawyers make more money outside of government too, but they still commonly do stints in public service, as well as other kinds of lower-paying public interest work. It is a respected and even prestigious part of their careers. My former boss Todd Park is just one example of the tech equivalent of this pattern: after founding two successful companies, he did almost eight years of public service in several high-profile tech roles, including CTO of the United States, before leaving to found a third company. Tech professionals, like lawyers, don't have to choose just one sector or the other.

Even more importantly, money is not people's only motivator. Silicon Valley workers may enjoy the famous perks of startup life—the free food, the chic office space, sometimes lavish off-sites. But many will see their work disappear entirely from the world. In government, if there are donuts in the office it's because someone brought them in from the corner store, and not even the coffee is free. But the developers and designers know that what they do will affect the lives of the people around them and that they'll get to build systems in the public interest. It's easy to complain about government but more satisfying to help fix it. As the USDS team is fond of saying, "Decisions are made by those who show up."

That's why there are so many highly skilled and effective technologists in public service—too many for them all to be anomalies.

Some of them, like Mike and Yadira, have been in government their whole careers. Others, like Natalie, came from outside government to do a "tour of duty" and never left. Any of them could land a job at a tech company and get a bigger paycheck or the chance to strike gold in an exit. And they might at some point. But they've stayed for years, or decades, for the simple reason that they like what they do, even if they don't always like how they are asked to do it. They may have to fight over ridiculous things like building a Facebook for Doctors, but their work touches millions of people. Mostly, technologists in government simply prefer the impact they have.

Finally, it's not clear that government and the tech industry are competing for exactly the same people. The biggest bidding wars among the tech giants and startups is for technologists who work with advanced technologies like AI and machine learning. Outside of national security and defense (where such skills are very much in demand), government is rarely competing for this talent pool. The skills most needed in government are good product management and service design. The work is hard not because the tech is complicated but because the environment is. Arrogance can be an asset in startups; in government, humility is not only necessary but soon acquired if one doesn't start out with it. While emotional intelligence matters in all jobs more than the Silicon Valley caricature allows for, it is critical in public-sector work, which is more about change and human responses to change than about technology. The same goes for ethics: a sense of responsibility to the common good and a willingness to think deeply about what harm might come from your actions are assets in any field, but if you're not already considering these factors, working in government will bring them front and center. When entrepreneurs say that government will never do tech well because lower pay means it won't get the best people, it's worth asking what they mean by "best."

...

HIGH-RANKING OFFICIALS IN government have themselves been complicit in promoting the narrative that skilled technologists don't belong there. That attitude originates, in some ways, with the Brooks Act of 1965, defining automatic data processing as a commercial activity and OMB's classifying it the following year as not "inherently governmental." That made sense then, but even as times changed and digital technology began profoundly reshaping our society and economy, White House leadership declined to reexamine its status as a commodity. When pushed—by Clinger and Cohen, among others—on the wisdom of consigning digital entirely to the tactical realm, the establishment rejected the notion that government might need digital competence, arguing that operations were irrelevant to the intellectual work of policy. Digital would remain something to be bought, like laptops or janitorial services. These decisions align neatly with Glueck's preferred narrative, right down to his admonishment to build "in-house government procurement expertise" while ridding government of tech "know-how." The resonance is striking, but I can't fault Oracle's lobbyists for that.

Today, though, there are many voices among government leaders eager to change this framing. Chief among them is Cecilia Muñoz, a recipient of a MacArthur "genius grant" for her work on immigrant rights, who served as the head of Obama's Domestic Policy Council. When the healthcare.gov crisis passed and the Obama administration turned its attention to proposals for immigration reform, Cecilia went out of her way to include our nascent White House tech team in the discussion. (Among the issues we highlighted was a service—once optional but now, in the proposed legislation, mandatory—that employers were required to use to verify the citizenship status of prospective employees; its clunky design meant that it would fail under the increased load.) Not only did Cecilia go on to champion the USDS but she encouraged her own team, and policymakers around government, to borrow from its practices of user research, agile iterations, and product management. For the early employees of the USDS, Cecilia's support meant everything: seldom had they seen that kind of validation of their approach, and now it was coming from no other than the Domestic Policy Council director. It also mattered on a practical basis. It was still conventional wisdom at the time that the White House should never get involved in implementation of any kind, and the USDS operated for its first years under the constant threat of being shut down. Championship from a senior policy official, assumed to have little connection to work that was "operational in nature," spoke volumes.

And whereas the message so often gets mangled—reduced to platitudes about the value of technology itself that inevitably lead to the unhelpful call for simply more of it—Cecilia's voice was always clear and on point. "We need to think bigger than bringing tech solutions to policy problems," she told the audience at a Code for America conference. Tech "solutions" to policy difficulties is exactly what Oracle and its ilk preach—that's how they make their money, though they rarely solve the problem. But as Cecilia noted it's not the tech, it's the tech *people*. "We need to bring technologists into all levels of government, so digital practices and concerns are built into policy decisions from the beginning. We need technologists to apply user-centered design to policy and put citizens and their needs at the center of the policy-making process." It turns out that if the tech people you bring in spend time understanding the problem instead of trying to apply predetermined solutions, government actually buys less tech, not more, and at a lower cost, while delivering better outcomes. Thus Oracle's counteroffensive.

I wonder, in retrospect, if Glueck's alarm at the "false narratives" taking hold in government was a reaction less to the USDS

and 18F and more to the language coming out of what had traditionally been strongholds of convention in the White House.
Even if your business is predicated on keeping tech expertise out
of government, a couple of hundred nerds getting together to
help a smattering of federal agencies is not going to upend an
enterprise as enormous and entrenched as public-sector tech. But
a fundamental change of attitudes, at the very institution that
had insisted on separation between the domains in the first place,
might at least stir things up.

If Cecilia alarmed some vendors, her message was a beacon
to government-curious technologists. Many of them had earned
their chops in startups or big tech, but the desire to make a difference drew them to public-sector work. After Mikey Dickerson
wrapped up seven months on healthcare.gov, he went back to
Google for a hot second. Back in Mountain View, planning to
pick up his tech career where he had left off, he realized that
"moving money from one billionaire's pocket to another" felt
empty. He called Todd (our tech recruiter in chief) and came
back to DC. The billionaires wouldn't miss him, but people trying to make the website work would. So would the people still
trying to get health coverage. That doesn't fit with Oracle's narrative or Silicon Valley's version of it. Mikey and thousands of
others like him are fine with that.

Oracle's narrative is not necessarily representative of the vendor community. Of particular note are the half dozen companies
that were started in the wake of the healthcare.gov recovery effort
by members of Todd's tech surge. Few of these founders had any
government experience, but working with CMS on the website
gave them the same taste of purpose and meaning that made
Mikey come back from Google. They came back too but saw that
sustaining the changes that were taking hold required not just
public servants practicing this approach but like-minded vendors
those public servants could hire. So before we go declaring that

Oracle defines the "vendor narrative," we should remember that there is enormous diversity among vendors. Some of them are among the greatest champions of change.

Many legacy vendors also welcome the shake-up. A few years ago, a state agency abruptly changed direction on a request for proposal that was about to be bid out, breaking the RFP down into several smaller projects that could be developed through agile processes and would focus more on user needs. It was a huge shock to the vendors, who had been preparing for years to be able to bid on the $600 million project and to be judged by the usual criteria. Agile development and user research were not what they were prepared to demonstrate in their bids. Everyone in the bureaucracy braced for retaliation.

It came, but it was nowhere near as bad as anyone had expected. Indeed, some vendors pointed out, with legitimate basis, that they'd been encouraging the state to take an approach like this for years. Others went even further. An executive from a company whose bid was ultimately not chosen approached a department head for a meeting. Such meetings are often tense. Vendors have more power than you might think in these relationships, since they can protest contract awards and delay a project by months or even years. But this executive wasn't there to protest or threaten. Instead, he wanted to offer thanks. He admitted that his staff didn't have the skills this opportunity called for, because government contracts had rarely asked for them. But what the RFPs had been asking for until then, in his view, wasn't good for anyone—not the agency, not taxpayers, not the people affected by the system. And they hadn't been good for his company either. His staff wanted to work differently, and this new RFP finally gave him the business justification to retrain them in user research, agile development, and product management. "We'll be back next year," he told the department head. "We're going to learn what we need to learn and proudly bid again. Thank you for changing the rules." Profit motives might make concrete boats seem attractive, but vendors can be as motivated by impact as any public servant.

Looking ahead, there promises to be plenty of the right motivation. A survey of over nine hundred randomly selected Stanford undergraduates asked students to rank priorities for their first job out of college. On average, students who intended to pursue tech jobs in the private sector ranked "your project's mission" below building skills, career growth opportunities, and compensation. Meanwhile, students who intended to pursue tech jobs in the public sector ranked "your project's mission" first and "compensation" seventh.[9] These are the graduates the government should be hiring. The best government vendors will be able to attract these grads too. These are the people who will define the narrative in the coming years.

■ ■ ■

THE PUBLIC-SECTOR WORKFORCE, current and future, will shift our national conversation about how we deliver on the promises of government. But there must also be a shift in what we as the public experience in our daily lives. Today, our low expectations for government services play right into Oracle's hands. But even that is starting to change.

On December 21, 2021, at the height of the Omicron wave of the pandemic, President Joe Biden announced that the federal government would be providing four rapid at-home COVID tests for free to every household in the country that wanted them. How would the administration know who wanted them? A website, of course. Biden even announced a date for that website: January 19, 2022. On January 18, covidtests.gov went live, a day ahead of schedule. Many people, eager to resume social contact with some assurance they were not spreading the disease, had been scrambling for tests, which were in short supply in many areas of the country. News of the launch quickly spread. "People discovered covidtests.gov like four hours ago and already my grandfather-in-law found out about it from his garden club group text," a journalist wrote. "It's some of the fastest transmission of not-officially-announced news I've ever seen."[10]

That day, thirty-nine million people clicked on the links friends sent them, eager to order tests but prepared for a minor ordeal.[11] I was among those who dropped everything and went to the site, though as much out of curiosity as out of need. I knew that the USDS had been working on this effort, so my expectations may have been higher than most people's.

I timed myself. Ordering the tests took me eleven seconds. My browser is set up to autofill my name and address, so I may not have been an entirely representative user, but I was not the only test seeker pleasantly surprised. Twitter filled up with shocked praise. "Based on many previous experiences with govt websites, I thought ordering my free federal COVID tests would be annoying," one user wrote. "But NO! This was truly among the easiest, most seamless web experiences I've ever had! Less than a min."[12] Another one even beat my time: "Truly a marvel of frictionless government website. Didn't ask for even one tiny fragment more information than they actually needed. Took me 8 seconds to complete."[13]

Sending people four COVID tests is pretty basic. It's never going to be anywhere near as hard as enrolling them in health insurance or determining their unemployment insurance benefits. It would be hard to make it a 212-question form, like California's previous SNAP application, even if you wanted to. But I couldn't help imagining all the ways this website could have gone wrong if someone had been asked to collect all the possible requirements and if stakeholders all over government had been able to add theirs. The tests were free, but so were COVID vaccines, yet most vaccine providers still asked for health insurance information; this service could have too. Because tests might turn out to be faulty, the form could have required reading a disclaimer and signing a release of liability. Household size, a notoriously difficult question for many to answer, could easily have been asked; same with household income. The site could have also asked about previous COVID infections, vaccination status, and other health questions. Users could have been required to agree to all manner of terms of service, like agreeing not to resell the tests. They could have been required to set up a username and password.

Some of these possible requirements seem like obvious over-kill for the benefit of getting about $90 worth of goods from the pharmacy—though you'd be surprised by how much information government often requires for one to receive benefits as low in value as bus fare. Some sound like they might have made the service better, such as sending more tests to larger households or to households with lower incomes. And these were probably debated among the team. But Clay Shirky's "litmus test for whether our political class grasps the Internet" comes to mind: "Can anyone with authority over a new project articulate the tradeoff between features, quality and time?"[14] The site launched in a matter of weeks and easily handled 750,000 concurrent users.[15] That's not much traffic for an Amazon or a Google, but it's huge for a government website—that day, it was more than for all other federal government websites combined.[16] It handled that volume with ease because the team had spent some of their precious time load testing instead of adding more features. Someone with authority had chosen speed of development, ease of use, and scalability as the things to prioritize, given the urgency of the need for tests.

I can almost hear other government agencies excusing their poor delivery relative to covidtests.gov. It was so simple! Their requirements were nothing! What we have to do is far more complicated! But that is exactly the point. Unlike Kevin at the VA, this team was not going to wait around while someone else came up with thousands of business requirements. Unlike healthcare.gov, this team decided what to do and not to do before it unleashed an army of project managers to track thousands of requirements. Unlike the California SNAP consortium, this team was empowered to make decisions in the interest of users and say no to stakeholders representing government needs. Unlike Mike at the FCC, they had enough in-house talent (and vendors on current contracts) not to blow nine months on procurement. The result was that everything in covidtests.gov made sense to a person.

The most important outcome, however, wasn't the performance of the site. It's that tests started showing up in people's mailboxes within days. Mine were on my doorstep by the end of the week. My daughter's roommate tested positive for COVID the next day, and I was grateful to have tests to give to her and their other roommate as they moved to isolate. Eleven seconds on the site is one thing, but if Clear My Record taught me anything, it's that the only thing worse than an inaccessible front door is a welcoming one that doesn't lead anywhere. More than any other agency, the US Postal Service is responsible for literal delivery. With covidtests.gov, it came through beautifully.

Among the appreciative responses, some criticism emerged. The website kept track of which households had requested tests and wouldn't allow a second request for the same address. But a few people, mostly apartment dwellers, were getting messages saying that tests had already been requested for their household even when they hadn't been. Each apartment was supposed to act as a unique address, but in a very small fraction of cases, one apartment dweller requesting tests would blacklist other units in the same building.

The problem, it turned out, wasn't with the programming of the site. It was that mail carriers had been compensating for incomplete data for decades. If you own a home and decide to subdivide it into apartments or add an in-law unit, you will go to your city's building department to get the permits, but you might never officially inform the Postal Service. You're not asked and you don't think of it. It's not a problem for your mail carrier, who gets one packet of all the mail for that address, sees three mailboxes, and simply divides up the letters appropriately. But it means that the USPS residential address database no longer quite corresponds to the ground truth. It's just that those gaps in the database had never mattered before.

The fix was simple. On the page that told people that tests had already been requested for their address, the team quickly added a little note asking anyone who thought this was an error to fill out a short form, and customer service teams reached out to clarify. It increased the burden on this small number of users, and unfortunately these users were disproportionately of lower income. But the Postal Service didn't just send them the tests—it also updated its database. Less than a month after the launch of the site, almost two-thirds of all households in the US had requested tests, so about two-thirds of the residential address database had been cleaned up. In the subsequent round of free tests, people who got this glitch fixed had no problem. If you'd tried to design a way to clean up that data, it would have been hard to come up with something this fast and comprehensive.

Even accounting for the apartment dwellers whose initial experience was flawed, two-thirds of all the households in the United States is a lot of people who got to experience a government service that was everything so many other services are not: clear, easy to use, and fast. Experiences like this make a difference to people's trust in government, as the MACRA team saw when doctors on the verge of revolt decided to stay with Medicare when the new program made more sense to them. They also make a difference to the public's expectations of government, and that shifts our public narrative.

The federal government is not alone in wowing the public

with easy-to-understand services. Lacking direction from the feds on how the public might verify their vaccine status, California launched a site that let you enter your personal information, looked you up in the state vaccine registry, and sent you a QR code you could keep on your phone to prove you'd been vaccinated. As with covidtests.gov, the process took between a few seconds and a few minutes. The team also decided to make the code freely available, and other US states and other countries have borrowed it. This means that when businesses were validating vaccination status, my California-issued QR code worked just as well at a restaurant in New York as it worked at the one down my street. It's radically simple but, again, that's the point.

Services like the digital vaccination card and covidtests.gov threaten companies like Oracle not just because they leverage more in-house tech talent. They're a threat because of how small they are. The combined USPS/USDS team got covidtests.gov ready in just three weeks. The initial vaccine record app took six weeks. In both cases, they kept it simple. No vendor wants a contract that small—it's not worth all the paperwork you'd have to do. Think of the VA website that lets veterans sign up for health care. That's a simple proposition too, but that team had managed to find thousands of requirements, and fulfilling them became a major operation. Projects of that kind, and more inherently complex ones, are what the companies known as the "Beltway bandits" want. Shifting the public's expectations of government services is not in everyone's interests. But the shift is happening, and it is opening up new possibilities.

■ ■ ■

THERE WAS ANOTHER criticism of covidtests.gov, one that I'm not sure we would have heard even a few years earlier. Obviously, the Postal Service has everyone's address. Why make each of us type it in at all? Why not just ship the tests to everyone?

Many governments outside the United States deliver services automatically, or at least do as much of the work for the public as they can. A few years ago, Ukraine built a multipurpose mobile app for its citizens that lets them access government records and various social benefit services. During the pandemic, the government offered financial support for those who got vaccinated, and it easily paid out the benefit within the app, checking each applicant's vaccination status automatically. When Russia invaded, being able to prove your Ukrainian citizenship without paper documents suddenly became a lifesaver for hundreds of thousands of refugees, and support became critical again. Ukrainians from combat regions could apply for income replacement in under a minute because the application checked their location and place of work automatically and deposited the money directly into people's accounts, saving time for both the government and the public. Ukraine's investment in this digital infrastructure was fortunate—it allowed the entire country to focus on job one: fighting a war.

Meanwhile, tax prep is all but automatic in many countries, including most of Europe, Japan, and New Zealand. Their equivalents of the IRS essentially prepare draft tax returns for review by each taxpayer. Filing taxes becomes just a matter of checking the government's data, making any needed adjustments, and hitting "submit."[17] That could be true here, too, at least for the average taxpayer. Almost all the information the IRS asks you to input when you file, from Social Security numbers to dates of birth for everyone in the family, is data it already has. When your employer sends you a W-2 form, it also provides a copy to the IRS; the same goes for statements of interest and other income. Yet Americans spend six billion hours a year collecting data and filling out tax forms. We spend $10 billion on tax preparation services like H&R Block and an additional $2 billion on tax preparation software like Intuit's TurboTax.[18]

There are many reasons given for our backwardness, including, of course, intensive lobbying by those same tax preparation companies, as well as the fragile state of the IRS's existing systems. But the situation might be changing, thanks to the recent demise of a long-standing agreement between the IRS and a consortium of companies called the Free File Alliance. Under that agreement, the companies had promised to provide free tax filing for people with low incomes, and in return the IRS promised not to build anything that would compete with consumer software products like TurboTax. In 2019, when investigative journalists revealed that the companies were intentionally hiding their free option—and in fact tricking people who would have qualified for it into using a paid product instead—the conversation started to change.[19] The consortium eventually fell apart, opening the door, theoretically, for the US to catch up with its peer countries and make things much easier for the public. The Inflation Reduction Act of 2022 includes $15 million for the IRS to study how it might implement such a system.

There is precedent in the US for just sending people what they need. In 2020, when schools across the country shut their doors in response to the pandemic, more was affected than just education. Many schools provide children from low-income families with free or reduced-price breakfast and lunch, and they are often the place for those families to pick up supplies from food banks and other charities. In response, Congress authorized a new program that was essentially an extension of food stamps: eligible families would receive an electronic benefits card that they could use at grocery stores to buy food, just like in SNAP. The feds left it to the states to decide how to administer the program. Some of them put forms online and allowed families to apply. Others, though, recognizing that the schools' free and reduced-price lunch rolls already had the data on who was eligible, decided to just mail out the cards. California did both: they sent out cards themselves, but also provided an online form for backup. If for any reason you didn't get a card automatically, that's where you went.

There are good reasons some services, like felony expungements and pandemic food benefits, should be delivered automatically while others, like COVID tests, should not. For one, when COVID tests are in short supply, sending them to people who wouldn't use them keeps them out of the hands of those who will. (Indeed, it's likely that a portion of the population would actively resent being sent COVID tests.) For another, the burden of "applying" for these tests was minimal, and there is value in reminding the public of the government's role. Government could use some good PR.[20]

But Jazmyn Latimer, who worked on the Clear My Record project, now dreams about getting rid of forms everywhere. In the same way that schools shared their free-lunch rolls with state departments of social services to deliver pandemic food benefit cards, other government entities could also build on one another's work. "Other agencies already rely on the IRS to verify applicant information," she points out. And the IRS already has data on low-income families who claim the earned income tax credit and the child tax credit. "What if we could use these programs to plug into the other programs? They already have all the information!"

Data sharing, however, is both operationally and legally difficult for agencies. Myriad existing laws regulate what can be shared and how it can be shared. As with the Paperwork Reduction Act, even when sharing is legally permitted, bureaucrats often disallow it in practice, citing the "better safe than sorry" doctrine. Advocates also frequently oppose broad data sharing for fear of further enabling a surveillance state. Jazmyn doesn't buy that. "If the FBI wants to find you, they're going to find you," she says, meaning that law enforcement agencies already get data from a host of actors. That shouldn't be an excuse not to use data sharing to benefit people. "People are afraid that automating services would be harmful. From what I've seen, *not* automating is *actually* harmful. All these forms drive people crazy. They ask the same information over and over again."

One California resident who found her marijuana conviction very difficult to remove from her record before automatic expungement noted that, when you're arrested, convicted, and sentenced, no one questions that everything gets done automatically. "It should be automatic for redemption as well," she told the *New York Times*.[21] In other words, today we have the worst of both worlds: automatic processes for punishing people and lengthy, burdensome procedures for helping them. While we work to reform the former, why not pursue simplifying the latter?

Sending out free COVID tests was probably not the right project for experimenting with eliminating forms, especially because covidtests.gov did such a great job of minimizing the burden. But it's a good sign that people were asking the question. If the public is starting to be able to imagine truly seamless service delivery, it is in part because they've seen what's possible. Perhaps experiences like covidtests.gov will not only meet people's needs and build public trust but spark the creative imagination that's so often been missing when service delivery is merely a matter of meeting requirements. That might open the door, even just a little, to a whole new world of possibilities.

· · ·

THE PROSPECT OF better service delivery is intimately connected to the question of government's core competencies. For the first six or seven years that I worked in this field, my colleagues and I would routinely find that users wouldn't believe that simple, clear, easy-to-use websites could be legitimate government offerings. When Mary Ann Brody let Dominic try the redesigned VA health care application, he responded that it was "so much better than the government one," despite having just been told it *was* the new government website. GetCalFresh routinely faced the problem that applicants were afraid the site was a scam because it couldn't possibly be from a government agency. We see this less and less frequently now. Perceptions are changing, and recent nationally visible successes are helping.

When you see government services that work this way, you might also consider how they came to be. You don't have to know much about how government works to guess that the key people behind the original VA health care application, the one Dominic described as "spikes and IEDs," were purchasing officers. The revised version Mary Ann's team built could only be the work of designers and developers. But if we can't picture those kinds of people working in government, it's hard to expect the kinds of seamless experience that covidtests.gov delivered.

Imagine you are introduced to someone and told they are a hotshot programmer. Where might you imagine that person belonged? Would it ever occur to you that the best use of their talents might be working alongside the head of the Domestic Policy Council in the White House? Could you picture them applying for food stamps and reinventing benefits enrollment? Or writing algorithms to clear outdated criminal records? If the first thing that came to mind was none of those but a job in big tech, fintech, or a startup, you wouldn't be alone. That's where many of us tend to think tech talent belongs. But we can think otherwise.

While there are many things that make it hard, most notably an excruciatingly slow and illogical hiring process, there is no law that says government can't have the tech talent it needs. Even when policies favor outsourcing tech development, nowhere do they instruct government to abdicate all responsibility to vendors. In no way do they prohibit public servants like Yadira Sánchez from deciding what to do instead of just handing the whole question off to purchasing officers. The product managers who work under Yadira, some of the best in the country, in fact largely manage outsourced teams who write the code and even design the interfaces. They do it well because they have the internal know-how and authority to create dialogue between policymakers and delivery teams, instead of just blindly following directives. They can hire contractors skilled in user research and agile development. Strong in-house talent is not a threat to government contractors as such, only to those who benefit from building concrete boats.

That is why what we think matters. So much of what drives how tech delivery works in government is not law, policy, or regulation but our expectations. People inside and outside government have made assumptions about where digital talent belongs, and doesn't belong, for too long. Every one of us can do our part by expecting digital competence from our government and by believing that the highest and best use of our country's most talented technologists is in public service. Oracle's narrative serves the company well, but it stopped serving the nation's interests decades ago.

Glueck's letter pushing that narrative also misses the point. He pits hiring contractors against having good in-house digital teams, but the two are not at odds. Each supports the other. Product management is key to avoiding the trap of "find all the requirements, fulfill all the requirements," but savvy vendors can and do provide excellent product managers—as long as there is an empowered and engaged "product owner" within government who can work with them to decide on and authorize smart tradeoffs. In fact, the best vendors won't take projects that don't have a defined product owner on the government side. And because there are so few public servants who know how to work in that role, some of these vendors expect that training their bosses is part of the service they will provide.

There are many valuable discussions to be had about how

software development within government should work. How do you break down barriers between policy and implementation teams so that you don't leave programmers guessing about policy intent? And who gets to decide what? Can someone like Natalie Kates insist that the law be interpreted to fit what makes sense to a person? Or must we resign ourselves to cramped "professional" thinking and the results it brings? Can government teams aim to serve the people in a way that builds trust and faith in the institution, or will they forever labor diligently and thoroughly to meet thousands of arcane requirements without fulfilling their actual purpose?

These are all good questions, but none of them is really the right place to start. The first thing we need to ask is: What is the nature of the capacity government needs today? And the next question is: How do we go about building it?

Our digital age is different from previous eras not because information is sent electronically instead of physically but because technology has changed people's needs, expectations, and behaviors. And native digital practices—user-centered, iterative, agile practices—allow for fast learning to keep up with those changing needs. The capacity government needs today is multifaceted, but one thing that's clear is that digital can no longer be an afterthought. To borrow from our British counterparts again: "You can no longer run a country properly if the elites don't understand technology in the same way they understand economics or ideology or propaganda."[22]

FOR AND BY PEOPLE

In 1994, the year before Senator Cohen cosponsored what became known as the Clinger Cohen Act, his staff put together an investigative report called "Computer Chaos: Billions Wasted Buying Federal Computer Systems." The only copy I could find looks like it's a scan of a photocopy of a print from microfiche.[1] It's blurry and flecked from dust spots, the pages are askew, and you can see holes from bygone staples in the corner. But the smudges and flecks are the only clues that the report is old. It complains about a modernization project at the IRS that had been underway for seven years at the time and had spent $7 billion. Today we have one that has been underway for twenty-three years and has cost billions more. It warns of agencies relying on such outdated hardware that they had to "buy vintage vacuum tubes from a manufacturer in Poland and search Radio Shack and junkyards for spare parts to keep the system running." I witnessed similar Nixie tubes being used by our military in 2017 and heard firsthand about the navy's troubles sourcing them. It complains that the Department of Defense has 161 different accounting systems. As of 2011, the department had 2,258 separate business systems, including 709 just for human resource management and 335 more for financial management.[2] It points out that "the government spends billions of dollars operating so-called 'legacy' systems, which are old mainframe computers from the 1960s and 1970s." We still do today.

Reading "Computer Chaos," it's easy to wonder what year it is. "Agencies do not spend enough time reviewing their processes and practices before undertaking these expensive automation programs," its authors say right at the start, as if they'd just stepped off the EDD task force. "Efforts by the government to provide greater efficiency and service to the American people will certainly fail unless the process for buying information technology is improved," they continue, as if they had witnessed the launch of healthcare.gov. "Management's limited vision of how it wants its business to work also contributes to poor planning," they conclude. It seems we knew almost thirty years ago that government investments in "technology modernization" were going off the rails, and we knew why.

Cohen's report focused primarily on the billions of dollars wasted. As time went on, it became ever more clear that the costs of not fixing this were more than just financial. We knew that government needed to deliver on its promises if it wanted to earn and keep the trust of the American people. We saw that as computing moved to the internet, digital technology would become not just how government stored and managed information but also how it talked to the public. But even as politicians kept speechifying about how they were making government serve the people, our benefits programs conveyed to clients that we thought they were criminals, and the VA left veterans feeling like we'd told them to go fuck themselves. As design and communication became central, the stakes grew ever higher.

"You can always count on Americans to do the right thing— after they've tried everything else." Winston Churchill didn't say that, contrary to popular lore, but my UK counterparts enjoyed quoting it when I was struggling with my task at the White House.[3] I don't know if our leaders have tried everything else, but we've tried a lot. We've tried giving agencies more money for bigger contracts, and we've tried starving them of money. We've studied and analyzed the issue again and again: the Congressional Research Service alone lists almost two thousand reports mentioning information technology. We've established checklists and forms and thousands of procedures to keep things from going wrong. We've increased oversight to the point where one tech leader at the Department of Homeland Security counted eighty-seven documents, eleven "stage gate" reviews, and twenty-one different oversight roles on a single project.[4]

And we have tried policy changes, though some would say not enough. We've increased the power of agency CIOs,[5] added alternate purchasing paths that are not subject to burdensome acquisition regulations,[6] introduced a "technology exchange program" for government staff to spend a year at tech companies to learn their practices,[7] and so forth. The latter two programs have gone largely unused, victims of a culture in which if even one person prefers safe over sorry, we're back to "the way it's always been done." Other policy prescriptions have backfired because they are deterministic, assuming that if you do X, you can get Y. If you measure administrative burden, it will go down. If you mandate interoperable architectures, agencies will be able to share data. But government is a vast, interconnected, complex, adaptive system made up of countless subsystems that connect in ways that are rarely fully seen or understood. Doing X often doesn't result in Y, because we fail to anticipate the ways each subsystem adapts to changes in the others and creates incentives we didn't intend. Deterministic policy solutions invite unintended consequences. The diagnoses from the "Computer Chaos" report are spot-on, but so far we have few effective cures.

With the unemployment insurance meltdown only now fading from public view, the catchphrase heard in state governments is "that can never happen again." It will. In fact, though the issue has all but disappeared from the headlines, the problem is still very present. State labor agencies remain in crisis even three years into the pandemic, still trying to differentiate between fraudulent and legitimate claims, still working through backlogs, still failing to measure their progress accurately and consistently. And although our leaders are debating how much money will be needed for fixes, what rules might need to change, and how they can provide better oversight, we are missing the most obvious problem.

After our EDD task force disbanded, as Marina Nitze and I were reflecting on what the future might hold for the agency, I lamented the fact that no more than a handful of people there knew how its systems worked. Marina corrected me. No, she said: a handful of people there knew how some individual pieces of the system worked. There was no one who understood how it all worked together. At the time, the EDD employed around five thousand people, not counting many more temporary contract workers. By 2021, that number was up to nearly ten thousand.[8] As far as I know, the EDD still doesn't have anybody who understands how the many fragile layers of technology in the department work together to verify a claim and turn it into an unemployment benefit.

"Software is made by people and for people," my colleagues on the Defense Innovation Board wrote in one of those innumerable reports that have recommended changes in government's approach to technology. But government doesn't have the people it needs on either legacy or current technologies. Today, we are in a fierce competition for assembly language coders to keep the Individual Master File alive at the IRS, and our deficit will only get worse as the people who know the many systems like it retire.

(Of the 7,500 IT employees at the Department of the Treasury, 63 percent are over fifty.)[9] As for developing the next generation of digital talent, while 16 percent of IT professionals in the US are under thirty, across cabinet agencies in the federal government only 4 percent of them are.[10] And we hamstring the technologists we do have by holding them accountable to two wildly different expectations: they are somehow supposed to follow processes that don't work yet deliver software that does. It is time we recognized that this is not at its heart a problem of more money, rules, or oversight, though changes in each area could be helpful. You cannot legislate competence. It is an issue of people—getting more of the ones we need and allowing them to do what we need done.

■ ■ ■

OUR ELECTED LEADERS keep thinking in terms of money, regulations, and oversight because those are the levers they have most immediately at hand. When they see a need for change, they push those levers. How much money will it take to solve the problem? What new rules can we put in place? How do we monitor failures more closely and punish poor performance? These levers can be helpful, but they need to be directed at the problem underlying our delivery failures: the lack of skilled technologists within government who are empowered to make the necessary decisions.

No amount of money will fix unemployment insurance as long as the number of people who understand how the complex, fragile web of technology works is between a handful and none. California's EDD had plenty of funding, but it fared no better than the states that had less to work with, and arguably worse. Now, states across the country are handing out megacontracts to megacontractors to "modernize" their unemployment systems once and for all. Sound familiar? The same thing happened after the Great Recession. The bewildering assumption is that more of what came before will get us different results. Perhaps with a bit more money, this hunk of concrete can be made to float.

Building the capability we need does take funding. But it should be spent on people before contracts, operating expenditures before capital expenditures. We need to create positions within government charged with digital strategy and product management, and we need to make sure those are filled by people with the proper expertise. I don't necessarily mean that we need to grow the government workforce overall: training our current public servants in digital skills is as important as hiring new talent. Still, this approach is politically unpopular, particularly with the right, which opposes most investment in the public-sector workforce. The left is less intrinsically opposed but prefers to strengthen state capacity by investing in legal functions like enforcement of civil rights laws. Both sides need to understand that investing in digital competencies will save far more money than it costs. The USDS tallied up $3.5 billion in savings and cost avoidance (that is, helping agencies find better, less expensive ways to address their needs) in 2019 alone. Given the unit's relatively small budget, that came out to a seventeenfold return on investment.[11] More importantly, it helped create less-intrusive government interactions and a lower regulatory burden. It's a government that feels smaller but gets more done.

Don't get me wrong. Unemployment insurance systems need money for contracts, as do IRS systems, benefits systems, immigration systems, local permitting systems (which suddenly need to permit vastly more residential solar construction), and pretty much every other government function. But the way those contracts are structured also needs to change. What we need is not more megaprojects but incremental, stage-based funding. Remember, the people putting together a request for proposal for a $600 million project are supposed to say with great certainty what development teams will be delivering ten to twenty years into the future. This is, simply put, impossible. No appropriation should ask for this kind of delusional plan.

While I'm not a fan of blindly adopting "private-sector practices," a largely unhelpful catchphrase in government, some parts of the venture capitalists' playbook are directly relevant. VCs fund startups to start small and learn quickly, then invest more when the startups get traction and show value. (That's the underlying concept, at least; in recent years the venture world has had more money than it knows what to do with, so funding has been less disciplined.) Incremental, value-based funding pairs perfectly with small, cross-functional teams that practice agile development and focus on understanding and meeting user needs. On the other hand, spending a decade preparing for a project, then approving $600 million to spend the next decade building it, pairs perfectly with giant waterfalls in which enormous teams check meaningless boxes to deliver on requirements that are fifteen years out of date. A big part of what keeps government from transitioning to agile, user-centered development is that teams are often trying to practice it in a megafunding framework. They are doomed before they even start.

Projects can fail under both the megacontract and the incremental models. And in both models they can restart and try again. The difference is that they can fail having spent $600 million over twenty years or a few million over just one or two. More importantly, the agency can go back to the drawing board and start gathering even more requirements, or it can launch its second effort with insights gained from the earlier attempt. But if we want the benefits of the latter approach, the people who control the money in government are going to have to do a lot of things very differently. Today, there is little affordance for funding and managing projects this way.

Throwing more money at bigger contracts is the first misguided solution our leaders go to. Writing more policy is the second. We constantly add to the laws, rules, regulations, and guidance that govern how agencies and departments at all levels build and buy technology. In practice, these policies tend to backfire, as with the legislation meant to reduce the paperwork burden on the public or the framework that foisted an ESB requirement onto software for next-generation satellites.

It's not that policy change cannot or will not help. But just as small-scale projects work better than gigantic ones, less may be more here. Removing mandates can have more impact than adding them. We desperately need to simplify and rationalize the policy that has accrued over many years and bogs down our systems, to clean up the sludge that decisions made decades or even centuries ago have left behind. This applies both to government services themselves—like the persnickety rules complicating the provision of unemployment insurance and food benefits—and to the procurement and hiring procedures involved in building them.

Less is also more when it comes to oversight, the third approach so often misused by politicians. Here, too, *how* is the question. Oversight bodies today judge tech projects on essentially two things: how thorough the initial plan was and how well the agency stuck to it. In the usual megaproject, such oversight makes teams double down on all the worst aspects of waterfall development: technically fulfilling requirements instead of shipping working software, locking in those requirements and not letting them change for decades, doing all the possible things badly instead of choosing the right ones to do well. Waterfall is a great fit for an institution without a core competency in digital, since it requires only complying with processes rather than exercising judgment. But it does not deliver software—or government—that works for people.

The oversight methods could also stand to borrow a bit from venture capitalists. VCs don't ask how well a team has stuck to a plan, especially one that was created years ago. They ask what the team has learned since it started implementing the plan. They don't ask for a report on how many formal requirements have been met on paper. They ask for the results of the latest user tests, and sometimes they log in and use the product themselves. They assume, to quote the agile manifesto, that "working software is the primary measure of progress." Neither the VA nor its over- sight bodies knew that the veterans' health care application didn't work, but hundreds of thousands of veterans knew, because they had tried to use it. Fixing that problem required people to value their judgment over some arbitrary checkmarks in a contracting document. Our oversight functions must reward that judgment, not the checkmarks.

The best solution of all would be to hold public servants accountable to outcomes over process. Many people smarter than me have tried to change this dynamic, and large-scale suc- cess remains elusive. Still, we must find ways to trust people in government to make smart tradeoffs in the service of meeting people's needs. They must be able to decide what to do, not just churn through endless checklists handed down from above. They must be empowered to make government make sense to a person.

■ ■ ■

BUILDING DIGITAL AS a core competency of government may take changes in budgeting, rules, and oversight, but it is largely a mat- ter of investing in people. This will not be easy, but there are existing efforts to build on. First, we must train and support the people we have. A promising initiative is the Digital IT Acquisi- tion Professional Program, which teaches federal contracting pro- fessionals how to help agile, user-centered digital teams acquire the services they need.[12] Second, we must hire new people with digital skills. There are a number of nonprofits that are dedicated to bringing a diverse set of technologists into the public sector, and they operate as a coalition under the banner of US of Tech. Third, we must put user-focused public servants in many roles where they can have an impact upstream, and we must connect them across disciplines. A great model is Cecilia Muñoz's championing of closer ties between policy and tech teams, disrupting the waterfall dynamics that disempower all parties. We need far more efforts like this in far more domains, across all levels of government.

It will be long, hard work, carried out mostly by public servants you rarely hear about. At first, it is going to feel unsatisfying—not least because it takes time to get good at something and you have to make mistakes along the way. It's not just one agency that has to adapt and learn but tens of thousands across federal, state, and local government. Nationwide, twenty-two million people work in the public sector, most of them at the state and local levels.[13] That's a lot of people who will have to accept a new competency into the core of their work. Having more technologists around, whether they are new hires or long-termers, is just the beginning. Their colleagues will have learn to include them when decisions are being made.

We know why this is difficult. Government leadership has typically seen implementation as a second-class job, and as the world moved into the digital age, the policy class mistook that profound change for a mere shift in the tools of implementation. But even the elites now have to acknowledge that implementation and policy cannot be so neatly separated. Few people read the tax code, or even part of it. What they know about tax policy they learn from filing their returns. Few people on assistance programs such as food stamps read and comment on proposed changes to eligibility rules; they discover them when they try to apply for or renew their benefit. And when the application or filing process is so hard to navigate that millions give up on understanding what they're entitled to, it becomes clear that the service people experience has at least as much impact on the success of a program as the rules that govern it. To most people, digital services *are* policy.

The reality is that in our system as it stands today, there is little incentive for elected leaders to build twenty-first-century state capacity. Politicians don't get reelected for simplifying and rationalizing the gargantuan maze of laws, policies, and regulations that govern service delivery. I struggle to imagine a candidate running on a platform of transforming how government funds and oversees tech projects, to say nothing of civil service reform. At the same time, politicians have many incentives to pass new laws and policies that (mostly inadvertently) wind up making delivery even harder and to publicly admonish bureaucrats for failures, which makes the bureaucracy even more risk averse.

If our elected leaders have the wrong incentives, perhaps there is one more layer up the chain to implicate. In our system of government, no sequence of causes can end entirely with our elected officials, in Congress or elsewhere. There is still someone above them, and in fact above all three branches of government: us. Yes, there is a staggering amount wrong with our electoral system and campaign finance laws, which has loosened the connections between what the public wants of its leaders and what it gets. But that doesn't give us as a public the right to absolve ourselves of all blame in our government's failures of delivery, nor does it let us off the hook for what role we might play in fixing them.

The question of our government's capacity is an afterthought in our public dialogue, if it is mentioned at all, and each of us can work to change that. Our media's coverage of the tax gap, for example—the billions of dollars the IRS is owed that it leaves uncollected every year—tends to focus on the personalities and politics of appointees at the Treasury Department, on whether they're progressive enough or conservative enough for a given taste. Those appointees matter, of course: whether they try to close the gap by focusing enforcement resources on taxpayers with the highest incomes or the lowest will make a big difference. But those debates are going to become academic if the Individual Master File, born in the 1960s and currently expected to keep serving as the IRS's core system until at least 2030, finally breaks. (I don't mean that the machines that run it will fall apart. The risk is in losing the knowledge needed to keep them functioning. Once again it is a people problem.) If that happens, and the way we raise funds to pay for everything the federal government does is at risk, we have a whole different class of problem. And there are places all around government where systems as core as this one are in danger.

In a sense, we are all Weaver, tracing the friendly fire of the ESB mandate up to the leaders in the highest ranks of government, whose well-meaning efforts to make technology work better wound up dooming his project. But we are also all Marilyn Tavenner hanging up on Mina Hsiang because we don't want to hear that healthcare.gov cannot be immediately made available in Spanish. We are the politicians deriding bureaucrats for taking decades to complete tech projects when those projects have to meet thousands of requirements and jump through thousands of hoops imposed by politicians. We are the activists who want to sue government at every turn and then condemn it for its risk aversion. We have an endless appetite for debating what government should or shouldn't do and little interest in understanding what it *can* and *can't* do. We want to talk policy and leave implementation to the mechanicals. That didn't work out well for the White House, and it's not going to work out for the American public.

...

WE SHOULD ALSO remember that the appetite for discussing policy and politics is not evenly distributed across the populace.

Debating politicians' latest ideas can be stimulating for those who look at the world from the top down, who believe that if we do X we will get Y, who see policy decisions as a way to achieve meaningful change. They are excited for their favored proposals to be passed into law and become magic.

But for much of the country, the magic has long since rubbed off. The shortcomings of government service delivery affect different parts of society very differently. If you can afford to pay someone else to handle your taxes, your car registration, your building permit, even your passport renewal, chances are that you will do so and that you won't notice the burdens they impose. At the same time, you'll be less likely to apply for social services, deal with child welfare agencies, be involved in the criminal justice system—all high-burden interactions, and all interactions that tend to erode trust in government.

For people who do have to deal with such interactions, delivery matters a lot more than politics. But politicians rarely get voted out of office for failing to clear the criminal records of former felons or making it hard for the needy to access food benefits. Instead, would-be voters who get burned in those ways tend to pull away from politics and government altogether. Their experiences teach them that the whole system is hopelessly broken and not worth their time or energy engaging in. They are not going to feel differently about government unless and until they experience something very different from what they have in the past. Delivery must come first. The only way to build trust with them is to earn it.

Those of us less alienated from government need to step up. But how? We can recognize the accountability trap our public servants are stuck in and do our best to support them. Better yet, we can participate in public service ourselves. Certainly I encourage anyone with tech and design skills to at least do a tour of service in government at any level. There are resources for you on this book's website, recodingamerica.us. But you don't have to be in tech to serve: our public institutions need all sorts of people who are patient, caring, and willing to fight to make government make sense to a person. Public service is hard, but you may get even more out of it than you give. You'll learn a ton, you'll meet people who will inspire you, and the world will never look the same once you've seen how the sausage is made, so to speak. It may be a brief interlude in your life or it may take you in directions you've never imagined. For my part, I found my year in public service deeply humbling. Looking back, I wouldn't trade it for the world.

One of the benefits of working in government is that it can put partisan politics into a different perspective. When you look at the world through the lens of left and right, it's easy to attribute all sorts of outcomes to political ideologies in action. We're wrong more often than you might think, as I discovered when Henry explained to me why some SNAP applications ask if you own a burial plot. We assume high-burden services are designed with an intention to make it hard for people to access them, and sometimes that's true: voter roll purges, for example, that require people to reregister can be a deliberate tactic to suppress voting rates. But that wasn't what drove Henry to write that question into the regulations, and it wasn't what drove California—a very pro-welfare state—to build a 212-question application form. Likewise, service designers at the State Department and US Citizenship and Immigration are working to streamline our painfully slow and clunky immigration system, especially in the aftermath of our military's withdrawal from Afghanistan. Many of our service members' most trusted Afghan friends and allies had started seeking US visas a decade earlier, but their paperwork moved through the system at such a slow pace that they were tragically left behind. Those public servants will tell you that the barriers to doing right by those Afghans are not primarily political—they are the government's long-standing rules and procedures, established largely in good faith, now working against us. Staffers from all ideological backgrounds want this system fixed.

People on the left like to talk about reducing administrative burden. They don't want families in need to have to struggle through a 212-question form to get assistance. People on the right like to talk about reducing regulatory burden. They want companies to be able to focus on their businesses, not on confusing, time-consuming government paperwork, like submitting an entire year's worth of documentation for a program doctors are going to be exempt from. Digital and service design skills in government address both these problems. The left and right may disagree about how much of a safety net the government should provide or what kinds of constraints it should put on private companies, but both are equally frustrated that interactions with it are so much harder than they need to be. And each will gain from the other's successes. Streamlined benefits processes can lead to lower administrative costs, which the right likes. Streamlined regulatory processes can mean higher rates of corporate compliance, which the left likes. Improving delivery won't resolve all our political tensions, but it gives us something to work on together. And working together helps us find more common ground.

We can't have it all, but we can have so much more than we have now, if we are willing for a moment to shift our collective focus. If we put aside, even a little bit, our political agendas, and work together on creating the capacities that government needs today, there's a lot to like about that outcome for everyone. We can get a government that delivers what the Miller Lite ads promise: tastes great, less filling.

There is already a lot to celebrate in government's progress toward better delivery. We can see it not just in accomplishments like covidtests.gov but in the beginnings of a consistent experience across government agencies. Visit the websites for Social

Security, the Global Entry program, USAJobs, or the VA, and you'll see an option to sign on through login.gov. If, like sixty million others, you take that option, you'll end up with a single username, password, and authentication mechanism that works for all of these as well as other government websites.[14] This kind of infrastructure can make all manner of government digital services both easier to implement and easier to use.

Leadership is infrastructure too, and as of 2022 we couldn't ask for better technology leadership at the federal level. Robin Carnahan is leading GSA, which now not only has 18F but also manages the Technology Modernization Fund, with $1 billion for projects that promise to truly modernize systems to achieve specific goals—not simply move meaningless, arcane processes to the cloud. Clare Martorana, the federal CIO within OMB, has worked with the White House to publish an executive order on customer experience, for the first time giving federal agencies a framework for changes that directly mean something to the public. Mina Hsiang has been hung up on by many executives but it hasn't dampened her enthusiasm for public service, and she's returned to DC to lead the USDS. Each of these women is a committed reformer in her own right. None of them is satisfied with the status quo. Their appointments give me hope.

Among these signs of progress, however, I worry. There are the outlines of a better path, but very few are choosing it. The top three tech jobs in DC may be held by skilled agents of change, but power in our government is extremely diffuse. Each federal agency makes its own independent decisions about technology development and pretty much all the other factors that go into getting implementation right. So do the states, where arguably the bulk of service delivery happens. The feds have little control over state governments; the states have little control of the operations of their counties and cities. And within each city, county, and state, mayors and governors and their OMB equivalents have less control than you'd think over each of their agencies and depart-ments. For the country to choose the path of digital competence, of user needs over government needs, hundreds of thousands of people in appointed and career positions across a wide variety of functions—including purchasing, finance, human resources, program management, oversight, and of course IT—would all need to decide to reject the status quo at approximately the same time. Wholesale change rarely happens so quickly.

So we are left with slow change and the question of whether it can accelerate fast enough to meet the moment, or accelerate at all. We should be on the lookout for bright spots, which I believe will continue to appear, but we should also be prepared for a lot of inertia. Ultimately, those of us who advocate for transforming government digital practices will need to take our own medicine. We advocate for incremental, user-centered, agile development; we must accept that change will also have to be incremental, to meet people where they are, to emerge from the work as we learn along the way. Top-down edicts will be helpful only insofar as they are met with changes in culture and practice from the bottom up. Finding and supporting the public servants like Yadira who can drive that bottom-up change takes time and effort. But any proposed solution that ignores this need is fantasy.

■ ■ ■

WHEN IT COMES to delivery, we think of the private sector as competent in digital and government as woefully behind. But of course the private sector has its own struggles. Big IT projects fail at companies too. So why are we all so outraged at government?

In part it's because we don't have an alternative. When the IT team at chocolate maker Hershey implemented a new order-taking and fulfillment system and the rollout went badly, the company missed shipping $100 million worth of candy in time for Halloween and saw a 19 percent drop in quarterly earnings.

Reputations were damaged, I'm sure. Perhaps a few people were fired. But no children were harmed in the making of this IT disaster. There were plenty of bite-size Snickers and other candies from Hershey's competitors on the shelves that year. When a government website goes down and the call center rings busy 24/7, there are no competitors to step in.

It's also not individually wrapped chocolate treats at stake but people's livelihoods. And in areas like child welfare, policing, and the courts, there is the specter of actual harm to children. Not only is government a monopoly but the services it provides are the ones that matter most. We're outraged because it matters. We should acknowledge that government carries a higher burden than the private sector, without letting that burden add to the risk aversion that makes delivery even harder.

Nor should we want government to simply "catch up" with the private sector, especially given some of the impacts that the digital revolution has had on our society. The commercial world has put many of the practices of digital delivery teams to use in the service of "dark patterns"—means to understand and serve users that result in products that deceive and entrap us. In many ways, the digital revolution has fed our worst selves. Government's move into the digital era can be better.

The internet was sold to us as a public good. Indeed, it started out as one, emerging from a project funded by the Department of Defense. Its early creators and early users saw its fundamental architecture, its lack of central management and control, as inherently enabling a set of values that included open access to information, free speech, and a framework for bottom-up collaboration among equals.[15] The good it would do in the world was inevitable. And it *has* done enormous good, but the structural reasons many believed it would always do so didn't hold. An internet dominated by companies answerable above all to shareholder value has also done enormous harm.

Many fear the tools of the digital age, and their power, in the hands of authorities. I recognize the harms that both the left and the right see in government, but I also see the good government does, and can do, for people. And I fear the growing asymmetry in power between the public and private sectors more. It's not just that social media companies have failed to take responsibility for actions that have undermined democracy, however unintentionally. It's also that some powerful tech figures disregard the value of democratically elected government in favor of a world of their own making. Consider Elon Musk's stance on the Federal Trade Commission's consent decree imposed on Twitter, the company he recently purchased, for the misuse of personal information. "Elon puts rockets into space," his lawyer is reported to have said. "He's not afraid of the FTC."[16] I want to push government forward in part because, while I am grateful for the conveniences of Zoom and the engagement of Twitter, I still want to live in a democracy. Rule by tech is just another form of oligarchy.

What if the way technology has played out in our society over the past decade, increasingly dominated by late-stage capitalism, was just a practice run and government's belated adoption of digital is what we were practicing for? What if, just as we most need institutions capable of bold collective action, we are at the beginning of the real digital revolution, the one that happens inside our public institutions? We've had a bit of bad timing so far in government's journey toward delivery competence. It was bad timing that digital got caught up in the 1990s mania for outsourcing government work and that White House leadership, having missed how fundamentally the internet was about to reshape society, cast the issue as a purchasing problem. If Clinger and Cohen's efforts to make the White House take tech seriously had come just a few years later, when the significance of these changes was more evident, we might not have had those "lost years" before Obama appointed the first federal CIO and CTO.

But it's been fourteen years since then and the foundation has been laid. The World Wide Web was born in 1990. It took fourteen years for us to get Facebook, Skype, Bluetooth, and blogging. Change takes time.

But this problem isn't just an issue of timing. It's also one of power. In his 1966 book *The Nerves of Government*, Karl W. Deutsch said, "Power is the ability to afford not to learn." When power flows one way—down the waterfall—from policymakers to implementers, from federal to local government, from those with high-priced lawyers and tax accountants to those without, even those the system appears to benefit lose out. Is it any surprise that the most powerful institutions within the most powerful country on earth have resisted the uncomfortable work of developing new and foreign competencies? If our timing is better in this moment, it may be related to our nation's loss of power. Our global standing isn't what it was in 1995. Our response to COVID was embarrassing, our tax system is the joke of the developed world, our military might is waning, and our health outcomes rank dead last among eleven peer countries. We can no longer afford not to learn new tricks.

Government may not have all the capacities it needs today, but now isn't the first time it's had to deal with its shortcomings. Throughout history, governments have created the competencies they needed to tackle the big challenges of their day. Roosevelt's New Deal and the United States' participation in World War II both required enormous leaps in the development of the administrative state. Laws were passed, agencies created, bureaucracies built. The nation pulled itself out of a depression, improved the quality of life for millions of people, and won the war. It wasn't linear, it wasn't easy, and it wasn't perfect, but we pretty much got the job done.

We face equally daunting challenges today. Wealth inequality, which declined dramatically during Roosevelt's presidency, has now been rising fast for four decades. Climate change, which we used to think of as a problem for future generations, is brutally present. The United States has even lost its military advantage on the world stage—we are consistently defeated in war games against China.[17] We should face these challenges with the same resolve as our predecessors eighty years ago, but we cannot face them with the same competencies and capacities they employed then. In fact, we will need to dismantle some of what our predecessors have built. We must both develop new capacities and clear out the policy clutter and ways of working that no longer serve us if we want an administrative state built for today's world.

The work is certainly teed up for that administrative state. Despite never-ending headlines about gridlock in our nation's capital, the 117th Congress (2021–22) is on track to pass well over two hundred laws, including such whoppers as the Infrastructure Investment and Jobs Act, the CHIPS and Science Act, and the Inflation Reduction Act (IRA). The implementation challenges of these and other legislative outputs nationally cannot be overstated. To take just a small slice, the IRA aims, among other goals, to limit global warming to 1.5 degrees. Will it? Perhaps, if we can dramatically streamline solar permitting in three thousand counties and almost twenty thousand towns and cities, navigate stakeholder input processes in the countless jurisdictions new power lines must travel through, get millions of consumers to take advantage of tax rebates for energy-saving investments, successfully administer tens of thousands of grants, and master dozens of other formidable tasks. Each of those tasks could be completed—all the boxes checked—in much the same cumbersome way that Medicare's value-based care programs were handled before MACRA. Or they could be done the way Yadira and her team worked, resulting in a service that made sense to a person (while still checking the boxes). The latter way is our only hope.

More hangs on this difference than we realize. "I think a lot about how, fifty years from now, I'm going to explain to young people what happened, when we're all huddled around a tire fire for warmth after the climate collapse," Lucas Merrill Brown told me. Lucas worked with Yadira as part of the USDS team assigned to the MACRA rollout and has gone on to environmental policy roles in the Biden administration, advising on the implementation of the infrastructure bill and the IRA. "Most days," Lucas says, "I'm convinced I'll have to tell them that lot of people worked really hard to build political consensus to fight the climate crisis. We passed half a trillion dollars in funding. And then we kept using fossil fuels because we couldn't figure out the permitting."

That's not the story most of us think of telling our grandchildren, and certainly not the legacy we want to defend. But the very fact that it sounds absurd makes this outcome more likely. The bill passed. We celebrated. What comes next is merely "operational in nature." If we want to escape that fate, on climate or any other existential issue we face, implementation can no longer be policy's poor cousin. It can't be beneath the attention of our most powerful institutions, and it can't be beneath our attention as a public.

We may have trouble imagining such banal reasons for our failures, but we seem equally bad at imagining the role of the details of delivery in our success. It is worth challenging our collective imaginations. What could a government that delivers at internet speed and scale achieve? And what role might each of us play in bringing that vision to life? If we lack that faith in government, perhaps we need to reframe the question. "Government is simply the name we give to the things we choose to do together."[18] We have chosen our battles. Now we must fight them.

SUGGESTIONS FOR FURTHER READING

See **recodingamerica.us** for more on how everyone can help recode America.

Practical guides for those in public service or considering joining government.

Belotti, Marianne. *Kill It with Fire: Manage Aging Computer Systems (and Future Proof Modern Ones)*. San Francisco: No Starch Press, 2021.

Carnahan, Robin, Randy Hart, and Waldo Jaquith. "State Software Budgeting Handbook, De-risking Custom Technology Projects: A Handbook for State Grantee Budgeting and Oversight." 18F, Technology Transformation Service, General Services Administration, August 2019. https://derisking-guide.18f.gov/state-field-guide/.

Digital Services Playbook, The. US Digital Service. https://playbook.cio.gov/.

Greenway, Andrew, Ben Terrett, Mike Bracken, and Tom Loosemore. *Digital Transformation at Scale: Why the Strategy Is Delivery*. London: London Publishing Partnership, 2018.

Harrell, Cyd. *A Civic Technologist's Practice Guide*. San Francisco: Five Seven Five Books, 2020.

Hopson, Mark, Randy Hart, Waldo Jaquith, Igor Korenfeld, Vicki Mc-Fadden, Rebecca Refoy, and Alicia Rouault. "De-risking Government

Technology: Federal Agency Field Guide." General Services Administration and 18F, September 2020. https://derisking-guide.18f.gov/federal-field-guide/.

Hunt, Bill. "Digital Policy Guide: A Digital Servant's Guide to U.S. Federal Information Technology Law and Practice." https://digitalpolicy.us/.

Kalil, Tom. "Policy Entrepreneurship at the White House: Getting Things Done in Large Organizations." *Innovations: Technology, Governance, Globalization* 11, no. 3/4 (2017): 4–21. https://doi.org/10.1162/inov_a_00253.

McGuinness, Tara, and Hana Schank. *Power to the Public: The Promise of Public Interest Technology*. Princeton, NJ: Princeton University Press, 2021.

Meyer, Erie. "How to Usability Test a Government Service." Medium, December 6, 2020. https://eriemeyer.medium.com/how-to-usability-test-a-government-service-e43d03834383.

Nitze, Marina, and Nick Sinai. *Hack Your Bureaucracy: Get Things Done No Matter What Your Role on Any Team*. New York: Hachette Go, 2022.

Pahlka, Jennifer. "Delivery-Driven Policy." Code for America, November 5, 2019. https://codeforamerica.org/news/delivery-driven-policy/.

"Qualitative Research Practice Guide." Code for America, Spring 2020. https://info.codeforamerica.org/qualitative-research.

Signals. Periodical from Public Digital, available at https://public.digital/signals.

"Software Acquisition and Practices (SWAP) Study." Report of the Defense Innovation Board, US Department of Defense, May 3, 2019. https://innovation.defense.gov/software/.

More on the gap between implementation and outcomes.

Bagley, Nicholas. "The Procedure Fetish." *Michigan Law Review* 118, no. 3 (2019).

Brose, Christian. *The Kill Chain: Defending America in the Future of High-Tech Warfare*. New York: Hachette, 2020.

Chapman, Jake. *System Failure: Why Governments Must Learn to Think Differently*. London: Demos, 2004.

Herd, Pamela, and Donald P. Moynihan. *Administrative Burden: Policymaking by Other Means*. New York: Russell Sage Foundation, 2019.

Lindsey, Brink. "State Capacity: What Is It, How We Lost It, and How

to Get It Back." Niskanen Center, November 2021. https://www
.niskanencenter.org/wp-content/uploads/2021/11/brinkpaper.pdf.

Stokes, Leah Cardamore. *Short Circuiting Policy: Interest Groups and the
Battle over Clean Energy and Climate Policy in the American States.*
New York: Oxford University Press, 2020.

Sunstein, Cass R. *Sludge: What Stops Us from Getting Things Done and
What to Do About It.* Cambridge, MA: MIT Press, 2021.

On bureaucracies.

Downs, Anthony. *Inside Bureaucracy.* Boston: Little, Brown, 1966.

Graeber, David. *The Utopia of Rules: On Technology, Stupidity, and the
Secret Joys of Bureaucracy.* Brooklyn: Melville House, 2015.

Scott, James C. *Seeing Like a State: How Certain Schemes to Improve
the Human Condition Have Failed.* New Haven, CT: Yale University
Press, 1998.

On social services and benefits delivery.

Burke, Ryan, Mikey Dickerson, Lauren Lockwood, Tara Dawson
McGuinness, Marina Nitze, Ayushi Roy, and Emily Wright-Moore
Burke. "A Playbook for Improving Unemployment Insurance Delivery." New America, June 22, 2021. https://www.newamerica.org
/new-practice-lab/playbook/improve-unemployment/.

Cottam, Hilary. *Radical Help: How We Can Remake the Relationships
Between Us and Revolutionise the Welfare State.* London: Virago, 2019.

NOTES

INTRODUCTION

1. US Commission on Civil Rights, "Collateral Consequences: The Crossroads of Punishment, Redemption, and the Effects on Communities," Briefing Report, June 2019, p. 1, https://www.usccr.gov/files/pubs/2019/06-13-Collateral-Consequences.pdf.
2. John Halamka, "A Deep Dive on the MACRA NPRM," *Dispatch from the Digital Health Frontier* (blog), May 5, 2016, https://geekdoctor.blogspot.com/2016/05/a-deep-dive-on-macra-nprm.html.
3. Robert Lowes, "Many Physicians Predict Mass Exodus from Medicare over MACRA," *Medscape*, June 30, 2016, https://www.medscape.com/viewarticle/865288.
4. Hana Schank and Tara Dawson McGuinness, "Why the Rollout of the $2 Trillion CARES Act Was a Colossal Mess," *Fast Company*, April 17, 2020, https://www.fastcompany.com/90491891/why-the-rollout-of-the-2-trillion-cares-act-was-a-colossal-mess.
5. Jason DeParle, "Hunger Program's Slow Start Leaves Millions of Children Waiting," *New York Times*, May 26, 2020, p. 1.
6. Kone Consulting, "Pandemic EBT Implementation Documentation Project," Prepared for Center on Budget and Policy Priorities Food Research & Action Center, September 2020, table 2, p. 15, https://www.cbpp.org/sites/default/files/atoms/files/10-7-20fa-kone.pdf.

7. Heather Long and Michelle Singletary, "Glitches Prevent $1,200 Stimulus Checks from Reaching Millions of Americans," *Washington Post*, April 16, 2020.

8. Glenn Thrush and Alan Rappeport, "About 89% of Rental Assistance Funds Have Not Been Distributed, Figures Show," *New York Times*, August 25, 2021.

9. Ryan Burke et al., "A Playbook for Improving Unemployment Insurance Delivery," New America, June 22, 2021, https://www.newamerica .org/new-practice-lab/playbook/improve-unemployment/; Julia Simon-Mishel et al., "Centering Workers—How to Modernize Unemployment Insurance Technology," The Century Foundation, National Employment Law Project, Philadelphia Legal Assistance, September 17, 2020, https://www.nelp.org/publication/centering-workers-how-to-modernize -unemployment-insurance-technology/.

10. "I'm Just a Bill," *Schoolhouse Rock!*, https://www.youtube.com/watch ?v=OgVKvqTItto. There are also millions of views for its *Saturday Night Live* parody, "How a Bill Does Not Become a Law," which is well worth watching (https://www.youtube.com/watch?v =JUDSeb2zHQ0).

11. For more on intentional sabotage of government programs in their implementation see Pamela Herd and Donald P. Moynihan, *Administrative Burden: Policymaking by Other Means* (New York: Russell Sage Foundation, 2018), and Leah Cardamore Stokes, *Short Circuiting Policy: Interest Groups and the Battle over Clean Energy and Climate Policy in the American States* (New York: Oxford University Press, 2020).

12. William Eggers and John O'Leary, *If We Can Put a Man on the Moon* (Cambridge, MA: Harvard Business Press, 2009), appendix B.

13. Joe Soss, "Lessons of Welfare: Policy Design, Political Learning, and Political Action," *American Political Science Review* 93, no. 2 (June 1999): 363–80.

14. Clay Shirky, *Here Comes Everybody: The Power of Organizing Without Organizations* (New York: Penguin, 2008), 160.

CHAPTER 1: ARCHAEOLOGY

1. Rebecca Rainey and Nolan D. McCaskill, "'No Words for This': 10 Million Workers File Jobless Claims in Just Two Weeks," *Politico*, April 2, 2020, https://www.politico.com/news/2020/04/02/unemployment -claims-coronavirus-pandemic-161081.

2. Legislative Analyst's Office, "Overview of Employment Development Department Response to COVID-19," Presented to Assembly Budget Subcommittee No. 4 on State Administration, Hon. Jim Cooper, Chair, July 30, 2020, https://lao.ca.gov/handouts/state_admin/2020 /Overview-of-Employment-Development-Department-Response-to -COVID-19–073020.pdf.

3. The Newsom administration called our group a "strike team," but I have used "task force" here because I think it is more descriptive of our work.

4. These four—Marina, Mikey Dickerson, Matthew Weaver, and Carla Geisser—had formed a company called Layer Aleph, and it was this company that the state hired.

5. Yolanda Richardson and Jennifer Pahlka, "Employment Development Department Strike Team Detailed Assessment and Recommendations," September 16, 2020, https://www.govops.ca.gov/wp-content /uploads/sites/11/2020/09/Assessment.pdf.

6. Howard Mintz, "California Courts Scrap $2 Billion Tech Project," *San Jose Mercury News*, March 27, 2012.

7. Gabriel Petek, "FI$Cal IT Project Update—Special Project Report 8," Legislative Analyst's Office, January 8, 2020, https://lao.ca.gov /Publications/Report/4132#Analysis_of_SPR.A08.

8. Office of Inspector General, US Department of State, "Review of the Bureau of Consular Affairs' ConsularOne Modernization Program— Significant Deployment Delays Continue," November 2021, https:// www.oversight.gov/report/DOS/Review-Bureau-Consular-Affairs% E2%80%99-ConsularOne-Modernization-Program-%E2%80%93 -Significant.

9. US Government Accountability Office, "Information Technology Cost and Schedule Performance of Selected IRS Investments," Report to Congressional Committees, October 2021, https://www.gao.gov /products/gao-22-104387.

10. James R. Thompson, "Fixing the IRS," *Government Executive*, April 1, 2012, https://www.govexec.com/magazine/features/2012/04/fixing -irs/41637/.

11. "The Individual Tax Processing Engine Project Is Making Progress," Report from the Treasury Inspector General for Tax Administration, September 14, 2020, https://www.treasury.gov/tigta/auditreports /2020reports/202020062fr.pdf.

CHAPTER 2: SEVENTEEN YEARS

1. This is one of many successful strategies Marina details in her book *Hack Your Bureaucracy: Get Things Done No Matter What Your Role on Any Team* (New York: Hachette Go, 2022), cowritten with Nick Sinai.

2. In 1975, *The Mythical Man-Month* by Fred Brooks described how adding people to a software project that is behind schedule delays it even longer. Everyone at the State of California who advocated for such accelerated hiring would have benefited from understanding this principle, known widely in the tech world as Brooks's Law.

3. T. R. Reid, *A Fine Mess* (New York: Penguin, 2017), p. 214.

4. Joseph Bishop-Henchman, "How Many Words Are in the Tax Code?," The Tax Foundation, April 15, 2014, https://taxfoundation.org/how-many-words-are-tax-code/.

5. Reid, *A Fine Mess*, p. 210.

6. Sophie Nieto-Munoz, "Lawmakers Spar with Labor Commissioner over Unemployment Problems," *New Jersey Monitor*, March 11, 2022.

7. US Department of Labor, Employment and Training Administration, https://oui.doleta.gov/unemploy/pdf/uilawcompar/2021/coverage.pdf.

8. California Employment Development Department website, https://edd.ca.gov/en/uibdg/able_and_available_aa_235/.

9. Work search was suspended in March 2020. Making people who had refused unsafe work eligible for Pandemic Unemployment Assistance happened in February 2021 under the new Biden administration.

10. A 2005 California law called the Dymally-Alatorre Bilingual Services Act (https://law.justia.com/codes/california/2005/gov/7290–7299.8.html) already required language access. The federal guidance is https://oui.doleta.gov/dmstree/uipl/uipl2k16/uipl_0216.pdf.

11. Legislative Analyst's Office, "Overview of Employment Development Department Response to COVID-19."

12. "A Playbook for Improving Unemployment Insurance Delivery," New America, 2002, https://improveunemployment.com/way_forward/#what-we-can-learn-from-arra.

13. Simon-Mishel et al., "Centering Workers—How to Modernize Unemployment Insurance Technology."

14. According to the budget of the state of California, the amount the state spent on the EDD jumped from $254 million in budget year 2019–20 to $1.3 billion in budget year 2022–23, a more than fivefold

increase. During this time, the EDD has continued to struggle with unprocessed claims and failed to modernize its systems.

CHAPTER 3: CONCRETE BOATS

1. Cyd Harrell discusses this in her excellent book *A Civic Technologist's Practice Guide* (San Francisco: Five Seven Five Books, 2020).
2. Clay Shirky, "Healthcare.Gov and the Gulf Between Planning and Reality," *The Health Care Blog*, November 26, 2013, https://thehealthcareblog.com/blog/2013/11/26/healthcare-gov-and-the-gulf-between-planning-and-reality/.
3. David W. Heron, *Forever Facing South: The Story of the S.S. Palo Alto, "The Old Cement Ship" of Seacliff Beach* (Santa Cruz, CA: Otter B Books, 2002); Ben Guarino, "Historic Concrete Ship S.S. Palo Alto Smashed in Half by Record Calif. Storm Waves," *Washington Post*, January 23, 2017.
4. Rob Bender, "A Brief History of Concrete Ships," ConcreteShips.org, https://www.concreteships.org/history.
5. "Improving California's Unemployment Insurance Program," Report from the Legislative Analyst's Office, August 8, 2022, https://lao.ca.gov/Publications/Report/4615.
6. Tim O'Reilly, *WTF?: What's the Future and Why It's Up to Us* (New York: Harper Business, 2017), p. 116.
7. Adam Beam, "California Unemployment Fraud Balloons to $20 Billion," KQED, October 25, 2021, https://www.kqed.org/news/11893715/californias-unemployment-fraud-balloons-to-20-billion.
8. The EDD had in fact been in a multiyear process of developing a procurement for a "business system modernization." The request for proposal for this modernization included a better way to verify claimants' identities, which means the problem had been identified years earlier, since the RFP had been in development for a long time. This is consistent with what's known as Whong's Law, after civic technologist Chris Whong: "Every government agency, everywhere is working on a 'new system'; it will solve all of their problems and will be ready to use in 18–24 months" (https://twitter.com/chris_whong/status/976816680256135169). It is *always* eighteen to twenty-four months away, no matter when you ask. This is illustrative of the dysfunction of government technology: instead of solving problems iteratively and learning as teams go along, government often tries to address all the issues at once. That tends to result in endless planning and a bureaucracy perpetually frustrated by a lack of appropriate tools.

CHAPTER 4: FRIENDLY FIRE

1. Tim Fernholz, "The Entire Global Financial System Depends on GPS, and It's Shockingly Vulnerable to Attack," *Quartz*, October 22, 2017, https://qz.com/1106064/the-entire-global-financial-system-depends -on-gps-and-its-shockingly-vulnerable-to-attack/.
2. United States Government Accountability Office, "Global Positioning System: Better Planning and Coordination Needed to Improve Prospects for Fielding Modernized Capability," December 12, 2017, p. 47, https://www.gao.gov/products/gao-18-74.
3. Nathan Strout, "Raytheon Rejects Report That $6.2B GPS Project Will Be Delayed Further," *C4IRSNET*, May 22, 2019, https://www .c4isrnet.com/c2-comms/satellites/2019/05/22/raytheon-rejects -report-that-62-billion-gps-project-will-be-delayed-further/.
4. This story is adapted from Matthew Weaver, "A Tale of Technical Policy," https://mjw.wtf/atotp.pdf (published only on the web).
5. Internet Engineering Task Force Datatracker, https://datatracker.ietf .org/doc/rfc768/.
6. UDP was created in part by Jon Postel (known during his lifetime as the "god of the Internet") while working at Information Sciences Institute, funded by the Department of Defense Advanced Research Projects Agency. See Stephen Cooper, "A Guide to UDP (User Datagram Protocol)," *Comparitech*, August 11, 2022, https://www. https://www.comparitech.com/net-admin/guide-udp-user-datagram -protocol/#Data_Security.
7. "Federal Enterprise Architecture Framework, Version 2," https:// obamawhitehouse.archives.gov/sites/default/files/omb/assets/egov _docs/fea_v2.pdf.
8. Charles Ornstein, "A Cheat Sheet for the Obamacare Hearings," *ProPublica*, November 25, 2013, https://www.propublica.org/article/a -cheat-sheet-for-the-obamacare-hearings.
9. Weaver, "A Tale of Technical Policy."

CHAPTER 5: THE KODAK CURSE

1. "Computer Chaos: Billions Wasted Buying Federal Computer Systems," Investigative Report of Senator William S. Cohen, October 12, 1994, Subcommittee on Oversight of Government Management, Senate Governmental Affairs Committee.

2. Kim Vicente, *The Human Factor: Revolutionizing the Way We Live with Technology* (New York: Random House, 2003), p. 74.

3. In China, by contrast, the government still played a key role in tech in the early 2000s, and it continues to play one today.

4. "A-76 Competitions in the Department of Defense," Congressional Research Service, updated June 2, 2020, https://crsreports.congress.gov/product/pdf/IF/IF10566/6.

5. Executive Office of the President, Office of Management and Budget, Circular No. A-76, August 4, 1983 (revised 1999), https://www.whitehouse.gov/wp-content/uploads/legacy_drupal_files/omb/circulars/A76/a076.pdf.

6. James F. Nagle, *History of Government Contracting* (Washington, DC: George Washington University Law School Press, 1999), p. 264. "Construction resumed when the war ended, but the final cost exceeded the original estimate by several million dollars. In 1921, after producing the first armor plates at a cost nearly double the price per ton charged by private producers, the plant closed quietly but ignominiously."

7. Charles S. Clark, "Reinventing Government—Two Decades Later," Government Executive, April 26, 2013, https://www.govexec.com/management/2013/04/what-reinvention-wrought/62836/.

8. Paul Glastris and Haley Sweetland Edwards, "The Big Lobotomy," *Washington Monthly*, June 9, 2014, https://washingtonmonthly.com/magazine/junejulyaug-2014/the-big-lobotomy/.

9. Susannah Patton, "Multiple Choice Answers," *CIO*, January 16, 2007.

10. Robert Plant, "A Kodak Moment to Reconsider the Value of IT," *Harvard Business Review*, October 12, 2011, https://hbr.org/2011/10/a-kodak-moment-to-reconsider-t.

11. Caitlin Dickerson, "An American Catastrophe: The Secret History of the U.S. Government's Family-Separation Policy," *Atlantic*, August 7, 2002.

12. Caitlin Dickerson, "Divided, Part 2: The Chaos of Reunification," *The Daily* (podcast), August 28, 2018, https://www.nytimes.com/2018/08/24/podcasts/the-daily/divided-migrant-family-reunification.htm.

13. Michael McQuade and Richard M. Murray (co-chairs), Gilman Louie, Milo Medin, Jennifer Pahlka, and Trae' Stephens, "Software Acquisition and Practices (SWAP) Study," report of the Defense Innovation Board, US Department of Defense, May 3, 2019, https://

innovation.defense.gov/software/. For commodity functions, "Unmodified commercial software should be deployed in nearly all circumstances. Where DoD processes are not amenable to this approach, the Department should modify its processes, not the software." In other words, enough with bespoke requirements. Stop telling your people to do a better, more thorough job of the wrong thing.

CHAPTER 6: OPERATIONAL IN NATURE

1. My colleague Cyd Harrell always says that a lot of websites are *about* the government, but we need them to *be* the government, doing the people's business.
2. Today, GSA takes an active role in digital strategy across government, in conjunction with the federal CIO in the White House. Two GSA administrators in particular have seen digital as strategic priorities: Dan Tangherlini, who served under Obama, and Robin Carnahan, under Biden.
3. Michael Garland, "A Brief History of IT Acquisition Reform," *Journal of Contract Management*, Fall 2015.
4. It's an old joke among feds that the *M* in OMB is silent.
5. Garland, "Brief History of IT Acquisition Reform."
6. J. E. Hodgetts, "Unifying the British Civil Service: Some Trends and Problems," *Canadian Journal of Economics and Political Science* 14, no. 1 (February 1948): 1–19, https://www.jstor.org/stable/137650.
7. Prior to Obama naming the first ever federal CIO, several people had served as administrator of e-government, a role that carries the same statutory authorities as the CIO position. In some ways, the federal CIO position is merely a rebranding of the administrator of e-government position, but a meaningful rebranding intended to send a signal about the increasing importance of technology in federal government.
8. "An Overview of 60 Contracts That Contributed to the Development and Operation of the Federal Marketplace," Department of Health and Human Services, Office of Inspector General, August 2014, https://oig.hhs.gov/oei/reports/oei-03–14–00231.pdf.
9. CGI held five of the sixty contracts, totaling about $220 million. See "An Overview of 60 Contracts."
10. Lydia DePillis, "Meet CGI Federal, the Company Behind the Botched Launch of HealthCare.gov," *Washington Post*, October 16, 2013.
11. Ezra Klein, "How the iPod President Crashed: Obama's Broken Technology Promise," *Bloomberg*, October 31, 2013.

CHAPTER 7: STUCK IN PEANUT BUTTER

1. Rachel Meeks Cahill, Jennifer Tracy, and Andrew Cheyne, "Ten Degrees of Decentralization: Overview of Snap Operations in County-Administered States," April 2018, appendix B, https://www.clasp.org/sites/default/files/Ten%20Degrees%20of%20Decentralization%20-%20CAS%20Narrative%20Report%202018.pdf.

2. Jacqueline Kauff, Emily Sama-Miller, Gretchen Rowe, Cicely Thomas, and Libby Makowsky, "Promoting Public Benefits Access Through Web-Based Tools and Outreach," Mathematica Policy Research, December 15, 2011, https://www.aspe.hhs.gov/sites/default/files/migrated_legacy_files/43721/index.pdf.

3. Jake Solomon, "How California SNAP Onboards Users," Citizen OnBoard, http://citizenonboard.com/snap/ca/.

4. Erie Meyer, "User Research Is Not Illegal, Uncle Sam," Medium, March 6, 2017, https://eriemeyer.medium.com/user-research-is-not-illegal-uncle-sam-51f2f92a280a.

5. Code of Federal Regulations, Title 5, Chapter III, Subchapter B, Part 1320, § 1320.3, https://www.ecfr.gov/current/title-5/chapter-III/subchapter-B/part-1320/section-1320.3.

6. Jane Edwards, "US Chamber of Commerce Report: Government Digitization Could Generate $1T Annually," *ExecutiveGov*, October 19, 2022, https://executivegov.com/2022/10/us-chamber-of-commerce-government-digitization-could-generate-1t-annually/. For population statistics, see Stella U. Ogunwole, Megan A. Rabe, Andrew W. Roberts, and Zoe Caplan, "U.S. Adult Population Grew Faster Than Nation's Total Population from 2010 to 2020," US Census Bureau, August 12, 2021, https://www.census.gov/library/stories/2021/08/united-states-adult-population-grew-faster-than-nations-total-population-from-2010-to-2020.html.

7. Shalanda D. Young and Dominic J. Mancini, "Memorandum for Heads of Executive Departments and Agencies" (M-22-10), Office of Management and Budget, April 13, 2022, https://www.whitehouse.gov/wp-content/uploads/2022/04/M-22-10.pdf.

8. "Agency Information Collection Activities; Proposals, Submissions, and Approvals," Notice for Docket CFPB-2022-0051, Consumer Financial Protection Bureau, July 27, 2022, https://www.regulations.gov/document/CFPB-2022-0051-0001.

9. George Shepard, "Fierce Compromise: The Administrative Procedure Act Emerges from New Deal Politics," *Northwestern University Law Review* 90, no. 4 (1996): 1557.

10. Edward Rubin, "It's Time to Make the Administrative Procedure Act Administrative," *Cornell Law Review* 89, no. 1 (November 2003), https://scholarship.law.cornell.edu/clr/vol89/iss1/2/.

11. For more, see David H. Rosenbloom, "Retrofitting the Administrative State to the Constitution: Congress and the Judiciary's Twentieth-Century Progress," *Public Administration Review* 60, no. 1 (January/February 2000): 39–46, https://www.jstor.org/stable/977412.

12. Angie M. Boyce, "'When Does It Stop Being Peanut Butter?': FDA Food Standards of Identity, Ruth Desmond, and the Shifting Politics of Consumer Activism, 1960s–1970s," *Technology and Culture* 57, no. 1 (January 2016): 54–79, https://dash.harvard.edu/bitstream/handle/1/27022907/57.1.boyce%202.pdf.

13. Quoted in Donald Moynihan, "Why Is American Administrative Capacity in Decline?" *Can We Still Govern?* (blog), June 9, 2022, https://donmoynihan.substack.com/p/why-is-american-administrative-capacity. For the original quotation, see Jon D. Michaels, *Constitutional Coup: Privatization's Threat to the American Republic* (Cambridge, MA: Harvard University Press, 2018).

14. Jarkesy v. SEC, Court of Appeals for the Fifth Circuit, May 18, 2022.

15. Moynihan, "Why Is American Administrative Capacity in Decline?"

CHAPTER 8: THE PROCEDURE FETISH

1. Ezra Klein, "Government Is Flailing, in Part Because Liberals Hobbled It," *New York Times*, March 13, 2022. Klein cites Paul Sabin, *The Attack on Big Government and the Remaking of American Liberalism* (New York: Norton, 2021).

2. Nicholas Bagley, "The Procedure Fetish," *Michigan Law Review* 118, no. 3 (2019), https://www.niskanencenter.org/the-procedure-fetish/.

3. Ezra Klein, "Liberals Need a Clearer Vision of the Constitution. Here's What It Could Look Like," *The Ezra Klein Show* (podcast), *New York Times*, July 5, 2020, https://www.nytimes.com/2022/07/05/podcasts/transcript-ezra-klein-interviews-larry-kramer.html.

4. Sheri Fink and Mike Baker, "'It's Just Everywhere Already': How Delays in Testing Set Back the U.S. Coronavirus Response," *New York Times*, March 10, 2020, p. 1.

5. Larry Kramer, *The People Themselves: Popular Constitutionalism and Judicial Review* (New York: Oxford University Press, 2004).

6. Scott Limbocker, William G. Resh, and Jennifer L. Selin, "Anticipated Adjudication: An Analysis of the Judicialization of the US

Administrative State," *Journal of Public Administration Research and Theory* 32, no. 3 (July 2022): 610–26, https://academic.oup.com/jpart/article-abstract/32/3/610/6380787.

7. "Federal Data Integration and Individual Rights: The Computer Matching and Privacy Protection Act," Congressional Research Service, February 23, 2022, https://sgp.fas.org/crs/misc/IF12053.pdf.

8. More recently, the left has—correctly, in my view—championed equity of outcomes across groups over mere equality of opportunity or equal treatment.

9. Chinchih Chen, Carl Benedikt Frey, and Giorgio Presidente, "Privacy Regulation and Firm Performance: Estimating the GDPR Effect Globally" (working paper no. 2022-1), University of Oxford, January 6, 2022, https://www.oxfordmartin.ox.ac.uk/publications/privacy-regulation-and-firm-performance-estimating-the-gdpr-effect-globally/.

10. "Helping People Achieve the Financial Stability They Deserve," Code for America, https://codeforamerica.org/programs/tax-benefits/getyourrefund/.

11. "States Could Do More to Ensure Historically Underinvested in Communities Benefit from Federal Drinking Water Funding," Environmental Policy Innovation Center, August 12, 2021, https://www.policyinnovation.org/blog/states-could-do-more-to-ensure-historically-underinvested-in-communities-benefit-from-federal-drinking-water-funding.

12. "Justice40: A Whole of Government Initiative," The White House, https://www.whitehouse.gov/environmentaljustice/justice40/.

13. See the UK's Government Digital Service's design principle no. 4: "Do the hard work to make it simple," https://www.gov.uk/guidance/government-design-principles#do-the-hard-work-to-make-it-simple.

CHAPTER 9: THE FAX HACK

1. "Reaching Those in Need: Estimates of State SNAP Participation Rates in 2011," Food and Nutrition Service, US Department of Agriculture, February 2015, https://fns-prod.azureedge.us/sites/default/files/ops/Reaching2012-Summary.pdf.

2. Genevieve Gaudet, Better Foundations, Code for America Summit, May 31, 2018, https://www.youtube.com/watch?v=RdUE9Z8iI8s.

3. Jacob Solomon, "People Not Data," *Civic Quarterly*, September 24, 2014, https://www.civicquarterly.com/article/people-not-data.

4. Hilary Cottam, *Radical Help: How We Can Remake the Relationships Between Us and Revolutionise the Welfare State* (London: Virago, 2019).

5. Dave Guarino, tweet, December 7, 2021, https://twitter.com/allafarce/status/1468248766708785157.

6. Rachel Edelman. The quotation is from a blog post of hers that is now down, but I quoted it on my Twitter at the time: https://twitter.com/pahlkadot/status/1128064707317960706.

7. Annie Lowrey, "The Time Tax: Why Is So Much American Bureaucracy Left to Average Citizens?," *Atlantic*, July 27, 2021.

CHAPTER 10: BYRNE'S LAW

1. See, for example, the work Code for America has done with the state of Minnesota: https://codeforamerica.org/programs/social-safety-net/integrated-benefits/.

2. Clients can continue despite the warning if they like, because it's important to not only inform users but give them choice.

3. Data from Feds Data Center (https://www.fedsdatacenter.com/federal-pay-rates/), which is compiled from public records released by the Office of Personnel Management and other agencies. Of the seven, four of those product management positions were at the Consumer Finance Protection Bureau, one of the newest federal agencies, founded in 2011, where several of the people in this book have worked, including Mike Byrne. The bureau is known for using technology and design in the service of its mission. USDS and 18F have been instrumental in bringing product management into federal government, while the digital services in Colorado, New Jersey, Georgia, and California have brought it into their states.

4. "Healthcare.gov: CMS Management of the Federal Marketplace, a Case Study," Report from the Office of the Inspector General, US Department of Health and Human Services, February 2016, https://oig.hhs.gov/oei/reports/oei-06-14-00350.pdf.

5. Mike Byrne, "The Fixie Federal IT Paradigm," *feoNotes* (blog), July 12, 2014, https://feomike.github.io/post/fixie-federal-it-paradigmn.html.

6. John Gall, *Systemantics: How Systems Work and Especially How They Fail* (New York: Quadrangle/The New York Times Book Company, 1977).

7. Clay Shirky, "How Willful Ignorance Doomed HealthCare.gov," *Politico*, November 24, 2013, https://www.politico.com/magazine /story/2013/11/the-willful-ignorance-that-doomed-healthcaregov -100290/.

8. From "Overview of 60 Contracts": "The original estimated value of these contracts totaled $1.7 billion; the contract values ranged from $69,195 to over $200 million. For 20 of the 60 contracts, the amounts obligated through February 2014 already exceeded the estimated value of the contracts at award. For 7 of these contracts, the obligated amounts exceeded the expected value by more than 100 percent."

9. Shane Donglasan, "The Lucky Life of Author Michael Lewis," *Your Oberver.com*, March 5, 2018, https://www.yourobserver.com/article /author-michael-lewis-sarasota-ringling-town-hall-2018.

10. Eric Ries, *The Lean Startup: How Today's Entrepreneurs Use Continuous Innovation to Create Radically Successful Businesses* (New York: Currency, 2011).

11. Kate Clark, "Bodega, Once Dubbed 'America's Most Hated Startup,' Has Quietly Raised Millions," *TechCrunch*, September 25, 2019, https://techcrunch.com/2019/09/25/bodega-once-dubbed-americas -most-hated-startup-has-quietly-raised-millions/. On Bodega's failure: https://en.wikipedia.org/wiki/Stockwell_(company).

CHAPTER 11: THE INSIDERS

1. CMS internal documents.

2. John D. Halamka, "The Quality Payment Program Final Rule," *Dispatch from the Digital Health Frontier*, October 19, 2016, http:// geekdoctor.blogspot.com/2016/10/the-quality-payment-program -final-rule.html.

3. The Agile Manifesto, https://agilemanifesto.org/principles.html.

CHAPTER 12: UP THE WATERFALL

1. Alan Barber and Cherrie Bucknor, "The Price We Pay: Economic Costs of Barriers to Employment for Former Prisoners and People Convicted of Felonies," Center for Economic and Policy Research, June 16, 2016, https://cepr.net/report/the-price-we-pay-economic -costs-of-barriers-to-employment-for-former-prisoners-and-people -convicted-of-felonies/.

2. State of California Department of Justice, "AB 1793—Cannabis

Convictions Resentencing," https://oag.ca.gov/fingerprints/record-review/ab1793.

3. California Legislature, "AB 1308—Arrest and Conviction Record Relief," https://leginfo.legislature.ca.gov/faces/billTextClient.xhtml?bill_id=202120220AB1308.

4. National Conference of State Legislatures, https://www.ncsl.org/research/civil-and-criminal-justice/marijuana-overview.aspx.

CHAPTER 13: WHAT WE BELIEVE MATTERS

1. Letter from Kenneth Glueck, senior vice president, Office of the CEO, Oracle, to Christopher Liddell, director, American Technology Council, The White House, September 20, 2017, posted at https://github.com/GSA/modernization/issues/41.

2. Deborah Collier, "The Risky Business of Federal IT," Citizens Against Government Waste, March 28, 2017, https://www.cagw.org/thewastewatcher/risky-business-federal-it.

3. That much of the tech industry stays away from government work is a problem in its own right. When the burdensome contracting process and other operational problems make tech companies averse to doing business with the government, that only gives more power to the incumbent vendors.

4. Eric Schmidt, Reid Hoffman, and Kurt DelBene stand out as particularly supportive, but there are many others.

5. Noah Smith, "Interview: Marc Andreessen, VC and Tech Pioneer," *Noahpinion*, June 21, 2021, https://noahpinion.substack.com/p/interview-marc-andreessen-vc-and.

6. Marc Andreessen, "It's Time to Build," *Future*, April 18, 2020, https://future.com/its-time-to-build/.

7. That's the GS-15 Step 10 rate, adjusted for DC's cost of living, according to https://www.opm.gov/policy-data-oversight/pay-leave/salaries-wages/salary-tables/pdf/2021/DCB.pdf.

8. Deborah Gage, "The Venture Capital Secret: 3 Out of 4 Start-Ups Fail," *Wall Street Journal*, September 20, 2012.

9. Nik Marda and Julia Ingram, Stanford Tech History Project, April 26, 2021, p. 42, https://techhistory.stanford.edu/report/.

10. Cristiano Lima, "Microsoft Has Avoided the Hot Seat for Years. Its New Mega Deal May Change That," *Washington Post*, January 19, 2022.

11. See https://analytics.usa.gov/. See also Tim Lowden (@tdlowden), "covidtests.gov saw ~39M visits Tuesday. I was livetweeting realtime

numbers, and max at one time on http://covidtests.gov was ~750,000,"
Twitter, January 20, 2020, https://twitter.com/tdlowden/status/148426
5327433326593.

12. Rachel Kurzius (@Curious_Kurz), Twitter, January 18, 2022, https://
twitter.com/Curious_Kurz/status/1483516260486979586.

13. Amanda B-S (@AmandaWorking), Twitter, January 18, 2022, https://
twitter.com/AmandaWorking/status/1483544062745624584.

14. Shirky, "How Willful Ignorance Doomed HealthCare.gov."

15. Tim Lowden (@tdlowden), Twitter, January 18, 2022, https://twitter
.com/tdlowden/status/1483522613347590150.

16. Mitchell Clark, "The US's Free COVID Test Website Has More
Visitors Than All Other .gov Sites Combined," *The Verge*, January
18, 2022, https://www.theverge.com/2022/1/18/22889769/us
-government-free-covid-test-website-massive-page-viewcount.

17. Jessica Huseman, "Filing Taxes Could Be Free and Simple. But H&R
Block and Intuit Are Still Lobbying Against It," *ProPublica*, March
20, 2017, https://www.propublica.org/article/filing-taxes-could-be
-free-simple-hr-block-intuit-lobbying-against-it.

18. T. R. Reid, interview by Paul Solman, *PBS NewsHour*, April 13,
2017, https://www.youtube.com/watch?v=qPKUjZzRirY.

19. Justin Elliott, "TurboTax Deliberately Hid Its Free File Page from
Search Engines," *ProPublica*, April 26, 2019, https://www.propublica
.org/article/turbotax-deliberately-hides-its-free-file-page-from-search
-engines.

20. For more see Amy E. Lerman, *Good Enough for Government Work:
The Public Reputation Crisis in America (and What We Can Do to Fix
It)* (Chicago: University of Chicago Press, 2009), which exposes how
biased the public is about public services. When told to rate services,
people consistently rate services higher if they think they were performed by the private sector and lower if they think the service was
performed by the public sector. When they rate a service well, they
tend to assume it came from private industry. If they don't like a service, they will assume it was the work of the public sector.

21. Jill Cowan, "Thousands of Californians Could Get Their Marijuana
Convictions Cleared. But It's Complicated," *New York Times*, September 5, 2019.

22. Tom Steinberg, "5 Years On: Why Understanding Chris Lightfoot
Matters Now More Than Ever," *mySociety*, February 11, 2012, https://
www.mysociety.org/2012/02/11/5-years-on-why-understanding
-chris-lightfoot-matters-now-more-than-ever/.

CONCLUSION

1. Thanks to Luke Rosenberger (@lukelibrarian), who answered my desperate post on Twitter with this vintage copy. Bill Hunt has since put the report up at https://digitalpolicy.us/info/cohen-report/.

2. "Financial Management and Business Transformation at the Department of Defense," Hearing Before the Subcommittee on Readiness and Management Support of the Committee on Armed Services, United States Senate, 112th Congress, First Session, July 27, 2011, https://www.govinfo.gov/content/pkg/CHRG-112shrg72524/html/CHRG-112shrg72524.htm.

3. The underlying phrase comes from Israeli diplomat Abba Eban, who said in 1967 that "men and nations behave wisely when they have exhausted all other resources," https://quoteinvestigator.com/2012/11/11/exhaust-alternatives/.

4. Mark Schwartz, AWS Cloud Enterprise Strategy Blog, October 16, 2020, https://aws.amazon.com/blogs/enterprise-strategy/announcing-the-delicate-art-of-bureaucracy/.

5. See the Federal Information Technology Acquisition Reform Act of 2014 (FITARA), https://www.cio.gov/handbook/it-laws/fitara-2014/.

6. Other Transaction Authority (OTA) is one path. Purchasing agreements made under this authority are not subject to the Federal Acquisition Regulation.

7. See Title 5, Part III, Subpart B, Chapter 37 of the US Code, https://www.law.cornell.edu/uscode/text/5/part-III/subpart-B/chapter-37.

8. California State Budget (enacted) 2022–23 Labor and Workforce Development Department Report (22–23 has the final 2021 numbers), https://www.ebudget.ca.gov/2022–23/pdf/Enacted/GovernorsBudget/7000/7100.pdf. The 2019–2020 headcount was 2,691.3, though it ramped up significantly at the end of that fiscal year; the 2020–2021 headcount was 9,286.2.

9. "Federal Tech Workforce Data Report," *Tech Talent Project*, data as of April 15, 2022, https://techtalentproject.org/improve-federal-cx/agency-hiring-data/dept-of-treasury/.

10. "Information Technology Professional Demographics and Statistics in the US," *Zippia*, https://www.zippia.com/information-technology-professional-jobs/demographics/; "Federal Tech Workforce Data Report," data as of April 15, 2022.

11. "Impact Report," United States Digital Service, Spring 2020, https://www.usds.gov/resources/USDS-Impact-Report-2020.pdf.

12. For more information, see https://techfarhub.cio.gov/initiatives/ditap/.

13. US Bureau of Labor Statistics, "Employment Projections: Employment by Major Industry Sector," September 8, 2022, https://www.bls.gov/emp/tables/employment-by-major-industry-sector.htm#1.

14. Login.gov Partners, General Services Administration, https://login.gov/partners/faq/.

15. David Weinberger, "The Internet That Was (and Still Could Be)," *Atlantic*, June 22, 2015.

16. Alex Health, "Elon Musk Is Putting Twitter at Risk of Billions in Fines, Warns Company Lawyer," *The Verge*, November 10, 2022, https://www.theverge.com/2022/11/10/23451198/twitter-ftc-elon-musk-lawyer-changes-fine-warning.

17. Christian Brose, *The Kill Chain: Defending America in the Future of High-Tech Warfare* (New York: Hachette, 2020), p. xii.

18. Attributed to Barney Frank, former member of the U.S. House of Representatives.

ACKNOWLEDGMENTS

My greatest luck with this book was that Grigory Tovbis, Sara Bershtel, and Riva Hocherman at Metropolitan didn't like my proposal. But they thought I had something to say, and they offered to work with me anyway, on trust. Grigory then shaped everything about this book, with unwarranted patience and exceptional wisdom. I could not be more grateful for all he and the team at Metropolitan gave to this. He and the team also managed to secure me (and I quote from a neutral third party) "the best copy editor who ever lived" in Roslyn Schloss. Calling her my "secret weapon" would put me in far better company than I deserve, but I can't help myself. Working with her was a treat I never expected to get, but one for which I will be forever grateful.

I'm also so grateful that Tim Duggan agreed to pick up this project and brought it into the world with such kindness and skill. What an enormous stroke of luck. Anita Sheih's patient and clear help has also been invaluable. My agent Zoe Pagnamenta has been an amazing champion and guide through all of this. Anand Giridharidas introduced me to Zoe, which was an act of kindness on his part. Many people encouraged me to write this:

Van Jones, Tom Kalil, danah boyd, Clay Shirky—your words meant more than you know.

Praise seems to be the only thing that Yadira Sánchez shies away from, and I thank her for letting me share her story despite the discomfort. I wish I had been better able to honor her desire to spread the credit more widely; she works with many inspiring colleagues and pushed hard for me to shine the spotlight on them over her. May this book inspire others to honor many more public servants for their tireless efforts to make our government work for all of us.

Advocates, too, worked tirelessly on some of the efforts described here, but out of the spotlight. One of those is Jenny Montoya Tansey, the originator of the Clear My Record project at Code for America and a central figure in records clearance in her previous role at Californians for Safety and Justice. I want to thank her for her important work and for her graciousness in contributing to the book. Many others, including Ben Golder and S. T. Mayer, also deserve credit for helping start Clear My Record, in addition to Jazmyn Latimer.

So many people generously shared their stories, read drafts, and/or provided much-needed feedback: Marci Harris, Donald Moynihan, James Anderson, Misha Chellam, Michele Evermore, Todd Park, Zach Graves, Dan Tangherlini, Max Steir, Meg Peters, Monica Chellam, Max Henderson, Lauren Lombardo, David Recordon, Dave Zvenyach, Waldo Jaquith, Gulsanna Mamediieva, Rick Klau, Yolanda Richardson, Alix Dunne, Dave Cole, Honey Dacanay, Mike Bracken, Dana Chisnell, Bill Hunt, Natalie Kates, Mike Greenfield, Mikey Dickerson, Margaret Levi, Sabrina Merlo, Cristine Soto DeBerry, Victoria Cuff, Genevieve Gaudet, Bret Taylor, Erie Meyer, Adrien Abrams, Becky Sweger, Lucas Merrill Brown, Shannon Sartin, Rohan Bhobe, Jake Solomon, Alan Williams, Dave Guarino, Jazmyn Latimer, Meilani Santillan, Alia Toran-Burrell, Tracey Patterson, David Newville, JP Sharp, Lainey

Trahan, Matthew McAllister, Mike Byrne, Michael Brennan, Robert Gordon, Kaitlin Devine, Mina Hsiang, Josh Marcuse, Angela Colter, Stephanie Cain, Chris Lynch, Steve Spiker, Eddie Hartwig, Jez Humble, Stephanie Grosser, Casey Burns, Eric Mill, Bill Hunt, Dana Chisnell, Mark Lerner, Tony Scott, Eric Schoonover, Cecilia Muñoz, Mary Ann Brody, Natalie Moore, James Myall, Mike Wilkening, Matt Lira, Eleanor Davis, Dustin Palmer, Will Slack, Charles Worthington, Marcy Jacobs, Kelly Taylor, Maria Cancian, Benno Schmidt, Kayenda Johnson, Meredith Broussard, and Samuel Unger.

Tom Steinberg graciously spent many hours with me generously getting me unstuck. Ashley Meyers was my partner and coconspirator in the early days of this book. Nik Marda, Daniel Zhao, and Cristina Chenal all helped with critical research and insights. Mark Hopson seriously overdelivered with stories, gems of insight, and complete citations.

There is a lot of Matthew Weaver in this book—most of chapter 4 is literally his story. But he also deserves much of the credit for helping me accept the abyss without fatalism or complacency. And then there's Marina Nitze. The abyss slinks away in fear when she appears. She and the amazing Nick Sinai wrote a book and then proceeded to coach me through my own process like new parents who'd had their baby ahead of me. I don't know what I did to deserve friends like these, but I'll take it and be grateful.

Speaking of chapter 4, though I have never met Dominic, he has been one of the biggest agents of change in one of the world's largest bureaucracies, and for that we all owe him thanks. And thanks to Emily Tavoulareas, Mary Ann Brody, Courtney Eimerman-Wallace, Paul Tagliamonte, Alex Gaynor, and others for lifting up his voice.

Haley Van Dyck is the true mother of the US Digital Service. The story of what she endured to set up this office has not been told, but should be. Getting to work by her side was an honor. Having her in my life is a joy.

Matt Cutts went above and beyond with steady guidance and a keen eye. But I am even more grateful to him for holding his ground those four long years. Because of him, Eddie Hartwig, Charles Worthington, and everyone else who stuck it out, it was still the people's government to me, and that meant everything. Thank you to *everyone* who stayed.

Amanda Renteria, Lou Moore, and Zeryn Sarpangel: your leadership allowed me to write this book. John Lilly: there never was and never will be a better board chair, mentor, and friend than you. And to everyone at Code for America, past and present, but particularly the originals: Meghan Reilly, Abhi Nemani, and Alissa Black. We made something good, didn't we?

I learned so much during my time on the Defense Innovation Board. I have DJ Patil's generous championship to thank for that, and for the chance to learn from the late Ash Carter, a man of enormous intellect, integrity, honor, and caring. I was fortunate to know him, and I was heartbroken at his passing, as were the thousands of others he touched with his inspiring leadership. I was equally fortunate to work with Josh Marcuse, Bess Dopkeen, Michael McQuade, Eric Schmidt, Milo Medin, Richard Murray, Trae Stephens, Neil deGrasse Tyson, Eric Lander, Gilman Louie, Marnie Levine, Adam Grant, Danny Hillis, Ben FitzGerald, and many others in and around the Department of Defense. Jordan Blashek and the team at America's Frontier Fund continue to inspire me as they tackle state capacity at the intersection of national security and economic revitalization.

Just when I thought I was retiring, I had the honor of working alongside many inspiring public servants at the State of California, including Yolanda Richardson, Amy Palmer, Amy Tong, and Mike Wilkening. Yolanda for president, please!

I am grateful to be part of (or get to watch from the good

seats) so many efforts to make government work better for people. Jessica Cole, Tina Walha, Alex Allain, and Jessica Watson at US Digital Response; Jennifer Anastasoff and Cassandra Madison at the Tech Talent Project; Michelle Shevin and Jenny Toomey at the Ford Foundation; Hashim Mtuezi at Code for America; Raylene Yung and Robin Carnahan at GSA; Cyd Harrell at the San Francisco Digital Service; and everyone involved with the For the People exchange: you all bring me joy and hope. A special shout-out to Chris Kuang and Caitlin Gandhi at the Digital Corps and Rachel Dodell and Ariana Soto at Coding It Forward for cultivating our next generation of public servants. And to Sabrina Merlo, my sometimes collaborator and always and forever friend: love you, and sorry I didn't skewer the vendors.

John Koskinen is a man of integrity, honor, and grace. Thank you for letting me tell the story my way and thank you for your remarkable service to this country. Dan Tangherlini, thank you for making me a better person. I have a ways to go.

To the Brits, without whom my journey to DC would have been very different. Mike Bracken, Ben Terrett, Tom Loosemore, Ade Adewumni, and so many others: thank you for showing the way and pulling me through. Martha Lane Fox and Francis Maude: may leaders everywhere follow your example.

To everyone who made the hardest year of my life also the best: Lynn Overmann, Hope Hall, Ryan Panchadsaram, Nicole Wong, Nick Sinai, Casey Burns, Charles Worthington, Cristin Dorgelo, Tom Kalil, Raph Majma, Erie Meyer, Cori Zarek, Mollie Ruskin, Sean Herron, Beth Cobert, Cecilia Muñoz, Tara McGuinness, Kumar Garg, Kara deFrias, Claudia Williams, Greg Gershman, Paul Smith, Hillary Hartley, Aaron Snow, Mina Hsiang, Dave Viner, Andy Ruff, Adam Bookbinder, David Recordon, Matthew McAllister, Randy Paris, Tom Power, Macon Phillips, Dan Correa, Andrew McMahon, Mark Schwartz, Bryan Sivak, Nani Coloretti, and many others. David Simas, I will never forget how you championed us. Brian Deese, I didn't know you, but I know what you did for USDS and I'm forever grateful. And to the memory of Jake Brewer, who always cultivated our *karass* and whose spirit of bipartisanship inspired this book!

The Volcker Alliance generously supported me as a fellow during the first year of writing this book. Thank you to Sara Mogulescu, Melissa Austin, and Emily Bolton. Amy Clark, Nadine Freeman, Michael Zakaras, Konstanze Frischen, and others at Ashoka have also been enormously supportive.

Then there's 7 Minute Women, my daily healing, strengthening touch point the past two years. Ayelet Waldman, you were already a genius but getting this group together was next-level. Semi Chellas, thank you for getting me to join, for "Keep Going," and for thiry-two years of love and support. Rachel Snyder housed, fed, and entertained me during my final push. Maile Meloy, you and I are like upside-down Catholics—twice a day every day and sometimes on Sunday. Thank you for your friendship. May we meet in person one day . . . or not! I love you either way. And to Lindsey Strasberg, Peggy Orenstein, Monique El-Faizy, and everyone else, two words: jumping jacks!

Thank you also to Matthew Lezama, Lynda Kravitz, Michelle Jurkiewicz, Leopoldina Matus, and Rhonda Block for caring for me and my family.

To the people of the little town of Washington (nope, different Washington!) but especially Phillip Copening, Mike Stewart, and Maya for welcoming me and my family to your wonderful community.

To my father, Bill Pahlka. Thanks for encouraging me to write, and for being my role model. I love you so much.

To my mother, Barbara Sellars. Thanks for always fighting for the things you care about. You're an inspiration.

To my sister, Amy, thanks for always being my champion,

having my back, and taking care of everything and everyone. Kendall and Kieran, I love you both so much.

To Meara, Isaiah, Arwen, Saul, Huxley, and Bronte: thank you for accepting me into your family. I love you all.

To my daughter, Clementine. Thanks for putting up with so much on so many fronts for so long. And thank you for writing what you wrote. Keep writing! I love you to the ends of the earth and back. Also, never forget to vote!

And finally, to my husband, Tim O'Reilly, the best partner in life and work a person could ever ask for. This book is the culmination of a journey we've been on together, ever since you declared government a platform and pushed me on stage to announce the nonprofit I wanted to start. Everything I've done since then has been with your unfailing help and encouragement. The work has sometimes kept us apart, but mostly brought us together, enriching our lives and giving them meaning. Thank you for putting up with that year in DC, for giving me the good office, and for always thinking of me. I love you.

INDEX

ABOUT THE AUTHOR

JENNIFER PAHLKA served as the United States deputy chief technology officer for government innovation under President Barack Obama. While at the White House, she cofounded the United States Digital Service. She also founded Code for America, an award-winning nonprofit that seeks to make government work for the people, by the people, in the digital age, and she chairs the board of another nonprofit, United States Digital Response, which helps public entities respond quickly to critical needs. She served on the Defense Innovation Board for the Department of Defense under Presidents Barack Obama and Donald Trump and cochaired Governor Gavin Newsom's strike team on unemployment insurance during the pandemic. Pahlka is the winner of a Skoll Award for Social Entrepreneurship and was selected by *Wired* magazine as one of the people who have most shaped technology and society in the past twenty-five years. She lives in Oakland, California, with her husband and their nine chickens.